THE UNIVERSITY LIBRARY IN THE UNITED STATES
Its Origins and Development

The library of the University of South Carolina, the first university library building in the United States.

ARTHUR T. HAMLIN

The University Library in the United States

ITS ORIGINS AND DEVELOPMENT

UNIVERSITY OF PENNSYLVANIA PRESS
Philadelphia
1981

The publication of this title has been partially
supported by funds from the Samuel Paley
Endowment Fund, Temple University Libraries,
Philadelphia, in recognition of the directorship,
1968–1979, of the author

Library of Congress Cataloging in Publication Data
Hamlin, Arthur T.
   The university library in the United States.

   Bibliography: p.
   Includes index.
   1. Libraries, University and college—United States—
History. I. Title.
Z675.U5H19   027.7'0973   80–54049
ISBN 0–8122–7795–3   AACR2

To the hundreds of librarians, mostly women, who devoted their lives
to the service of scholarship in secondary positions with little
recognition and often at bare subsistence salaries, in the first half of
the twentieth century.

Contents

Preface

The genesis of this book was a casual conversation with Maurice English, my friend and college classmate who was then director of the Temple University Press. "What," said he, "needs to be published in the field of librarianship?" I thought for a moment, then replied, rashly as it turned out, "A history of university libraries in the U.S." This interested him and we discussed it. The question then was, who should do it? My recommendation was Robert Downs, and shortly thereafter a letter went from English to Downs. The reply triggered the event, for it was a polite refusal, coupled with the suggestion that Temple had on its own faculty just the man for the job. By this time the seed was planted and investigative work began.

The demands of a senior administrative post are such that progress was slow until the university granted a study leave for 1976–77. A major portion of this book was completed in those months. The material was then left "fallow" for some twenty months until I took early retirement in order to complete it.

This history is written for the academician outside the library profession who is a user of libraries and interested in them. It is also written for younger members of the profession, both prospective and already committed, who want to know the general background of growth and development. It lays no claim to being the definitive history. It is rather the story as viewed by one individual who has read extensively in background material and who has been, over a period of forty-eight years, a staff member of six of the largest research libraries in the country (Harvard, Columbia, the New York Public, University of Pennsylvania, University of Cincinnati and Temple University). As executive secretary of the Association of College and Reference Libraries in the fifties I visited literally hundreds of campuses, and came to know the leaders in the field, and was then and subsequently, personally involved in many professional developments.

This material, then, is based in part on personal experience and observation. It is also based on a considerable reading of university histories. "It wonders me," as the Dutch say, that so many otherwise reputable historians can write extensive histories of their alma maters with hardly a reference to the library except possibly that a building was built, or a director appointed. Athletics, social events, parking provisions, inaugural addresses of presidents, and a host of petty matters all too frequently crowd out any reference to "the heart of the University." Robert Vosper once wrote, "The powerful and steady growth of book collections in individual American university libraries, particularly during the mid-twentieth century, has been a major achievement in American cultural and educational history. It has both matched and fostered the ebullient and questing intellectual life of the universities themselves, and it has been a marvel to many foreign observers." It is well known that every distinguished complex university also has a library equally distinguished for its collections and its library services. Yet the library, which is vital to the attraction of a superior faculty and for its function, rates little or no mention in a majority of institutional histories. But there are exceptions, and here and there one will find a whole chapter, a glorious, thoughtful, constructive review of the building of the library. To such as so write, all praise.

Most of the source material used has been strictly the literature of librarianship. A small number of doctoral dissertations and Brough's *Scholar's Workshop* give detailed historical data on such major universities as Harvard, Yale, Columbia, Ohio State, Illinois, Indiana, Chicago, California at Berkeley, and Texas. Other dissertations and many masters' theses deal with other institutions and with particular aspects of librarianship. In addition, many brief histories of university libraries have been issued, some as separate volumes of some length, others as articles, usually in a library or university publication. Many, but by no means all of these have been examined. Finally, of course, there is the journal literature; particularly useful have been the *Library Journal, Library Trends, College and Research Libraries,* and *The Library Quarterly.* The findings here are based on this literature, not on examination of trustees' notes, annual reports of directors, or minutes of committees.

Footnotes are given only when considered essential and as briefly as necessary for identification. Reference must be made to the bibliography for the full citation of any footnote. The section on sources is intended to give the principal authorities used for each chapter. In several cases this section is also used to refer readers to other material which is believed to be especially important or because it presents a different view.

University names are generally abbreviated and reference is generally assumed to be to the library of the institution. Thus it is "Columbia" from the very early days, not its first designation, "King's College," and it is Duke, not Trinity. Further, state universities are often referred to only by the name of the state; a full form is used where necessary for clarity. Thus it is Pennsylvania and Oregon for the University of Pennsylvania (Philadelphia) and the University of Oregon (Eugene) and it is Penn State (State College) and Oregon State (Corvallis).

The bibliography is limited to publications referred to in this work. It would be foolhardy to duplicate the excellent work of Michael Harris and Donald Davis, Jr., whose *American Library History, a Bibliography* (University of Texas Press, 1978) fills this need.

The literature of librarianship in recent years has become distinguished for its obscurity. Alas, some of the younger members of the profession are so learned that their published findings are beyond the comprehension of their seniors. In England a decade ago, the director of a university library in whose office I sat opened a new issue of *College and Research Libraries* and read to me a few paragraphs of the lead article. "Arthur, what kind of writing is that!" he exclaimed. Neither of us could make any sense of it. More recently I took something, recommended as essential for every library school student, to a fellow director for elucidation. No help. Then to a dean of a library school. He was equally nonplussed. These are by no means unusual cases. The literature of librarianship has its full measure of jargon, and this is a reflection on us all. The matter is mentioned here in defense of the terms used in this book, which may seem unnecessarily simplistic to some of my learned colleagues. I hope and pray that the exposition is reasonably clear to any and all with collegiate level backgrounds, regardless of special interest.

The presentation of the university library is given here first with a chronological overview, then with chapters on some principal topics. There is necessarily some duplication, but every effort has been made to hold it to the minimum. The chronological approach includes relatively full treatment of some topics which did not seem to fit in the later chapters.

Certain topics, treated here as chapters, can obviously only be handled properly with book-length treatment. This is particularly true of Cataloging and Classification, of Library Buildings, and of Technology.

To continue with these apologies, a word of warning about the statistical tables. Data on the size of libraries, their budgets, and other essential information varies enormously. Does the figure for volumes represent all collections in a university? The truth is, "almost never." Is it a really reliable figure in other respects? Again, seldom, if ever, because of variant methods of counting, unrecorded losses, clerical errors, etc. Then does the volume count include material in microform? Some reports include it, others do not, and in the large library this count runs into six figures. Financial figures also vary. In my own experience the annual expenditure for a major departmental library was reported by its librarian to one professional journal as nearly $950,000.00; for the same year it was recorded on the comptroller's books as just under $700,000.00, while the figure sent to the federal government (HEGIS) was an official $558,000.00.* Which figure does a responsible person use? In academe the explanations generally lie in a welter of obscurations that seek to justify such wide variation. Figures for university enrollments are equally treacherous. Do they include all branches of the university? Do they include all who took a course at any time during the year or are they figures for enrollees at a particular time? Are they full-time equivalent? The variations are quite considerable. The figures used in this history are believed to be as accurate as obtainable. I have held the statistical presentations to a very few because of chances of misuse.

Generalizations as to what was happening in university libraries as a group at a particular point in time cannot reflect the situation in the emerging institution. A considerable number of great university libraries, as represented in the select membership of the Association of Research Libraries, have grown to maturity in recent years. Their libraries of a few decades back might not have done justice to a junior college of that time. So the generalizations given here usually apply only to the well established.

A considerable number of acknowledgements for permissions and for aid and assistance are a pleasant obligation: to Temple University for a study leave at half salary to pursue the work; to the University of Illinois Press for permission to reproduce the statistical table from Brough's *Scholar's Workshop;* to Robert Downs and Richard De Gennaro for critical comment on portions of the manuscript and for encouragement; to Charles Churchwell and H. Glenn Brown for data on Brown University Library; to Donald Davidson for information on the University of Califor-

*Approximate figures used so as to obscure identification of the institution.

nia at Santa Barbara; to Walter Woodman Wright for material on Dartmouth; to Kendon Stubbs of the University of Virginia Library; to William Carlson for data and for a copy of his history of the Oregon State University Library; to Edward G. Holley for many favors; to Gerhard Naeseth of the University of Wisconsin at Madison; to Hendrick Edelman for permission to reprint his tables on university libraries and for much informal discussion of history; to Harold Billings for material on the building-up of the University of Texas collections in the last twenty-five years; to Ernest Earnest of Temple for advice on the history of higher education; to Rutgers University Library for courtesy borrowing privileges; to Beverly Feldman of the Harvard College Library for information; to E. L. Inabinett for answers to queries on the early history of the University of South Carolina, and particularly to Kenneth Toombs for many courtesies regarding data on that institution; to William C. Roselle for data on the acquisition of the American Geographical Society Collection by Wisconsin at Milwaukee. Alas, this list includes none of my own staff at Temple's Paley Library, who were always ready to help, but their very number precludes such designation.

Newcastle, Maine
March 1981

Part I
Chronology

CHAPTER 1

The Collegiate Libraries
of the American Colonies

There are approximately 150 universities in the United States which have professional schools of some stature and a variety of respectable study programs at the doctoral level. Both aspects of university work require sophisticated library services and extensive library collections for the progress of students, for the vitalization of teaching, for the research essential to dissertations, and for the extension of knowledge carried on independently by the faculty.

These libraries now gather their collections from all over the globe and routinely handle material in scores of languages. The enormous growth of knowledge of the last several decades has resulted in a similar growth in publications of research value, which must be acquired, recorded, and serviced. With all this goes a dependence on technology that would have bewildered the librarian of the 1920s: microreproduction of many types, reading machines, telex, reader-printers, a wide spectrum of audio-visual aids, laboratories for paper and film conservation and restoration, and finally and dramatically, the computer with its multiplicity of services for use and misuse. The handling of programs of such magnitude and complexity requires budgets in the millions and staffs numbered in the hundreds with language competencies and technical knowledge of high order.

It was not always so. Our institutions of higher education were all on the collegiate level until late in the nineteenth century, when the true university began to develop, and these collegiate institutions depended on libraries which, for the most part, were limited to a few thousand poorly selected volumes and virtually no service programs. Libraries were increasingly emphasized in university growth in the fifty years following the founding of Johns Hopkins in 1876, but their real growth has come within the lifetimes of librarians still professionally active. It is only a slight exaggeration to say that the growth of these research libraries which are the foundation of the modern university has been as dramatic

3

and far-reaching since World War I as the growth of air travel. While all
this seems to have developed with bewildering speed, it is not at all
unlikely that similarly dramatic change lies in store for research libraries
in the two decades remaining in this century.

Enough of this speculation; let us turn to first beginnings. The
"seed" of a university library was sown with the founding of Harvard
College, on October 25, 1636, when the General Court of Massachusetts
voted "to give 400£ towards a schoole or colledge, whearof 200£ to be
paid the next yeare and 200£ when the worke is finished, and the next
Court to appoint wheare, and what building." It was at least as late as the
summer of 1638 before any collegiate instruction was inaugurated. A firm
date for its origin is established by a letter written by one Edmund
Browne in September of 1638 in which he reports: "Wee have in Cambridge heere, a College erecting, youth lectured, a library, and I suppose
there will be a presse this winter." That same month another wrote,
"Newtowne now is called Cambridge. There is a University house reared,
I heare, and a prity library begun." John Harvard enters the picture, also
in September of 1638, when he died at the age of thirty and left one-half
of his estate, estimated at 1,700£, towards the erecting of a College, and
all his library. Word of this reached New England some months later and
on March 13, 1639, the General Court, "ordered, that the Colledge
agreed upon formerly to bee built at Cambridge shalbee called Harvard
Colledge." The "prity library" mentioned in the two letters undoubtedly
refers to books given locally, recorded in a contemporary document as
"the Honoured Magistrates and Reverend Elders gave. . . . out of their
libraryes' books to the value of £ 200."[1]

Readers who are librarians will agree with the writer that surely the
first university library antedates the university, this out of loyalty rather
than solid historical fact. In any case, the first university did indeed begin
its first very feeble movements with a sizable collection of books. Aside
from the gifts mentioned above, John Harvard's bequest added 329 titles
in more than four hundred volumes. To this beginning were shortly
added other works so that by conservative estimate the holdings in 1655
had increased to eight hundred titles in about nine hundred physical
volumes.

We know that a "prity library" was provided before the John Harvard
donation, but there is no record of the number or nature of the books.
We only know that the educated people of the colony had been dunned
for books. Harvard's first building, which lasted scarcely a generation,

had a small room termed "library" on the second floor. Closed to students, it was a locked room to house the book collection. Was this the "prity library," housing a hundred or more miscellaneous volumes?

In any case, the shelves were soon filled with the bequest of the Reverend John Harvard, sometime Minister of God's Word at Charlestown, who had arrived, with his library, in the Bay Colony just the year before his death.

This was a gentleman's library. About 65 percent of the works were theological, mostly in Latin. But it was broad in scope and included some Catholic, indeed even Jesuit, authors. The classical authors were represented in the original and in some of the famous translations, such as Chapman's *Homer* and North's *Plutarch.* Bacon was there and Descartes, Poliziano, and Erasmus, a goodly number of grammars and dictionaries, some English poetry, a very little classical drama, and a few medical books. It was a catholic collection and, if theology predominated, we must remember that this was the principal interest of the educated men of that time. It was quite contemporary since more than a quarter of the books had been printed after 1630. It is of interest that so extensive a library was shipped safely to the new colony at such an early date.

Other gifts followed. President Dunster found time from his oppressive lecturing schedule and other duties to appeal in 1647 to the New England Confederation on behalf of the library. It is the mark of the man that he recognized, as few others did in that day, the need for books in all branches of learning. In particular he noted that the library was defective "in all manner of bookes, especially in law, phisicke, Philosophy and Mathematickes, the furnishinge whereof would be both honourable and proffitable to the Country in generall and in speciall to the schollars, whose various inclinations to all professions might thereby be incouraged and furthered."[2]

While this appeal fell on stony ground, gifts began to come with some regularity from other sources.

A touching picture both of concern for the Harvard library and of how it operated is given in a 1663 document by one Jonathan Mitchell.

1. Forasmuch as a Compleat & well-furnishd Library is altogether necessary unto eminent degrees of Learning in any Faculty. And to Have at least one such in yᵉ Country is needfull for yᵉ publike & Common good, as well as for the (p)rofit of particular scholars. It is [er]go a needful & would be a N[oble?] work to Inlarge the L(i-

brary of t)he Colledge at C[ambridge] [torn] And should it please
any to contribute either particular summes, or any Annuity to that
end It would be a worthy & renouned service to ye publike. provided Alwayes that the Trustees abovesayd doe with ye Help of the
President & Fellows take a speciall & extraordinary care for the
Keeping & well-ordering of ye Library, & to prevent all Abuses
therein; & that (as soon as may be) the Bookes may be chained as
they are in other places. In ye mean time y^t the president and senior Fellow with some one or two of ye Trustees, doe every quarter
goe into ye Library & take a strict account of ye Library-Keeper y^t
no Book may be so lent out or disposed as to be in Hazard either
of being lost or abused.[3]

Just as later colonial libraries to a degree were patterned on Harvard
practice, Harvard's first library conformed to the experience of the leaders of the Bay Colony, who were mostly Cambridge University men. Of
those who came before 1650, one hundred were Cantabrigians as contrasted with thirty-two Oxonians. And of the Cambridge colleges, Emmanuel had by far the greatest number of these students. No less than
ninety-eight colonists were ministers of the gospel in New England. Obviously, then, this little group of leaders in the New World thought of the
college they were founding principally in terms of Cambridge, just as
later on the founders of Yale, mostly Harvard graduates, thought in those
terms.

Instruction at Cambridge University was very largely in the hands of
the tutors, as it was at Harvard. In the former it was extremely flexible,
dependent on the interests, taste, and conviction of the tutor, whereas in
the New World it was anything but flexible. The key to instruction until
the nineteenth century was the tutor. Of a Cambridge tutor in the early
seventeenth century Morison writes:

A college tutor at that time had almost absolute control over his
pupils, with whom his relation was more than paternal. He seldom
had more than six pupils, and usually less; for he was supposed to
spend much time on his studies. He might be highly conscientious,
or otherwise. . . . He might teach his pupils in a class, or individually.
But in any case, one or more pupils shared his chamber, his compen-
sation was a matter of personal arrangement with their parents, and
he was responsible to the College for all their bills . . . Simonds
d'Ewes, on leaving the University, notes: "My loving and careful
tutor, Mr. Holdsworth, accompanied me home, not only to perform
the last loving office to me, but to receive some arrearages due to him
upon his bills."[4]

At that time at Cambridge University the pupil rose in time for a five o'clock chapel followed by a breakfast of bread and beer. Then came lectures or recitations and some study until an eleven o'clock main meal "in hall." This was followed by an hour for recreation and supposedly by several hours of study. Then more bread and beer in the afternoon, supper at five or six, relaxation, and finally, if the tutor was conscientious, an hour of "improving conversation" before early retirement. Evening reading was not expected because of obvious limitations in lighting.

Libraries played no part in this program. In 1610, Emmanuel College had 503 books, of which 30 were reported missing! In 1637 the number had grown to "about 600." These were for the tutors, should they be inclined to study. The entire library came by gift, and was largely theological in nature.

Instruction at Cambridge, as later at Harvard, William and Mary, and the other colonial colleges, was based on the seven liberal arts as laid out by Martianus Capella in the fifth century. These were the Trivium of Grammar, Rhetoric, and Logic and the Quadrivium of Music, Arithmetic, Geometry, and Astronomy. Six of the seven, together with the three Philosophies brought in by the twelfth-century Renaissance, and the Greek literature introduced in the later Renaissance, remained the backbone of the undergraduate course in European and American universities well into the nineteenth century.

Throughout the centuries the study of grammar remained fundamental. Of course, it was Latin grammar, although Benjamin Franklin was partly successful in introducing English grammar at the University of Pennsylvania. Rhetoric, whether verbal or written, was the art of persuasion. Logic was a principal preparation for both the pulpit and the bar. Whereas rhetoric encouraged interest in belles-lettres, logic exercised a stultifying influence on originality and scientific investigation.

The basic preparation for these studies was a sound knowledge of Latin and a smattering of Greek, which any boy could acquire in the early days of the New World from his clergyman. Thus while seventeen was a usual age for acceptance in a college, English or colonial, some students were matriculated much younger.

The daily life of the colonial student conformed to the English pattern. It remained basically the same until the early nineteenth century. For example at Harvard the student gained admission by a brief examination at the college to show thorough grounding in Latin and some knowledge of Greek. In effect he then entered college, which meant he was assigned space in the single building where he would sleep, eat, attend class, in fact do everything for the next four years because there was only one building, except for the college "office," the polite term for the outdoor privy. As a freshman he might sleep in a dormitory but he soon would have a "chamber" with several other lads. He would sleep two in a bed for warmth, and on a trundle bed at that. But he would have a "study" to himself, a tiny cubicle partly partitioned off inside the chamber where he could keep his personal belongings and study in some privacy and where he had a window for light. He would be up with the sun if not earlier, wash probably at an outdoor pump, and attend prayers at his tutor's chamber. Then breakfast similar to his Cambridge University counterpart (bread and beer), served over a counter to be carried to his chamber. Following this, a morning lecture and study until eleven, when dinner was served in the main hall (used for classes and sundry other gathering purposes). Basic food was bread, beef, beer. There was some free time after this, then disputations or recitation generally based on the lecture of the morning, a leisurely supper and recreation period beginning at 7:30 P.M., and evening prayers. Students were to be in their chambers by nine.

This program seems much more confining than that of Cambridge. Of course, the student's tutor could make all sorts of alterations. There is record of students taking long jaunts in term, then as now. However, there were no real recreational facilities other than those that nature affords. And in theory Saturday afternoon was the only free time for sports. Then there were pranks and serious disorders, as there always have been for boys in their teens.

The Harvard curriculum of the mid-1600s generally offered one subject each day, introduced by a lecture and followed by study of the topic, then recitation based on the lecture and subsequent study. Some classes had their study period early in the morning and lecture later. Greek was studied throughout. There was a smattering of Hebrew, Aramaic, and Syriac. Rhetoric was emphasized along with "Divinity Catechetical." In general the Trivium and Quadrivium mentioned previously were followed. The president carried the entire burden of instruction of all four classes, a program quite possible with a student body of fifteen or twenty students. There were no written examinations. For three weeks prior to commencement the upperclassmen had to be available for "visitation" several hours each day. They were there to be examined "by all Commers in the Latine, Greek and Hebrew tongues and in Rhetoricke,

Logike and Physics," to quote the Harvard statute of 1650. The "Commers" were normally only a few of the overseers of the college.

In addition to the B.A., which took four years, many students took an M.A. This graduate degree was granted after three years to those who prepared a paper on any subject of choice or fulfilled some other minor requirements. No residency or formal study was required although many did spend part of the time at the college.

As at Harvard, student bodies of the other earliest colleges remained small, often fifty or sixty and seldom more than a hundred, until the middle of the eighteenth century. Since he was sheltered under the same roof in the closest proximity to his charges, twenty-four hours a day, no tutor or president could be quite a hero to the student body.

Like many a college president of later years, Nathaniel Eaton, Harvard's first president, had all the proper credentials for the office but none of the talent. In addition, he soon proved to be a thorough scoundrel and escaped the Bay Colony only by pushing a constable into the harbor and sailing immediately for Virginia. He was destined to die many years later in an English prison within a stone's throw of the former home of John Harvard.

As the choice of Eaton was singularly unfortunate, the selection of his successor was exactly the opposite. The college, which had been closed in the fall of 1639, reopened a year later under Henry Dunster. The details of his contribution has no place in this history of libraries. Suffice it to say that,

> Dunster found Harvard College deserted by students, devoid of buildings, wanting income or endowment, and unprovided with government or statutes. He left it a flourishing university college of the arts, provided with several buildings and a settled though insufficient income, governed . . . by a body of fellows and officers whose duties were regulated by statute. The Harvard College created under his presidency and largely through his efforts endured in all essential features until the nineteenth century, and in some respects has persisted in the great university of today.[5]

New England's First Fruits, written in 1643 largely as a promotion piece to assist fund raising, emphasizes the religious or clerical element in the founding of Harvard College. "One of the next things we longed for, and looked after was to advance Learning and perpetuate it to Posterity; dreading to leave an illiterate Ministery to the churches, when our present Ministers shall lie in the Dust."[6] Too much has been made of this.

While an immediate and pressing concern was the education of the clergy, "to advance learning" was a principal, long-term need and objective. Theology did not exclude other branches of learning. Although not expressed in these terms, "polite learning" or the education which a gentleman should have, was accepted by the early leaders of the colony. This was a recognized feature of the English university which had once been primarily church oriented, but had come to recognize that education should develop the whole man, and lay a foundation for development in any useful direction, as a gentleman and a man of action. As will be pointed out later, the earliest librarians of Harvard, like their fellow graduates, by no means all ended in the pulpit. The distinguished historian Samuel Eliot Morison points out,

> No pledge expressed or implied that he would enter the ministry was required of any student entering Harvard; and it is obvious that many of the students never had the slightest intention of becoming ministers. Other documents of the first generation point to the same conclusion: that Harvard was founded for the advancement and perpetuation of learning, in the broadest sense of that term.[7]

Nearly thirty years after its founding Harvard took the decisive step of appointing a librarian and adopting the "Library Laws of 1667." These specify that only seniors and M.A. candidates can borrow books and that only the fellows may study in the library. Certain materials are not to be loaned out at all. There are penalties for damaging books, rules about the key, requirements about records, sale of duplicates, and so forth. The hours for borrowing and returning books were specified as eleven to one and the loan period as one month.

This first American librarian known to history by that title was Solomon Stoddard, who graduated from Harvard in 1662 and took an M.A. three years later. In November, 1666 he was made a tutor at Harvard and on March 27, 1667, the corporation voted, recording that "Mr. Solomon Stoddard was chosen Library keeper." Stoddard functioned as librarian probably for not much more than three years. We next hear of him accepting a pulpit in Northampton, Massachusetts in February, 1672. This he occupied for nearly sixty years. It is a pleasure to record that he was one of the leading clergymen of the Bay Colony.

For nearly a century, the Harvard librarianship was held by a succession of young men, most of whom left after one to three years. Approximately one-half followed callings other than preaching. Thus Stoddard's successor was Samuel Sewall, the famous diarist and chief justice. He was one of the judges who presided over trials at which several were condemned to death for witchcraft, an action for which he later made public confession of sin. Sewall set an example for all librarians to follow by marrying money, in his case the daughter of the mint master. His successor in turn became a clergyman, and the next one a doctor.

So it went for over a hundred years until, in 1772, James Winthrop was appointed librarian and retained the post for fifteen years. This gives him a certain claim to the distinction of being the country's first professional librarian. He was a man to admire for his patriotism (wounded in the Battle of Bunker Hill), his learning (a scholar of distinction in the natural sciences and languages), his selflessness (little or no salary during the difficult war years), and his stewardship in his assignment to care for a book collection that was dispersed widely to neighboring towns in order to avoid capture or destruction. Possibly he should be given more credit for bringing it back together again, for this was accomplished with little loss.

A later contender for the title of "first professional" is Samuel Shopleigh, librarian of Harvard from 1793 until his death at age thirty-five in 1800. Unlike Winthrop, who earned his living as register of probate since Harvard paid him virtually nothing, Shopleigh devoted his full attention to the library, for which he earned an annual salary of $360.00. On his death he left nearly all his property to Harvard for a fund to buy books.

Although the intellectual fare was strictly textbook, recitation, and discussion and although the college library was not easily accessible to most students until late in the eighteenth century, students did somehow find time to read recreationally, and some of their reading was light. A record of the reading of two seventeenth century Harvard students shows access to Spencer, Herrick, Witt, Warner, and some rather erotic verse of Sir Philip Sidney. There were other works of a decidedly secular nature available, possibly from parental libraries. Books would be loaned about. Later on, the literary society libraries were formed to meet these needs for current literature, which eager young minds crave and will find, one way or another.

Naturally, such reading interests did not meet with universal approbation. Cotton Mather disapproved of them because youths who entered college as pious young men graduated as skeptics or even heretics. He claimed that students filled their rooms "with books which may be truly called Satan's library." He asked for an investigation as to "whether the books mostly read among them are not plays, novels, empty and vicious pieces of poetry."[8]

In all academic processions the representative of William and Mary marches second after Harvard by virtue of the commonly accepted date of founding, 1693. William and Mary actually has some claim to primacy because of a 1619 Virginia Company grant of ten thousand acres to found a college. There were other similar actions later in the century but it was only in 1693 that a royal charter for a college was secured. A main college building was begun in the following year and instruction started in 1697. There was the surprisingly large enrollment of nearly one hundred students. And while William and Mary is today a college rather than a university and so technically outside the scope of this work, it once had more claim to the title of university than any other American institution, for in the late eighteenth century it had separate schools of law, medicine, and modern languages. In respect to faculty, resources, student body, and indeed influence, William and Mary was the leading institution of the pre-Revolutionary period.

> It contributed more great leaders in the Revolution than any other college. Numbered among its sons were seven of the eleven members of the Committee of Correspondence appointed in 1773, and six of the eleven members of the Committee of Safety appointed by the Virginia Convention in 1775. Eleven of the thirty-one members of the Declaration of Rights Committee of the State Constitution were William and Mary alumni. Further, of the seven Virginia signers of the Declaration of Independence, four attended the Virginia College and the author himself, Thomas Jefferson, was a member of the Class of 1758.[9]

The list continues: Peyton Randolph, the first president of the Continental Congress, John Tyler, Virginia's first governor, Edmund Randolph, the attorney general and secretary of state, John Marshall, the chief justice and many others. In many respects William and Mary was innovative and modern. And from the very first it had a responsible faculty of seven to divide the teaching load, one for divinity, one for mathematics, one for philosophy, one for languages, one for history, and one for the humanities, which in that day meant Latin literature. President Blair was relatively free from teaching.

War and natural disaster dealt severely with the institution, but most tragically with its library. In October, 1705, a fire destroyed all except possibly one of the volumes of the brave beginning of its collection.

Another fire in February, 1859 wiped out the library again, and three and a half years later the new collection was in large measure lost in a Civil War action. Few records survive.

Both Henry Compton, bishop of London, and Gilbert Burnet, bishop of Salisbury, are known to have given books to William and Mary before 1699. Robert Boyle left a considerable sum for charitable purposes when he died in 1691, and much of this was assigned to the college. Books are assumed to have been involved. A large collection, well over two hundred volumes, came about 1698, from Colonel Francis Nicholson. William and Mary is undoubtedly the first to use college funds for a library, for a record which has survived shows a sizable expenditure in February, 1697. Another big purchase was made with £50 of funds from Dr. Thomas Bray's Associates. With these purchases and presumably many other gifts William and Mary had accumulated at the time of the fire what Thomas Hearne, Bodley's librarian at Oxford, termed "a library . . . which in all probability would in some time have grown very famous."

The library was housed in the main college building, probably designed by Sir Christopher Wren, apparently in a room on the second floor. The room was presumably furnished with wooden cases or presses, plus necessary tables and stools. The library is believed to have served merely as a reading room. In any case, its use was restricted to the college masters.[10]

Disaster struck on the night of October 29, 1705 when fire consumed the entire library, a collection estimated to number between seven and eight hundred volumes. Very little is known of the second library, which grew over a period of more than a century and a half.

The strong start of William and Mary was followed in only a few years by Yale, which dates the beginning of both university and library from the fall of 1701 when ten clergy met, by prearrangement, in the parlor of the Reverend Mr. Samuel Russell in Branford, Connecticut. Each of the ten brought a number of books and one by one left them on the center table with these words, reminiscent of the prayer book, "I give these Books for the founding a College in this Colony." Reportedly, forty folios were collected.

This account of the founding by no less authority than Thomas Clap, Yale's first president, is heavy in romance but of very doubtful historical authenticity. All solid data, reinforced by common sense, indicate that the ten ministers (nine of them Harvard graduates) met a great many times to plan the founding of the college. At one time or another in the first

year or two, most or all of them gave books. And, of course, donations
of books and money followed.

That same fall of 1701, the General Court passed "An Act for Liberty
to erect a Collegiate School" wherein "Youth may be instructed in the
Arts & Sciences who through the blessing of Almighty God may be fitted
for Publick employment both in Church & Civil State."[11] Instruction
began promptly at Killingworth in the residence of the minister. It moved
in a few years to Saybrook and in 1716 to New Haven, where the first
collegiate building was completed in 1718.

Gifts of considerable value were received in these first few years. The
principal credit belongs to Jeremiah Dummer, a Harvard graduate who
had advanced degrees from Leyden and Utrecht, became a London agent
for the Massachusetts Bay Colony in 1710, and two years later switched
employment to Connecticut. Support for the new college was dear to his
heart and in this work he was most astute. For example, in preparing the
way to win over one Dr. Daniel Turner, he suggested that the trustees
send Turner a doctoral diploma. This was dispatched with alacrity by the
trustees. As one historian piously wrote, "It had probably never occurred
to them that one of their diplomas could be exchanged for gifts." Such
thoughts have since occurred to many a trustee group! In September,
1714, the trustees received a shipment of more than eight hundred
volumes collected by Dummer. The collection included the best in English thought on all major subjects, "from theology and medicine to
literature and travel." That same year the trustees printed the first catalog
of a collegiate library ever issued in the U.S.; unfortunately no copy
survives.

By the year 1718 the library had grown to a respectable thirteen
hundred volumes. Then disaster struck, not in the usual form of fire, but
in civil strife. New Haven had finally been chosen as the permanent site
and a collegiate building had been erected. But the library was lodged in
Saybrook and an aroused citizenry would have no truck with any relocation. There followed orders by the governor and council, denials that
there were any books by otherwise honest citizens, warrants to arrest,
appearances in court with more refusals, a fight between the citizens of
Saybrook and the sheriff's men at the home of the librarian, the door
broken down, the books seized, loaded in carts, sabotage of carts and of
bridges on the route. In short, to quote President Clap's account, "in this
Tummult and Confusion, about 25 percent of the most valuable Books,
and sundry Papers of Importance were conveyed away by unknown

Hands, and never could be found again." In the light of all this the reader must decide for himself whether or not to honor with the title of Yale's first librarian Daniel Buckingham, who had custody of the books, and whose door was flattened in the action.

The Yale library flourished in these early years. In 1733 it received some thousand volumes, the private library of George Berkeley, bishop of Cloyne. Another catalog was printed in 1743, which listed twenty-six hundred volumes. Shortly before the Revolution it had the largest collegiate library in the colonies but it suffered heavily during the war years with the result that the catalog of 1791 could list only twenty-seven hundred volumes.

By any standard of judgment this colonial library at New Haven was extensive and varied. It contained the principal works on the natural sciences and represented all shades of theological doctrine. In theory, according to the trustee minutes, it was for the students. From the very first it was ordered, "that undergraduates Shall at the Discretion of the Rector have the Benefit of the Collegiate Library for their assistance in their Studies." Obviously the need to get the rector's approval in order to borrow limited the traffic. Later rulings tightened, then loosened, the regulations. In 1718 only the trustees could borrow, except with rector's approval. Five years later seniors and graduates in residences were permitted books. One book a month was the limit for some time. Records of considerable use of the library do exist today in the form of notations, signatures, and graffiti of these users, for Yale was most fortunate in being spared the fires which destroyed the early libraries of other institutions. The Yale historian of this early period sums up the role of the library thus:

> The library, then, had both its serious and frivolous users. A few students obviously used the library to complement their studies and a few more to expand their intellectual horizons. Others borrowed books for extracurricular reasons. On the whole, however, the library was not an integral part of the college course of study. Tutors used some books in preparation for their teaching but they rarely made additional assignments in library volumes to supplement classroom work. So in assessing the Yale curriculum from 1701 to 1740 the library is a relatively insignificant factor.[12]

Unlike Yale, Princeton University, founded by royal charter in 1746, claims no solemn conclave as the origin of its library. In fact, the first historical reference (1750) is not to books, but to a bookcase, which is at least an indication of interest in, and quite possibly ownership of, the small beginnings of a library. Seven years later the bequest of Jeremy Belcher brought 474 volumes, just in time to be housed in the new collegiate building, Nassau Hall, which had a "spacious room" on the second floor designated as a library. The Belcher bequest was heavy in the orthodox, moralistic writing of that period, and in classical literature. In addition it had modest holdings in history, biography, law, geography, navigation, and physics. It was strong in the more recent masters of English literature, such as Defoe and Dryden.

Princeton was blessed with effective fund raisers, which made library purchases possible. By the time the catalog of 1760 was published the library contained 1,281 volumes. This catalog has a most unusual preface, written by President Samuel Davies, which emphasizes the importance of independent use of books by students. To quote small portions, the library "is one of the best Helps to enrich the Minds both of the Officers and Students with Knowledge; . . . to lead them beyond the narrow Limits of the Books to which they are confined in their stated Studies and Recitations, that they may expatiate at large thro' the. . . . Fields of Science. If they have Books always at Hand to consult . . . it will enable them to investigate TRUTH thro' her intricate Recesses . . ." Davies died shortly after this was published but the emphasis on free inquiry and investigation by students in the use of the college library continued at Princeton for some years.

The library contained two thousand volumes when war struck in 1775. Princeton suffered grievously as Nassau Hall was occupied by American troops, then by the British, then again by the Colonials. Neither army respected the building, which was left a shambles, nor the library, to whose contents soldiers of both sides helped themselves, thereby effectively destroying the fine beginning. It was only due to the great talent and devotion of President John Witherspoon that building, endowment, faculty, and library were later restored and the college put once more on a sound operating basis.

The University of Pennsylvania was first chartered as a college in 1755. With Benjamin Franklin an influential founder, library needs were sure to receive considerable attention. An appeal for books to serve the publick academy, predecessor of the college, was made in 1749 and this was followed in a few months by authorization to spend up to £100 sterling for "Latin and Greek authors, maps, Drafts, and Instruments."

There was not in Philadelphia the urgent need for a university library that existed elsewhere. Indeed, the academy was offered the gift of a lot next door to the library of James Logan, one of the trustees. Logan was the possessor of the foremost private library in the thirteen colonies and offered its use to the masters and scholars of the academy. Also close by was the Library Company established in 1741. While the constitution of the academy recognized a responsibility to furnish "books of general use, that may be too expensive for each scholar," there is no evidence of the accumulation of a library of any size or importance until after the Revolutionary War. This despite various trustee actions in the first decade that bear witness to an interest in financing the purchase of books.

Kings College, which became Columbia University, dates from 1754, the year of its charter, and that same year was bequeathed a fine library, among other things, by the Honorable Joseph Murray. From London came another early bequest of fifteen hundred volumes. There were many small donations, so that by 1763 the board of governors felt the need for a librarian and a printed catalog. During the Revolution, British troops pillaged the library and some six or seven hundred books were lost. To the credit of that army, a proclamation was issued by the commanding general requiring the restoration of the books. Curiously, a large cache of them turned up in St. Paul's Chapel thirty years later.

When the College of Rhode Island (Brown University), was founded in 1765 it too applied to English friends for funds and books. In the competition for location, the rival towns of Newport and Providence both stressed an existing library which would serve the students. The size of the college library when hostilities broke out is not known. It was moved to the country for security. Later, when peace was restored, President Manning wrote, "Our library consists of about five hundred volumes, most of which are both very ancient and very useless, as well as very ragged and unsightly."

The seventh decade of the century saw the founding of two more colleges, Rutgers and Dartmouth, whose libraries will be mentioned only briefly here. In the case of Rutgers, chartered in 1766, there is really no record of a library or book collection until 1792. The university archivist is authority for the following:

> For two or three years, the College was housed in a temporary location, i.e., the "Sign of the Red Lion." When the Revolution began the College was evacuated from New Brunswick and it is

therefore not likely that any but the most rudimentary collection of library materials was accumulated and these probably were in the possession of the tutors connected with the College at that time.

Dartmouth, on the other hand, began assembling books seven years before receiving its charter in 1769. Many of the early gifts secured by Eleazar Wheelock, the founder, prior to the charter, were primers, Bibles and textbooks in theology for the use of the Indian children. Two important early donations came in the form of bequests of money and books from Theodor Atkinson, Sr. (1770) and the Reverend Diodate Johnson (1772). Wheelock brought an important library of his own to the institution and emphasized the importance of the library throughout his presidency.

In 1772 tutor, later professor, Bezaleel Woodward was named librarian and the collection placed in his house. Five years later it was moved to Old College Hall and regulations for its use prepared. For various reasons the books were moved a number of times before the century was out.

In its early days, Dartmouth adopted the questionable practice of supporting the library by charging students according to their use of it. A quarto cost more than an octavo! This practice did not foster a love of library books in the young men. The income from circulation was largely applied to book purchases, which indicates Dartmouth alone of the colonial colleges had a regular appropriation for library acquisitions. By an action taken in 1793 one-quarter of income from this source went to Professor Smith (librarian from 1779 to 1809) and three-quarters to acquisitions. This canny librarian also operated a book store in his house.

> The library was opened in 1793 to the two upper classes on Monday, and to others on Tuesday, of each week from one o'clock to two. In 1796 the arrangement was changed so as to admit seniors and sophmores on Mondays, alternately, and the juniors and freshmen on the corresponding Tuesdays, between the hours of two and three. No more than five were admitted to the library chamber at once, and no one was permitted to handle a book except by permission from the librarian.

Dartmouth was well removed from Revolutionary War hostilities. At the close of the century the library numbered approximately twenty-nine hundred volumes, but nearly a thousand of these were duplicates of doubtful utility.

In the colonial period no library received a regular appropriation for any purpose except through student fees charged at several institutions. It must be remembered that the only expenses of the period were for staff and books. And staff consisted only of the casual duties assigned to a faculty member whose salary was not thereby increased. So the only expense that survives as historical record is for the purchase of books. Generally speaking, these funds came through occasional action by the trustees, the few and far between gifts of money from friends, and, as noted, student fees. It is clear that the majority of the libraries of the colonial colleges went for long periods without a cent to spend.

Most support for the libraries came, then, not in funds through which selection could be made, but in gifts of books and bequests of private libraries. Shores estimates "the proportion of accessions acquired by direct purchase was probably less than a tenth of the total, especially when it is considered that many purchases were the result of private donations."[13]

The first really important sum given to a college library was the £1,170 given to Harvard by Thomas Hollis in 1726. Six years later William and Mary received benefit from the Brafferton estate, of which £300 was authorized to be spent on the library. Several years after the destruction of the Harvard library in 1764 a subscription of £554 was received by the college from John Hancock for the purchase of books. Shortly after the Revolution, Mr. John Brown, treasurer of what became Brown University, offered to match any gifts given by his trustee colleagues, and thus was raised nearly £700 for the benefit of the library and, as the phrase read in those days, "for philosophical apparatus." Yale's first sizable recorded gift in currency for the support of the library was 333 pounds, 14 shillings from the Reverend Samuel Lockwood, received in 1789.

There must have been other gifts, probably minor, and some donations to the colleges without statement of purpose which were in part used for the purchase of books. However it is clear that gifts for library purposes were extremely infrequent.

Equally infrequent were appropriations by the trustees. These institutions of a few score students and a handful of faculty had little money for purchases of any equipment. The need for a single book was therefore a proper matter for trustee deliberation. Exceptions to practice were the eighteen hundred dollars voted by the New Jersey legislature in 1796 to Princeton for repairing the buildings and the increase of the library, and the £750 voted by the Columbia trustees in 1792 for books for the library.

As one might suspect, the possibilities of a library fee occured to

several of the institutions early in their history. After the Revolution
Princeton instituted a charge of two shillings and six pence per quarter
for library support. At one time the sum of two shillings per quarter was
assessed at Dartmouth. The same practice was apparently followed at
William and Mary, as evidenced by a 1779 faculty vote that "at the
ceremony of Matriculation shall be a pecuniary contribution to the Library from every student when he enters the College, & annually after-
wards, on which his name together with his Contribution shall be entered
in a Book kept for that Purpose by the Bursar, & he shall be entitled to
the use of the Library."[14] Three years later the amount of the fee was set
at ten shillings.

There were ingenious methods of collecting revenue for books. Back
in 1734 the Virginia General Assembly voted to the college proceeds of
a penny per gallon tax on imported liquor and provided "that some part
thereof should be spent on books." Dartmouth once took a chance on a
lottery for the benefit of the library, but was not the winner so did not
repeat the venture. At the University of Pennsylvania a 1752 rule levied,
on behalf of the library, a fine of one shilling on trustees who were absent
from meetings, and on students granted holidays, a charge of ten shillings. About the same time graduation charges were levied on Bachelors
(fifteen shillings) and on Masters (one pound).

These occasional small rivulets of support did leaven the rather
heavily theological quality of the collections. A careful analysis of the
books listed in the printed catalogs of the colonial colleges, from the 1723
of Harvard to the 1793 of Brown shows these libraries to be very similar.

> A subject analysis of these catalogs reveals that only about one-half
> of the titles were theological and that books on history, literature,
> and science comprised from 32 to 45 percent of the titles. With the
> exception of the 1793 Brown catalog, the distribution of subjects was
> remarkably similar despite the differences in size, and a time span of
> seventy years. A bibliographical review of the more important titles
> indicated that the range of subjects was impressive and that the
> significant authorities were available in many fields.[15]

It is also noteworty that in the Harvard 1790 catalog 73 percent of the
titles were in English and only 19 percent in Latin. French came third and
Italian fourth.

As we look at these institutions as a group it is clear that in the years
immediately prior to the Revolutionary War the majority of college students had access to a considerable choice in reading, but there was

relatively little encouragement of such reading. The boy rose early, he went to class to recite, he studied a single text for each subject; he had opportunity for games and sports and minor hell-raising. Since the whole student body might number scarcely a hundred, or at the very most four hundred, he knew them all. He lived in close proximity to the very few men that comprised the faculty and so knew them equally well. His studies were in the medieval tradition but in the middle and later decades of the eighteenth century mathematics and science did receive gradually increasing attention. Also there was a slow but steady decline in the ministry as the chosen profession.

It is quite clear that few if any students, whether preparing for the ministry or with interests in other subjects, really had to use the library. The difficulties were such that only a minority did make appreciable use of it. Access was generally only a few hours a week, and access did not necessarily mean access to the shelves, even when only a few hundred volumes were involved. The rules were extraordinarily explicit in "No-nos." At some institutions only upperclassmen could borrow. However, young men with strong motivation find ways to surmount such obstacles, and there is abundant evidence of use by students as well as faculty. But use must have been very limited at such institutions as Brown, Dartmouth, and Rutgers where, at this time, the collections consisted of no more than a few hundred miscellaneous volumes. Harvard had the largest library, then as subsequently. At the time of the fire in 1764 its collection numbered some five thousand volumes. This number was replaced in relatively few years. The Yale library was only slightly smaller as the eighteenth century wore on. Pennsylvania students could use the extensive library of James Logan. Columbia and Princeton offered at least some reading in science and literature as well as theology. While these facilities were absurdly poor judged by modern standards, they must be viewed in the light of the times, when library service of any type or dimension was unusual both in the colonies and across the Atlantic, where the practice of chaining books to the shelves still prevailed.

CHAPTER 2

Growth and Development, 1790–1876

As the new nation recovered from its war of independence and moved into the nineteenth century there was tremendous expansion in the number of collegiate institutions but relatively little in their size. Until the middle of the century the colleges remained, with few exceptions, clusters of several buildings serving perhaps one to two hundred students, many of whom might be in the preparatory stage. For example, the three well-established universities, Pennsylvania, Harvard, and Yale, had enrollments in 1841 of one hundred, slightly over two hundred, and four hundred respectively.

Similarly, the period from the establishment of the Republic to the 1870s is one of continuance of traditional methods of instruction and of little change in the role of the library. New colleges were established, book collections were increased, a scattering of buildings designed solely for library purposes was built. With few exceptions leadership of these libraries was in the hands of a faculty member whose duties were primarily instructional and whose tenure as librarian was short. But the seeds of change were germinating in the minds of those few leaders who were primarily librarians as well as of a small group of college presidents. So at just about the precise moment of birth of the true university in America, the library movement also formed into bud. The magic year was 1876, the date of the founding of Johns Hopkins, of the American Library Association, of the *Library Journal,* and just a few years before or after appointments to presidencies of a group of forceful leaders who were to transform the whole picture of higher education. The giants to come were Eliot of Harvard, Barnard of Columbia, White of Cornell, Angell of Michigan, and Gilman of Johns Hopkins. Radical modernization of library services took place at Harvard in the seventies and at Columbia in the eighties. Then 1876 is also the date of the publication of *Public Libraries in the United States,* a quite startling publication to come from a governmental body, since it emphasized a responsibility to make books convenient of access to students, the importance of availability of the collection for consultation in the evening and on Sundays, reference service, and other less dramatic innovations. This complete about-face, from stress on guarding the collection to the exclusion of use, to one of emphasis on use even at some risk to preservation, is the single most important event in the history of the American academic library. It did not take hold everywhere at one time, but it spread gradually after the Civil War and grew solidly over the following several decades.

With the expansion of the new republic in population, in wealth, and in area came an increasing concern for education and the gradual emergence of collegiate institutions in all parts of the country. This was as true of New England as of the Middle West and to a limited degree of the South. In Vermont, for example, the Universities of Vermont and Middlebury were both founded by 1800, and in Maine, Bowdoin. By the same date the Universities of Georgia and North Carolina were established as were several colleges in Pennsylvania, New York State, Massachusetts, and elsewhere. Furthest west was Transylvania, born in 1780 in Danville, Kentucky, and soon to move to Lexington. The dawn of the new century saw nearly thirty institutions in operation either at the collegiate level or in the cocoon stage as academies which were soon to have degree-granting status. Growth in numbers was steady throughout the 1800s. An 1850 report of Charles Coffin Jewett provided data on 133 college libraries. In 1870 the commissioner of education reported 369 colleges in the United States. The Bureau of Education's report of 1876 lists 305 college or "university" libraries which claimed library collections of three hundred volumes or more. However, the latter publication considered only seventy-one of these libraries sufficiently large and important to warrant designation as "Principal College Libraries"; of these, the majority had less than fifteen thousand volumes.

And while several great institutions in the South date from the late eighteenth and early nineteenth centuries, there was considerable opposition to the concept of state-supported higher education, partly because this was conceived by the planter class as a responsibility of the church. Growth south of the Mason-Dixon line was therefore slower. The earliest in effective operation was the University of North Carolina, with 1793 as its date of founding. The University of Georgia came into being a few years later. An historical note on that institution vividly illustrates the difficulties of those days. Powell comments:

> When Meigs came into office [as president] in 1801 he found an institution without buildings, faculty, funds, or students. Although

the first students were admitted in 1801, no building for the college was completed until 1806. Rent from its land provided most of the early support of the University.[1]

From the southernmost institution turn to the northernmost, the University of Vermont, and consider the burden borne by its president at the turn of the century. In order to keep body and soul together he earned money by preaching each Sunday. During most of the first decade (1800–12) he was the sole instructor. Then he had to help erect buildings, clear the land, plough and cultivate crops in order to raise food to feed the students. When a man bears such burdens he may be forgiven for lacking a proper attention to building up a scholarly library for his institution.[2]

The picture is much the same in the West. The State University of Missouri, founded in 1839, was conceived as an institution to which and for which the state government had no responsibility for direction or support. These responsibilities were assumed only gradually, long after the population had flowed across the Appalachians and into the western territory following the Revolutionary War. South Carolina is the only state in which the legislature met a responsibility for annual financial support of its fledgling university from the very first. Miami University was launched in southwestern Ohio in 1809 with a grant of two townships of land. The same was true of the University of Missouri, Indiana University, and a number of others. Grants of public lands for educational purposes were not uncommon before the Civil War. They were authorized by various state and federal legislation. The big step of this nature came in May of 1862 with the Morrill Land Grant Act to spur collegiate level studies related to agriculture and the mechanical arts. The conversion of this land into hard money was all too often hedged in by legal restrictions. Its value was therefore limited. The University of Maryland sold its 210,000 acres from the Morrill Act for a paltry $112,504.00. The land grant was of some assistance, but its value was limited by the urgency of need, political pressure, and, on occasion, by dishonesty on the part of trustees.

Among the important factors which encouraged the founding of collegiate institutions were the needs of educational facilities at hand as the frontier moved west, the recognition of the inviolability of endowments and trustee control as determined by the famous Dartmouth College case of 1819, and the initiative of church groups.

Many of the institutions began as academies, as had the University of Pennsylvania a hundred years before. They assumed instruction at the collegiate level later, and the two departments, secondary and degree-granting, went hand in hand for many years. Service as preparatory schools was essential in many parts of the country until public responsibility for secondary education became firmly established. Enrollment figures of the day and institutional statistics of all sorts often include the total institutional picture, not just that at the collegiate level.

For nearly a century after the Revolution the curriculum remained basically what it had been for the preceding one hundred and fifty years. It was textbook study and class recitation, with regurgitation of the book in most cases, heavily classical, moralistic, and pedantic. The University of Pennsylvania, led by Franklin, had tried to break out of the mold, but failed. Experiments at William and Mary and at the University of Virginia were short-lived. There were modest innovations toward the middle of the nineteenth century, as chemistry, physics, botany, history, and even modern languages received some attention, but the main emphasis continued to be classical. Science was admitted toward mid-century at Harvard and Yale, but only through the backdoors by establishment of the Lawrence and Sheffield scientific schools. Law and medicine appeared as separate studies, often in separate institutions. It is a dull, dreary picture, much as though the scholasticism of the Middle Ages had somehow hurdled the Renaissance and settled comfortably in the New World under a few new headings. As a young man teaching mathematics and interested in chemistry, Charles W. Eliot chafed at the traditionalism of Harvard. He estimated that the bright college student of the period before the Civil War could comfortably handle all academic requirements in four hours daily, of which three would be class attendance. A dull scholar might need an hour or two more. But the only relief from this set pattern was a course, traditional at most colleges and usually taught by the president, often called moral philosophy. It was at least a respite from ancient languages and mathematics and might include some rudimentary instruction in science as well as heavy doses of ethics and religion. In any case it was given by lecture, dealt with the modern world, and required some reasoning on the part of the students.

The historian of Rutgers University wrote of this early nineteenth century collegiate scene:

> The formal educational program prescribed by the Trustees and the faculty, intended as it was to strengthen the mental faculties and

provide the students with a highly ornamental store of knowledge,
allowed little scope for genuine intellectual inquiry nor did it afford
adequate opportunities for creative self-expression. The heavy diet
of classics, mathematics, and theologically-oriented philosophy,
didactically presented by teachers of limited pedagogical skills, was
scarcely intended to excite interest or arouse curiosity; neither did
it appear to have much relevance to everyday concerns. Occasionally,
in the colleges of that era, a daring president or an inspired group
within a faculty sought to introduce innovations in the standard
curriculum, but the heavy weight of authority and collegiate inertia
usually brought defeat to such efforts; and the old tradition remained. Because they made so little in the way of concessions to the
new society that was emerging in America after 1815, the colleges,
although they multiplied in numbers, continued to find remarkably
little demand for their services. In New Jersey, Princeton rarely had
as many as 250 students prior to 1850, while Rutgers' enrollment
never rose above 85.[3]

In the light of all this one may well wonder why any attention was
given to the formation of libraries. Most boards of trustees and presidents
paid at least lip service to the importance of libraries, as has continued
to be the practice down to the present day; it has always been the proper
thing to do. Some leaders were candid. W. W. Hudson of the University
of Missouri, while in an acting presidential capacity, stated in an 1849
report to his board that "of course they understood that a library was of
very secondary importance in the development of the University, scientific equipment being far more important." And later President Woolsey
of Yale commented to Daniel Coit Gilman, on his resignation as the
university's librarian:

> In regard to your leaving your place my thoughts have shaped
> themselves thus: the place does not possess that importance which
> a man of active mind would naturally seek; and the college cannot,
> now or hereafter, while its circumstances remain as they are, give it
> greater prominence. With the facilities you possess . . . you can in
> all probability secure for yourself . . . a more lucrative, a more
> prominent and a more varied, as well as stirring employment. I feel
> sure that you will not long content yourself . . . in your present
> vocation, and therefore I regard it better, if you must leave, to leave
> now, better I mean for yourself . . .[4]

The other side of the coin is the dedicated zeal of a few college
presidents, boards, and faculty to build a strong library, apparently in
anticipation of broader studies and in any case as an important aid to

faculty in their teaching. The first book bought for the University of Michigan Library was the enormously expensive Audubon's *Birds*. President Tappan went to great personal effort in soliciting library funds from the citizens of Ann Arbor in the fifties. The same was true of Brown's President Francis Wayland in the 1830s. The short-lived emphasis on library support at Virginia, led by Thomas Jefferson, is another instance. The University of South Carolina stressed library development from the very first and continued to do so during most of the six decades preceding the Civil War.

All the above is overshadowed by the example of Harvard, which from the very first had not only emphasized the importance of a strong library, but maintained that interest and zeal pretty consistently for two centuries until John L. Sibley arrived on the scene in 1841 as assistant librarian (librarian in 1856) and gave it greater force. Sibley was indefatigable in building the collections, enormously resourceful in attracting gifts and had never a doubt as to the vital importance of amassing the published and written record of all events and discoveries, great or small. Sibley was primarily a collector and a conservator. He took little interest in casual readers and had no tolerance for the abuse of material or infraction of rules. He was interested in helping the serious scholar. His resignation came in 1877, just one year after the dawn of the new day for the development of libraries in the service of higher education.

But what were the libraries like? At most institutions, as the eighteenth century gave way to the nineteenth, and later as new institutions passed through their infancy, the library might be housed briefly in locked cases in a classroom or presidential office. It would soon graduate to a room of its own, but one used for other purposes as well, in the central building. And when the institution became sufficiently prosperous for separate buildings, and the collection of a size to warrant something better, it was likely to find itself occupying one large room over the chapel. An early student at Indiana University recalls

> In that one building . . . was the library, the whole of it in one small room. There were no departmental libraries. A busy member of the faculty, Professor T. A. Wylie, acted as librarian, the library being open one forenoon a week, on Saturdays, after the students had had their weekly drills in declamations, essays, orations, and debates; . . . The little library room of the time was crowded and cluttered. There was no reading room, no chairs to tempt the stu-

dents to linger and read, and stack permits to enable them to browse among the books were as unnecessary as the practice was unknown. So far as I can recall there were no periodicals to induce the interest of students in current affairs. The students went in (or a few of them did) only long enough to return a book and to take out another for a week.[5]

At the University of Delaware the library was housed in a tiny room in College Hall until the Civil War. This room also served as a guard room, reception hall, and office of the professor temporarily next in command below the president. At another time it was the faculty meeting room and the president's office. At Brown the library was located in University Hall, "an apartment . . . crowded to excess, unsightly, and wholly unsuited for the purpose to which, from necessity, it was devoted." This was the situation until a combination chapel and library building was erected in 1835.

While the earliest buildings erected solely for library purposes had some space where books could be consulted, the concept of the reading room as known today, a place for general reading and study, was slow in developing. In fact the term "reading room" was first applied to quarters stocked with current journals, often attached to a tavern, and used only after payment of a fee. The demand for it arose, of course, principally from the scarcity of newspapers and their cost.

The need for reading rooms was particularly acute in the South, and continued there longer than in the North because the general impoverishment of universities following the Civil War. Powell comments on the situation as follows:

> The provision of such general reading materials as newspapers, periodicals and current books was so late in coming that special facilities for this purpose were established at six universities before their general libraries assumed the responsibility. Perhaps it should be recorded here that the first wave of student criticism against libraries was directed at their neglect to provide these general reading materials—materials not required in the preparation of daily assignments. This led to the establishment of reading rooms, many of them independent of the library, but some closely related to it. Most of them were administered by students. In examining the records of these reading rooms, one should remember two facts which appear significant; their book collections were provided at a time when university funds were low, and they prospered in institutions where society libraries had not become important.[6]

It was the University of South Carolina that led the way with the first building to be planned for and solely devoted to library purposes (1840). It was in every way a fine building which avoided mistakes made by Harvard (1841), Yale (1846), Williams (1846), Amherst (1853), and others. A number of these early libraries were built without provision for heat, and with little if any thought to light; they were plagued with dampness and structural faults.

To match the provision of quarters for these libraries, the collections were distressingly small and generally ill suited to student needs or interests. At mid-century only Harvard could claim a college library of more than fifty thousand volumes; Yale, Georgetown, and Brown had collections in the low twenty thousands, not counting the student society libraries. These were the big ones; Columbia followed with twelve thousand, five hundred and Princeton with nine thousand.

There were two exceptions in the South. That admirable institution which is now the University of South Carolina was approaching the twenty-thousand-volume mark when war cut it off; more importantly its scholarly collection was carefully selected with much history, literature, travel, and science as well as the customary theology, classics, and antiquities. The University of Virginia got off to a marvelous start, thanks to the absorbing interest of the aged Thomas Jefferson, but this impetus vanished when he died.

To quote a perceptive study of "College Libraries in the Mid-Nineteenth Century,"

> Eighteen college libraries in the states of North Carolina, Georgia, Alabama, Mississippi, Louisiana and Tennessee averaged 3,140 volumes. Five Kentucky institutions had an average of 5,100 volumes each; and seven in Ohio 2,957. Transylvania University had 12,000, Kenyon and Western Reserve 4,500, Indiana University 5,000, and the University of Missouri 675 . . . Excluding the University of Pennsylvania, seven Pennsylvania institutions averaged 2,839 . . . Georgetown College had 25,000 volumes and St. Mary's College, Baltimore 12,000; but these were exceptionally large collections; the 2,500 volumes at Delaware College, Newark, Del. and at St. James College, Hagerstown, Md. were more typical of this section of the country.[7]

Despite the enormous destruction of property in the South wrought in the Civil War, only two college libraries were destroyed or completely dispersed (at the Universities of Alabama and Louisiana). The principal loss was of book collections in private hands, many of which would presumably have come to the institutions later.

If these nineteenth-century libraries were weak in other respects, they more than matched modern ones in the length and explicitness of the regulations governing their use. The Statutes and Laws of Harvard College of 1854 contain seventy-three paragraphs of regulations governing the operation and use of the library. One of these states, "The books most suitable for the use of undergraduates shall be separated from the rest, and kept in the librarian's room, where they shall be accessible to the students and may be borrowed by them."

It was not unusual to forbid students to take volumes from the shelves: only the librarian could do this. The rule at Wesleyan (1837) reads:

> At the regular hours of opening the library, those wishing to take books will not be permitted to enter the room within the counter; but will hand to the librarian a strip of paper containing his own name, together with the *number* and *letters* of the work wanted, and the book will be handed him at the counter. No unregistered book, folios or quartos, and no translation of a classical textbook can be taken from the library without special permission.

One librarian is quoted in the 1850 Jewett report to the effect that "books are sometimes lent out to be read but the practice is discountenanced at present on account of former abuse of the privilege." A unique control of period of loan was in effect at DePauw University, where the length of books determined the period of loan; a two-hundred-page book could be borrowed for one week and a book of more than five hundred pages for three.

While the Yale University Library was, at the outbreak of the Civil War, well established and progressive in comparison with many other collegiate libraries, the regulations of the day could not be termed enlightened. For example, only juniors and seniors could borrow books. And while the library was open from eight to one and "during a considerable portion of the year it is open again in the afternoon," said juniors and seniors "shall have the liberty of drawing and consulting the books of the Library only on Mondays and Thursdays." Freshmen and sophomores were not permitted across the threshold! Present-day librarians will applaud the proviso that "no person shall without permission lend to another a book which he has borrowed," but not "no person shall . . . carry a book belonging to the Library out of the town of New Haven." Students could borrow only three volumes at a time, and for each such loan a charge of from six to twelve cents was levied, the amount depending on the size of the volume. Furthermore, before any borrowing of books a bond must be executed or a deposit of five dollars paid over. And pity the poor wretch who might be charged with injury to a volume while in his care; the regulations covering that problem go on interminably.

Another glimpse of college libraries at mid-century comes from Professor Otis Robinson, librarian of the University of Rochester:

> I have seen a college library of 25,000 volumes or more, all in most beautiful order, everything looking as if just fitted up for critical examination, where the reading room was entirely apart, and the books could be seen by students only through an opening like that of a ticket office at a railroad station. . . . At another college, which has good claims to rank among the first in the country, a friend residing as a student, after complaining of the great difficulty of using a library by means of a catalogue and with no access to the shelves, writes that he knows it contains plenty of good books, for he got in through a window one Sunday and spent the whole day there.[8]

In contrast, the University of South Carolina *Rules* of the 1840s are basically quite modern although the language is at times quaint. The faculty had access to the library at any hour. All students could borrow and the normal limit to be withdrawn at any one time was three, but this could be exceeded under certain circumstances. Students could loan books to each other, but not to outsiders. Antiquated, but very practical was the injunction "The Librarian is strictly enjoined never to carry, or suffer to be carried, into the Library, a lighted lamp or candle, except in case of necessity."[9]

The enlightenment of the 1840s at South Carolina had been preceded by a different philosophy. In the early period students paid a two-dollar library fee. Its historian reports:

> Students were admitted by classes when sent for by the librarian, and did not enter beyond the librarian's desk. No book could be taken out unless it was covered with clean, thick paper. . . . Strictest decorum was required while books were being drawn on penalty of one month's deprivation from use of the library.[10]

These restrictions are mild compared to those required of most Italian research libraries as specified in the *Codice delle Biblioteche Italiane* (Rome, 1949), which takes 724 pages to specify just how libraries are to be operated and used. However, Italians are adept in determining which governmental regulations to observe and which may be ignored; possibly some of the same philosophy was current in our colleges with regard to these sometimes weird requirements.

Nearly all collegiate libraries were open for use only a very few hours a week until the 1850s, principally for the withdrawal of books. Consultation of materials within the library was virtually forbidden, if not by statute, by the lack of space, the lack of tables and chairs, and, in winter, the lack of heat. Carlton's article on college libraries at mid-century summarizes the picture:

> In 1850 the times at which the libraries of various New England colleges were open were as follows: Bowdoin, one hour three times a week; Colby and Wesleyan, one-half hour twice a week; Middlebury, one hour a week; Amherst and Trinity, once a week, hours not given. At Brown the hours were 10 A.M. to 2 P.M. daily; at Yale, 10 A.M. to 1 P.M. and 3 to 5 P.M. daily. . . . Similar conditions prevailed in the Middle States. The Columbia library was open twice a week from 1 to 3 P.M.; Hamilton, one hour twice a week; Colgate daily from 1:30 to 4 P.M. except Saturday; Princeton was open one hour twice a week; . . . In the South the situation was much the same except, as usual, at the progressive South Carolina College, which opened its library daily from 9 A.M. to 1 P.M. Westward the hours were even less. The library of Central College, Ky. was accessible on two afternoons in each month; that of the University of Missouri one hour every two weeks. . . . Ohio State University, Ohio Wesleyan University and Kenyon were open one hour each week. Hobart College had "no regular time of opening," but at Maryville College, Tenn. the library was "opened whenever application was made for books."[11]

When Sibley became librarian at Harvard in 1856 the laws provided that freshmen and sophmores could charge out books one hour a week; juniors and seniors, two hours a week. Since this seemed to him to be unreasonable he informally lowered the bars at other times. Similar benevolent action must have been followed at other institutions. In any case, Sibley was an organized character and he proposed extension of the hours of opening. They were increased to eight hours weekly and again in 1860 to seven hours daily, Monday to Friday, "except when the sun set earlier." Saturdays and college vacations must, Sibley insisted, be kept free for tasks, such as cataloging, which had to be done without interruption. Through the sixties, the hours were further extended.

Collegiate libraries generally had the benefit of career or professional librarians, indeed staff of any nature, only late in the nineteenth century. There were, of course, exceptions. As the largest library, Harvard was the first to have a conscientious and talented leader for a number of years in the person of William Harris, a distinguished entomologist who devoted himself to the library from 1831 to 1856. He was followed by John Langdon Sibley, who served until Justin Winsor came in 1877. Harvard owes as much to Sibley as to any of his successors. At Yale there was continuity in office from 1805. Three incumbents filled the position of librarian from that date until 1856, when Daniel Coit Gilman took office. All three devoted principal attention to professorial duties and made no great impact as librarians. For Gilman, this was the beginning of a great career in higher education, and within the limitation of support and wartime restrictions he did much for Yale in the nine years that he held that post. His successor in 1865 was Addison Van Name, who held it until 1905. Van Name emphasized the book collection and paid little attention to service to the student body. Columbia's first "professional" librarian was Beverley Robinson Betts who came in 1865 and served until Melvil Dewey's arrival in 1883. History records few if any favorable comments on Betts as a person and his years as librarian. Virginia was fortunate to have fifty years of service as librarian from William Wertenbaker, who was given the position in 1826 when in his mid-twenties. Wertenbacker held several other positions during much of this period, a necessity because of the low salary. But typical of most institutions was the youthful Longfellow's appointment at Bowdoin as librarian and professor of modern languages, with emphasis on his teaching duties. I record with pleasure the fact that Cyrus Hamlin, my grandfather, served as assistant librarian under Longfellow while a Bowdoin undergraduate. Carlton cites two instances of the practice of combining the office of librarian with that of instructor in the 1800s.

> At Amherst the bibliothecal post was held through fifty years by the following succession: the professor of Latin and Greek; the professor of rhetoric, oratory and English literature; the professor of mathematics and natural philosophy, and the professor of romance languages. At Colby the office of librarian was attached to that of the professor of modern languages from 1873 to 1892, when the entire time of the librarian was assigned to library and registrar work with a professor's salary. At Bowdoin the post was for many years associated with the professorship of modern languages.

Carlton further comments:

> The smallness of the libraries and the slight required use of them in
> connection with undergraduate instruction, combined to render un-
> necessary in all but a few instances a librarian devoting his whole
> time to the care and administration of the collection. Hence there
> arose very naturally the custom of an instructor uniting his teaching
> work with the duties of librarian. It was both an obvious and an
> economical arrangement, and does not altogether deserve the re-
> proaches that have been in later days bestowed upon it. It was no
> more incongruous in its time than the variety of subjects often taught
> by one professor. Where the dual office has been maintained long
> after both library and educational conditions call loudly for the
> whole service of a special official, a certain amount of censure is
> perhaps legitimate. But again it must be remembered that our col-
> leges throughout the greater portion of their history have led a hand
> to mouth existence, and the need of a special officer was possibly
> often fully realized but the means to fill it absolutely wanting.[12]

Virtually all the colleges printed catalogs of their library holdings at
some time before 1850. In those days when additions to collections were
few and far between, there was less concern that the list might go out of
date! The entries for each volume were very brief, often just the last name
of the author, brief title, or the cataloger's assigned equivalency, size, and
fixed location. What more was needed for collections of a few thousand
volumes? The librarian carried this information in his head and he personally handed out the books. There was no accepted system for shelving
books but most libraries were arranged in some fashion by very broad
subject or by literary form, such as poetry, sermons, etc. Division by folio,
quarto, octavo etc. was often used. One library arranged books by donors
and another by date of publication. Most printed catalogs were issued
before the mid-fifties and very few appeared after the Civil War.

The innovation which finally led to the modern form of card catalog
came at Harvard where Joseph Green Cogswell, librarian from 1821 to
1823, abandoned the traditional printed listing and put the catalog on
loose sheets filed in boxes. Thus he achieved basic flexibility. Each sheet
carried the name of a single author followed by his works. When Cogswell
left, Harvard reverted to the traditional method and printed one more
catalog (1830), then a supplement (1834). But in 1848 the growth of the
collections forced the staff to adopt a more flexible method. This time
they used cards, but kept the record away from public consultation. Only
in 1861 was the card catalog made available to the public. This was

both an author catalog and classed subject catalog in separate alphabets.

A card catalog was in existence at Yale before 1860. It was only in the 1880s that Columbia, under Dewey's leadership, went to cards. In 1876 publication of *Cutter's Rules for a Dictionary Catalogue* revolutionized the whole process of recording library materials.

As a general rule the collegiate libraries had very little regular financial support. Additions to the library came principally in the form of gifts of books. Money was available only as it came from a donor, a rare legislative appropriation, or the occasional allotment from general funds. In many cases a small library fee charged to students brought in a trickle of hard cash. All this of course went to the purchase of library material, as the salary expense was handled otherwise; far distant were the days when librarians undertook professional travel, or bought furniture and equipment!

At mid-century, Brown and Yale were the most affluent in book fund endowment. At the former institution President Francis Wayland had led a successful drive in the 1830s for twenty-five thousand dollars. Brown had another source of income, at least for a period when a fee was imposed for each book charged out, certainly no encouragement to student use of the library. The smaller the book, the smaller the fee. Thus it was ten cents for a folio, eight for a quarto, and so on down to four cents for a duodecimo! To cap this curious arrangement, from about 1828 to 1855 25 per cent of the money so collected went to the librarian, the remainder to the book fund.

By 1860 a number of small book funds at Yale totalled slightly over twenty-six thousand dollars. These produced an annual income of about fifteen hundred dollars which was all that the library normally had for books and journals. To quote the librarian, this was "a sum far from adequate to the wants of so large an institution as Yale College."

Harvard had been receiving small sums for a very long time, but in more than two centuries, by 1841, these totalled only about five thousand dollars, which produced an income of two hundred and fifty dollars. By 1877 the five thousand had grown to a capital fund of one hundred and seventy thousand, largely due to the efforts of John L. Sibley.

At the University of Michigan, in the fifties, President Tappan solicited funds for the library from the citizens of Ann Arbor and raised fifteen hundred dollars with which twelve hundred volumes were purchased. More typical was the situation at the University of Misouri, where virtually no funds were assigned for the purchase of books for the first ten years of its existence. Then in 1849 the library was allotted $1,250.00. Later it received very small sums from the sale of public lands; this had brought in only $2,666.77 by 1855. At Indiana University the first recorded library appropriation was seventy-five dollars in 1834, six years after its founding as Indiana College.

Like Brown, Dartmouth at one period charged students according to their use of the library. History records, "The system of library charges had become so odious . . . that it was common pastime to abuse the books by throwing them down stairs, and by other indignities . . ."

The University of South Carolina was virtually unique in having the regular support of the state legislature. Before the institution opened its doors in 1805, the state legislature permitted the expenditure for books and apparatus of funds earlier allocated for salaries of the faculty. It directed that these funds be made available until such time as the salaries should commence. About three thousand dollars was spent for library material before the college opened its doors.

Most colleges charged a library fee in the 1800s. At mid-century this seemed to vary from a low of one dollar for the year to the high of five dollars at the University of Georgia in the seventies.

An extraordinary ruling is that of the trustees of Indiana University in 1837: The librarian "shall exact from students for the use of the library fifty cents per session; or if the student shall wish to take out a single volume, he may have that privilege by paying for it in proportion to the size of the volume, and the time for which he has its use."[13]

Library fees were generally applied just to the purchase of books and journals. One suspects that portions were sometimes borrowed for other pressing collegiate needs. When queried for the 1850 report on libraries, prepared by Jewett, a number of institutions claimed average expenditures of two to six hundred dollars. These are all estimates, in round figures, and probably on the high side.

Generalizations on the nature of the collections are difficult because only a few analyses of them have been made. Obviously the collections were mostly small and therefore offered little choice. Since the college relied heavily on gifts of books, the quality must have been questionable much of the time, just as the same source is questionable today. The frequent lack of any annual budget for books and journals precluded the purchase of much modern literature. There was very little attempt to buy journals. An analysis of the early University of Delaware library shows twenty seven volumes in English literature and fifty four in history as contrasted with forty eight in Latin authors, fifty eight in philology and rhetoric, fifty two in theology and so forth. There was a conspicuous lack of American and foreign authors who had written within the past thirty years.

On occasion an institutional library would achieve distinction because of some very unusual bulk purchase or the gift of an important personal library. Thomas Jefferson's selection for his university is an example of this. President Tappan of the University of Michigan went to Europe in 1853 and bought nearly a thousand volumes: from what is known of his educational philosophy these must have included much of the best in science, history, and belles lettres. These selections were in addition to the nearly four thousand volumes purchased for Michigan by Asa Gray, the noted botanist, just a few years before.

President Caldwell of the University of North Carolina was authorized to spend six thousand dollars on books while in Europe in 1824, but actually used only half that sum for 979 volumes. This was the only significant purchase in the first sixty years of the life of that university. The University of South Carolina and Harvard were of course notable exceptions: the former had funds regularly from the start and Harvard's current book selection picked up enormously after the building of Gore Hall in 1841.

In the early years of most institutions such book selection as was done was in the hands of a committee of the trustees. This responsibility was usually passed on to a committee of the faculty in relatively few years. Neither the president nor the librarian participated in book selection except as members of that committee. These grave gentlemen were more concerned with the traditional subjects and authors, and were all too often uninterested in the contemporary authors emerging into greatness and in the record of stirring events of their own time.

Patently, not all the tradition in the world could place blinders on young eyes to keep them from seeing, and taking interest in, the problems of the world around them. Could the orations of Cicero claim exclusive attention when the halls of Congress reverberated with eloquence on the national bank, nullification, restrictive tariffs, and slavery? Could the Latin poets completely divorce students from Scott and Irving, from Byron, Keats, Shelley, and William Cullen Bryant? The ivory tower might have kept these young people in isolation if their days had been fully occupied with their studies; but such definitely was not the case nor were there sports, fraternities, dramatics or other special interest organizations to hold their attention. So, to fill this void there came into being the literary societies, first in the later eighteenth century at the colonial colleges and thereafter on virtually every campus soon after instruction was first offered. No record of higher education is complete without due recognition of these societies and no history of university libraries without similar consideration of the society libraries. As an historian of Dartmouth wrote of the two on that campus, "It [the library] appears to have been in both [societies] at first merely an incident to the primary objects of the association, which were literary composition, oratory and debate, but from force of circumstances it soon grew to be in both the central point of existence, and at last the only element of life."[14]

It was in these societies that much of the intellectual growth took place through the first half of the nineteenth century and well into the eighties. Some of these libraries equaled the university libraries in size and far exceeded the institutional holdings in use and in educational role. Finally, as changes in curriculum and outlook brought the decline of the societies, their libraries were, one by one, transferred to the parent institution.

Throughout the course of history, universities have educated young people as much by providing a climate of learning as by providing pure instruction. The contribution of the faculty and other resources in comparison with student reaction to fellow students varies greatly according to time, location, prevailing concepts, and other factors, but many students have learned as much from their fellows and from their environment as from the classroom. This is as true today as it was centuries ago.

Until the Civil War the literary society dominated student life. It was frequently the only recognized extracurricular activity. Since the formal educational process had little or no relation to present-day interests and needs, the students were left to their own devices to develop their interests and the innate desire to know. While these societies were primarily forensic and debating in organization they were also social fraternities where varied interests and knowledge were transmitted and where the debate of the evening bull session was as important in student development as the formal contest with a rival society. So, in almost every college two rival literary societies were born shortly after the birth of the institution itself. Their very names haunt us: Philomusarian (Harvard), Philermenian (Brown), Philomathean (Pennsylvania), Philalethean (Hanover), Philomesian (Wake Forest). One can only wince and wonder at such names as Clariosophic and Eurodelphian, Calliopean and Euphradian

(University of South Carolina). How did St. Joseph's College (Ohio) ever come to choose the name Philopedian Society, or the State University of Iowa the Zetagathian? Among the best known to history are the Linonian and the Brothers in Unity (Yale), United Fraternity and Social Friends (Dartmouth), Dialectic and Philanthropic (North Carolina), so not all were "Greek" in name and focus.

A sidelight on student attitudes is the relationship of the two societies at Dartmouth. The Society of Social Friends (1783) and the United Fraternity (1786) kept a joint library until 1799, supported by a tax on members and by donations. Then, as might be expected, tempers flared over recruiting new members, and this dissension led to separation of the libraries. This fostered such rivalry that within a year each library possessed an astounding two thousand volumes or more, more than twice the number of the combined collection before the split.[15]

It seems hardly necessary to note that in content the collections of these societies were almost entirely in English, as opposed to the Greek and Latin fare of the daily recitation. Belles lettres, particularly fiction and drama, predominated. The social sciences were well represented by history, political science, biography, travels, and voyages. The collections were scholarly and classical in tone, in that Shakespeare, Hume, Plutarch, Voltaire, Milton, Gibbon, Dryden, Malthus, and Jefferson were standard fare. Subscriptions were maintained for the popular journals and back files preserved. Virtually all had reference collections of encyclopedias, dictionaries, and related tools. The most popular authors prior to 1850 were Sir Walter Scott, James Fenimore Cooper, and Lord Byron. Only the natural sciences seem to have received scant attention on most campuses. The members of these societies taxed themselves heavily to support their collections, at least in the early nineteenth century. Furthermore, the libraries were quite freely available, normally to members of rival societies, often to all students and faculty, and sometimes even more widely to alumni and townspeople. If the hours during which books could be drawn and the number to any one person were limited, these restrictions were in keeping with the tempo of the day. Fines were levied for late return. There were the same problems of theft, mutilation, lack of care, etc. that have plagued all libraries since the beginning of time.

I happen to own the manuscript of a report written in 1832 by my grandfather, Cyrus Hamlin, while president of the Peucinean Society, one of the two literary organizations at Bowdoin College. The problems discussed here are believed to be typical:

The Society is in debt for books purchased on the strength of subscriptions which will doubtless all be paid but delay has embarassed us and injured our credit. There are now due to the Treasurer about $160.00 yet we cannot collect money enough to pay for a desk to keep our records in or for the wood and oil burnt at our anniversary. During the past year but little more than two hundred dollars have been contributed to the Library while in order to maintain the spirit of those who have gone before us we should have contributed more than four hundred.

The student who was largely dependent on these association libraries of the nineteenth century had certain advantages over his successors in later ages. For one thing, books, students, and indeed librarians were mostly sheltered under the same roof. Meetings were held in the room that housed the collection. Therefore, the student was in close physical contact with the books and could not help knowing what was available, and only with difficulty could he avoid being seduced into some extracurricular reading. Then too, they were *his* books. He and his friends selected them and paid for them. How much better, therefore, they must have seemed than the contents of some institutional bookstack. The very requirement of direct, monthly payment for the library must have been an incentive to get some return on the investment. The importance of the effect of these societies on the intellectual climate, so sterile in other respects, cannot be overemphasized. It was only as change in institutional emphasis came after the Civil War that the importance of the societies and their libraries began to decline.

At mid-century a revolution in higher education was brewing, and the Civil War helped bring into play forces which caused the rapid decline and eventual death of the societies, at least as forces in education. The natural sciences were at last recognized as important for the curriculum; graduate instruction was begun and the elective system gave students new vistas. In the next thirty years came an entirely new breed of institution—Cornell, Hopkins, Clark, Stanford, and Chicago. Eliot revolutionized studies at Harvard. This was an altogether different situation.

Indicative of the change is the record of eight northern states where the libraries of the literary societies declined in holdings from 1859 to 1876, while college libraries showed a considerable increase.

With the change in emphasis and the revolution in instruction came many new features of collegiate life. Athletics developed from mere games on the campus into organized teams for intercollegiate sport.

Students with like interests, scientific in nature, religious, academic, or whatever, got together and formed clubs, study groups, or initiated other activities. The whole concept of the role of the college library was altered so that some collections were open for use all day and a few even in the evening. Regular support was gained for the purchase of contemporary literature and for full-time staff. Regulations were liberalized and assistance to students emphasized in the seventies and eighties. The curriculum was gradually liberalized to include public speaking, which deprived the societies of one of their major justifications for existence. The literary magazines, which had been edited in some of the societies, were taken over by independent student boards. Finally, there was the burden of maintaining the library, a considerable expense to each member, which became less and less necessary as the institutional library was improved. In short, the college libraries began to provide basically the same collections, with better services than the societies could afford. The social aspects of student life were absorbed by the new Greek letter fraternities and the libraries were, one by one, taken over by the parent institutions.

While the average student made little if any use of the early nineteenth century college library, those who were highly motivated, the Thoreaus and the Emersons of that day, borrowed books regularly and were given considerable assistance. Among such students was Thomas Worcester, Harvard 1818, who left us this picture of the Harvard Library:

> Upon my return to college, after I had begun to read Swedenborg, I went to the library the second time to see if I could find any of his works. The librarian looked into the catalogue again, and found the alcove and shelves where they ought to have been; but they were not there. Then we began a thorough search. We looked through the whole library, in place and out of place, but could not find them. Then we began to think of other rooms. At that time the library was in the second story of the west end of Harvard Hall. In the east end was a large room, which for want of a proper name was called the "Museum." It was filled with rubbish, old curiosities, cast off, superseded, and obsolete philosophical apparatus, and so forth, all covered with dust. We could see no reason for hunting here, except that we had hunted everywhere else, without finding what we wanted.
>
> There was a long table in the room. Upon it, and under it, were piles of useless articles; and beyond it were shelves against the wall, where various things were stored away. On the under shelf, as far out of sight as possible, I saw some books. I told the librarian, and he went round and worked his way until he got at them, and found that

the large books were volumes of the *Arcana Coelestia.* There were also several other works of Swedenborg, all of them covered with dust. I immediately got an order from President Kirkland, giving me authority to take the books and keep them in my room; and this I did for the rest of my college life. By what means or for what purpose these *Heavenly Doctrines* were cast out of the library of Harvard College must be left to conjecture. Of the 50,000 or 60,000 volumes then belonging to the library, these were the only ones that were treated in this manner. The fact seems to represent the state of the New Church at that time.[16]

The University of Virginia had a distinguished library in 1826, thanks to the great perception and painstaking efforts of Thomas Jefferson.

He planned the library building, chose the initial collection, arranged for its purchase, classified the materials and played a large part in the selection of the first two librarians . . . Jefferson was also concerned about how the university library would be serviced. With this in mind he personally formulated the rules for its governance and supervised the cataloging of books. The library began with an appropriation of $10,000.00 and soon thereafter Jefferson ordered another $15,000.00 worth of materials from Hilliard. In addition the library subscribed to all the principal American and English reviews and owned the standard sets in law and medicine. Other innovations brought about by Jefferson included a library committee, a central location on the campus for the building, and the concept of a collection with authoritative coverage in all fields.

Unfortunately, much of the enthusiasm for such an approach to education ended with the death of Jefferson. After 1826, the library at the University of Virginia went into decline because of lack of income, attention, and interest. With such elements missing, the program was soon curtailed; and, because the initial outlay for library materials and facilities was substantial, low priority was given to further acquisitions. Even the personal library of Jefferson did not find its way to the college, for the majority of it went to creditors. Ultimately, the university did receive 6,800 volumes of this collection, but this was the last contribution of any size until 1836 when James Madison left part of his library and $1,500 in money to the library as endowment.[17]

Here is the Columbia library, described by a professor as it was in 1876, shortly before Melvil Dewey took over:

The library of the college, as I first saw it, was a very great disappointment to me. The college was already more than a hundred years old, and its library did not consist of more than twenty-five thousand volumes, few of which were rare and none of which were modern. . . . It was housed in an old tinder-box building with no conveniences for study or reading. It had nothing but a very inadequate author-catalogue; and it was adminsitered by a single person as librarian, the Rev. Beverly [*sic*] R. Betts, who crept up to the building about eleven o'clock in the morning and kept the library open for the drawing of books about one hour and a half daily. He generally seemed displeased when anyone asked for a book and positively forbidding when asked to buy one. He used to boast that the trustees appropriated fifteen hundred dollars a year to the library and that he turned back nearly half of it at the end of the period . . .[18]

More typical of college libraries is the description of the University of Delaware library, as recalled by a student fifty years later (1885):

The library occupied a room at the right of the entrance to the second story of what is now Old College. It was about fifteen feet square and about the same height with shelves on all sides reaching to the ceiling. These shelves were mainly filled with reports of the various departments of the national government. There were a few books of science and engineering, a very few of history and biography, a good collection of the Latin Classics; but an entire absence of books of literary value. These books usually contained the label "Newark College Library." As the title of "Newark College" was changed to "Delaware College" in 1843, these books were seemingly bought in the early years of the college.[19]

The 1850 survey of libraries by C. C. Jewett highlighted the situation at thirty three college libraries, those which supplied relatively full data and presumably ones that were, on the average, somewhat stronger than the other ninety three libraries covered. By piecing together the data a rough composite median library of the thirty three institutions was created by Kenneth Brough:

This fictitious library had in its combined college and society collections a total of 10,300 volumes. On the average it spent $200.00 for books and added 200 volumes annually. All students could use the library, but they had relatively little opportunity to do so since it was open only twice a week, one hour each time.

Small and undernourished as this fictitious library may appear, probably the great majority of the college libraries of the time were not its equal. Even if one accepts at face value the estimates of size and support made by the college officials, he must still reckon with

the fact that the 33 institutions here considered include a dispropor-
tionate share of the stronger colleges of the period.[20]

Another "composite" was furnished by James Hulme Canfield, the
former president of the University of Nebraska and of Ohio State University, who turned librarian by taking that title at Columbia. As a former
university president his 1902 statement has special impact:

> The changes which have come in all phases of college life during
> the last half-century constitute almost a revolution. But of all these
> the changes in library constituency and in library management are
> most notable. Fifty years ago the college library was almost an aside
> in education. Indeed, it was like the sentence which we enclose in
> brackets: to be read in a low tone, or to be slurred over hastily, or
> even to be entirely omitted without making any serious change in the
> sense. With rare exceptions, the position of the librarian was a haven
> for the incompetent or the decrepit. The appropriations for mainte-
> nance were pitifully meager. The expenditures for expansion were
> even less worthy. The efficiency, or the inefficiency, was, naturally,
> quite proportionate.[21]

Canfield might well have referred to these changes as all having
come, not in "the last half century," but the last twenty-five years, for
1876 brought dramatic events which radically altered the concept of the
library as well as the university which it must serve.

CHAPTER 3

Emergence of the Research Library, 1876–1920

The year 1876 will always be remembered for the great Philadelphia Centennial Exposition and the celebration of the country's hundredth birthday. Otherwise it featured less savory events such as the great Yellow Fever epidemic, the last of the President Grant scandals, the troublesome Hayes-Tilden presidential election, Custer's disaster at Little Big Horn, and the shock of Huxley's lectures on the theory of evolution. Despite this there was abroad a great spirit of optimism, a sense of destiny. Education at all levels was receiving critical comment with a view to expansion and improvement. In short, this was a time to do things, a time to act. And act the few librarians of the country did. This year of 1876 was their annus mirabilis, for it brought a truly remarkable series of events that were to transform library service in the United States and later throughout the world. The most important of these are: the birth of the American Library Association, which provided librarians with an organization through which to examine problems and find solutions cooperatively, to publish professional literature, to speak for the profession to the nation, and gradually to develop the complex activities and useful service that characterize the great modern professional associations; the birth of the *Library Journal,* the first and for many years the only journal for the publication of library news, statistics, and articles of professional merit; the launching of the Library Bureau, a commercial enterprise to manufacture equipment for libraries that endures to the present day; the publication by the Bureau of Education of *Public Libraries in the United States of America: their History, Condition, and Management,* nearly 1,300 pages of exhaustive statistics, description, and enlightened and sometimes trail-blazing articles, an extraordinary achievement for any governmental body at that or any other time; the publication of the outline of the Dewey Decimal system of classification, the most widely adopted scheme of classifying books by subject, which has had worldwide influence; publication of Cutter's *Rules for a Printed Dictionary Catalogue,* which did for librarians roughly what

45

Systema Naturae of Linnaeus had done for botanists a hundred and fifty years earlier, and, unlike Linnaeus, had immediate acceptance. Such events were not just the harbingers of Spring to the profession; it was as though all at once the crocuses, jonquils, the daffodils and dogwood had burst into bloom. And while it was indeed the year of destiny, it was not a time of revolution. Change came slowly; 1876 was the turning point.

The next half-century, roughly the period to 1920, which marks the end of World War I burdens, were years of adolescent growth for most libraries of those universities which had established firm foundations of research activity by the end of the nineteenth century. All generalizations about this period must necessarily ignore the constant birth of new universities, such as the University of California at Los Angeles, Wayne State University, Temple University, and Brandeis University, which went through the same process of birth, childhood, and growth to maturity at later periods, but at a generally accelerated speed.

Of overriding importance to university libraries were the changes in higher education. The country saw a new age dawning after the Civil War, with opportunities of great variety; it was essential that higher education turn from its classical traditions to the practicalities of present needs.

Of the major influences, first chronologically was the Morrill Act of 1862 which provided endowment for colleges to teach "agriculture and the mechanical arts," subjects certainly remote from virtually all colleges at that time. The federal government would provide thirty-thousand acres of public lands for each senator and representative then in Congress. This pump-priming had little effect in the midst of war, but it was largely responsible for the founding of new institutions and the reorientation of others in the late sixties, the seventies, and later. At first some of the instruction was purely at an elementary, vocational level. There were no textbooks for agriculture, and very few qualified instructors in either agronomy or any of the "mechanical arts." There was confusion over the very terms. Was "mechanical arts" to be construed as training of mere mechanics and technicians, or was it to include engineering in some or all its branches? Instruction was maintained at a basically "training" and vocational level for decades at some institutions; at others the level rose as fast as permitted by the paucity of adequate literature and corps of instructors. In later decades additional assistance was given by more federal legislation, notably the Hatch Act (1887), creating agricultural experiment stations, and the Second Morrill Act (1890) which provided direct appropriations to land grant institutions.

The growing industrialization of the country, greatly speeded by the needs of war, now demanded a college curriculum in tune with its needs. And the veteran, back from war and in need of education, was far too mature to accept blindly the stultifying drudgery of purely classical studies. Then too, industry made its influence felt through its pocketbook. The industrial barons of the day became increasingly liberal in their support of higher education. In the two decades after 1862 came the large gifts to education, eventually totaling more than a million dollars each, which memorialize the names of Ezra Cornell, George Peabody, Edwin Stevens, Paul Tulane, Matthew Vassar, and Cornelius Vanderbilt. And with their money these men gave advice and instructions for its use.

The outstanding example of such support was the bequest in 1873 by Johns Hopkins of three and a half million dollars to found a university. Under its first president, Daniel Coit Gilman, it took the German university as its model and emphasized research to a degree new to the country. Its success made it a model for change elsewhere.

Research had been a virtually unknown activity in the university; scholars of the early nineteenth century, mostly historians, among them Parkman, Motley, Bancroft, and Prescott, were well-to-do amateurs with no university connections. They had to have money to form their own libraries, travel abroad, employ copyists, and pay for related services. They published with commercial firms. Now, under the influence of the German model, research became a primary university objective. The seminar and lecture took precedence over textbook and recitation. Scholarship became institutionalized. No longer need the scholar work independently at his own expense. The new university provided a center of concentration, the association of other scholars, research materials, laboratories, and means of publishing. Scholarship, rather than teaching, became the vital core of the new profession.

As usual, change came slowly. Many institutions clung stubbornly to the traditional subjects and teaching methods; others gradually adopted the new emphasis. But a few joined with Johns Hopkins as the pacesetters. Chief among them was Harvard under Charles William Eliot, where the graduate school was set up in 1872; Cornell, founded in 1865, where President Andrew White established an elective system offering courses in such unheard of subjects as sociology and American history, and which drew on nonresident experts as lecturers; Columbia, whose talented president, F.A.P. Barnard, was handicapped by a conservative board of trustees, and for a time at least the University of Minnesota under President William Watts Folwell ("I do not want to be instructed but to be informed."); finally, to an extent, the University of Michigan during the presidency of James B. Angell. The influence of these men was enormous in turning higher education, to quote one observer, "from a classically oriented and culturally elitist posture, to a more vocational, scientific and democratic stance."[1] In so doing they created the need for truly research libraries to serve research-oriented goals.

Thus the library gained increasing recognition as essential to the new academic role. The phrase "heart of the university" came into vogue, even on campuses where there was reluctance to give it the financial support essential to a strong and steady heartbeat. And with this recognition generally came rapidly increasing annual budgets for books and journals, for employment of library staffs headed by professional librarians, and for the erection of costly buildings designed not only to hold large collections but to provide good working conditions for students, scholars, and librarians.

Whereas few institutions had separate libraries before the Civil War, most of those with pretensions to university status had sizable library buildings by the end of the century. With the Pennsylvania and Cornell buildings of 1891 came recognition of the particular needs of a research library for separate book stacks, reading rooms, seminars, adequate staff quarters, and many minor functional operations. As institutions grew in size and complexity the trustees gave up virtually all supervision of library operations. This became more and more the role of faculty committees, which were in many cases basically administrative, but became advisory when working with strong and competent library directors.

The dramatic events of 1876—the Conference, the birth of the *Library Journal,* the great publications by Dewey, Cutter, and the Bureau of Education—were all of benefit to the library profession as a whole. These, combined with the needs of an entirely reoriented academic world, brought during the next forty years a revolution in university library operations, notably in the following respects: (1) a shift in emphasis from conservation and protection of the book to one of putting material to effective use in the hands of faculty and student body; (2) a recognition of responsibility to provide effective personal service in the use of the library and, more particularly, the efficient use of reference material; (3) recognition of the library's role as an educational force not only as a resource for the curriculum but also apart from it, to a very real degree independent of the curriculum; (4) the absolute necessity of classifying books according to subject and not to fixed shelf locations, which had to be changed as collections grew in size and movement became necessary; (5) the need to record each book with adequate bibliographic description and to make this information easily available to users by author, by subject, and, within limitation, by title, form, series, and other approaches appropriate to individual items; (6) acceptance of the role of departmental libraries within certain practical limits; (7) the advantages of cooperation with other libraries principally in the loan of material.

These recognitions were accompanied by a number of changes in university library operations. Hours were extended and facilities improved to provide students with a reasonably comfortable working environment from early morning to late evening at least five days a week and often for some hours on the weekend. Financing the library operation became an accepted annual responsibility of the parent institution in order to provide staff and to guarantee a regular flow of books and journals.

The selection of material for purchase became routine with the establishment of policies, often unwritten but generally known and accepted. There was slow recognition of the uses of types of literature previously considered unsuitable. Book selection was still controlled largely by faculty, but librarians began to have some influence. The literary society libraries were absorbed by the university library.

Among other practices soon accepted were those of putting books on reserve when intensive use was anticipated and of assigning books to seminar collections within the library building for the use of small groups of advanced students.

While Johns Hopkins provided the dramatic leadership in breaking with tradition and emphasizing research as a principal university responsibility, it was not Hopkins under its librarian-president, but rather Harvard and Columbia that pioneered the new role of the library. Change began first at Harvard under Justin Winsor, appointed librarian in 1877; Columbia's revolution came in 1883 when Melvil Dewey took control of that library. At Harvard it was evolution, at Columbia, revolution. Dewey moved so far and so fast with innovation both in the library and his library school that he lasted only five years. But his program was sound and, in essence, it endured.

Actually the seeds of change had already been sown at Harvard under the aging John Langdon Sibley, a great librarian but one whose principal focus was on building the collection, not its use. The library was open only during daylight hours, Monday to Friday (theoretically forty eight hours weekly most of the year) and undoubtedly would have been open longer had it not been for the university trustees' deadly fear of fire. This fear continued to rule out evening hours until 1895 when Winsor finally persuaded them to install electric lights in Gore Hall.

Henry Adams had protested restrictions against consultation of books on the shelves and as a result Sibley had set up a limited system of reserve books, a collection segregated to make its consultation convenient to groups of students studying a particular subject. Winsor took as his motto the creed that a library justified its existence by use, that the purpose of a book was to be read. Both the new elective system at Harvard and the ferment in higher education brought changes in instructional methods that encouraged students to consult authorities and compare them. The reserve book system was extended at once. Winsor also came out strongly in his first report for the practice of loans between libraries, and a sizable traffic soon developed. By 1879 Harvard students were selectively being given permits to enter the book stacks. The cumbersome delivery system was greatly improved. While Harvard was the first library to have a public card catalog of authors and subjects, once the desired entry was located by a student, he had a dreary routine to follow in getting access to the book. First he tipped the card up in the tray. Then he called a library page, who memorized title and shelf mark. The page went off to find the volume and all too often returned to report the book not available, a report as often prompted by memory failure or careless work as by the actual absence of the book. And if indeed the book was located and brought, borrowing it required an elaborate entry in a ledger and student signature. To remedy this Winsor introduced a simple call slip of a type continued in library operations for generations.

In these and other ways Winsor humanized the library in a fashion unique in research library history. Any librarian could be proud to claim Winsor's 1893 achievement, that only forty one undergraduates out of a student body of 1,449 had made no recorded use of the library in the previous year.

Winsor was fortunate to have a president who shared his views. As early as 1871 President Eliot had confirmed the centrality of the library to the university, not only physically, but for the goals of the institution. Eliot is probably the first university president to refer to the library as "the heart of the university" (1873).

Columbia, like Harvard, had both a progressive president and a bold librarian. When Dewey took command of the Columbia library in 1883 he took over a very backward operation. However, a new library building had just been erected and in F. A. P. Barnard he had the cooperation of a president who was eager to build a strong library in support of a progressive academic program. Of added assistance was a leader of the faculty, Professor John A. Burgess, an equally enlightened scholar.

Dewey moved at once with a program worthy of an operation dated a century later. The hours were extended from the pitiful ten hours weekly of the late seventies to eighty-four. Students were permitted direct access to the shelves. A modern card catalog was begun. Lectures were given on the use of the library. In setting up the first organized reference department, Dewey inaugurated a major advance in library service, one that spread slowly but surely elsewhere. Dewey's reference librarians were to "counsel and direct readers." This was a major feature of his dominant concern that the library serve its readers. Then there were the little gestures which are so important in setting tone: writing paper was made available. So was ice water! There was an area in the library where readers could talk together. A suggestion box invited comment. Dewey claimed that book orders marked "rush" would be handled so quickly that the volume would be ready for circulation one hour after receipt in the building. If Dewey really achieved his one-hour delivery he accomplished a speed record that has seldom been equaled. Presiding over all this were six attractive, intelligent, library assistants, all recent graduates of Wellesley, now known to fame as "the Wellesley half dozen." Such employment was a startling innovation in a period when young women were just beginning to win collegiate level education and to emerge from the home into responsible positions. In one respect only were Dewey and Columbia traditional: for a considerable time Dewey maintained a policy against home loans in the belief that it was more important to be able to produce any book at any one time for use in the library.

Dewey's contribution to Columbia in five short years was neatly acknowledged fifty years later by President Nicholas Murray Butler at the 1934 dedication of what was later named the Butler Library. Referring to Dewey's appointment in 1883, he stated that the Columbia library was almost precisely fifty years old in all but name. Said Butler, "It was then and only then that the present fortunate conditions began to develop and to develop rapidly."

While Harvard and Columbia are the two universities which made dramatic advances in the seventies and eighties, naturally there was progress elsewhere. Cornell opened its doors in 1868 and five years later had a respectable research collection of nearly thirty-five thousand volumes. Its first president went to Europe to buy books before students were enrolled. And it was Cornell which could claim, along with the University of Pennsylvania, the first large library building planned for research university service (1891).

Otis Robinson of Rochester was an eloquent spokesman for modern attitudes of service to students and faculty. His article on college library administration in the 1876 survey of libraries by the Bureau of Education is entirely modern in its emphasis on the role of the library, stress on student access to the shelves, home loan, reader assistance, building collections for research, and related matters. Unfortunately Robinson was a professor of mathematics as well as librarian, and had two masters to serve.

At Indiana University Lemuel Moss, appointed president in 1875, stressed at once the importance of a free library, with liberal hours. "If our students are to get the highest benefit from their studies here, they must learn how to handle books, to consult them constantly, and bring together the results of their examinations," said President Moss. He recommended to the legislature a book appropriation of ten thousand dollars and an increase in the student fee for building up the library. A full-time librarian was appointed at Indiana in 1880.

When James McCosh became president of Princeton in 1868 he expressed shock at the condition of the library. "It should be a place of activity for both professors and students . . . How could there be a truly intellectual life among the undergraduates if their reading was confined to textbooks?"[2]

President McCosh brought Frederick Vinton from the Library of Congress. The library was opened every day except Sunday. Emphasis was placed on collection building so that in a fifteen-year period the fourteen-thousand-volume collection of 1868 had quadrupled to sixty thousand.

A study published in 1893 summarizes the state of the book collections as follows: "About 8 percent of the college students of the United States have access to college libraries of more than 50,000 volumes. Another small section of them, 9 percent, have access to college libraries numbering 25,000 volumes but less than 50,000. Forty percent look to libraries with less than 25,000 volumes but more than 5,000. Forty-three percent have for their college libraries those that contain less than 5,000 volumes."³

Only in the South, crushed by the burden of the war, was there no discernible progress. There were of course many northern institutions that were decades behind in recognizing the place of the library, as there were others, particularly in the West, which lacked the financial resources to move in any responsible way. Even the Harvard Library, notable in other respects, had no reference service worthy of the name until the late 1930s.

Curiously, it was Johns Hopkins, the one institution universally recognized as the leader in turning the American university toward research, that lagged in establishing a research library. Instead it relied on the resources of other libraries in Baltimore and put its funds into departmental collections. In later years this proved a serious handicap to its teaching and research.

In fact, the departmental library, which was emphasized at Hopkins at the expense of the central library, became a source of concern on virtually every campus as institutions expanded. It has been a topic of endless debate ever since. Hopkins followed the German emphasis on the seminar library. President Gilman believed in "placing those books which are most likely to be needed, or which specially bear upon the work, within the easy reach of the worker's hand."

While there is much to be said for that philosophy, there are many drawbacks, such as the expense of duplication, restrictions on the use of the books by scholars not in the department, the needs of research that cross departmental lines, the expense of providing professional staff for each collection, to name only a few. Virtually all universities then, as in later years, provided some departmental libraries, but the emphasis varied. Early in its history the University of Illinois adopted statutes which provided for control of departmental library operations by the central library. The University of Chicago attempted, not too successfully, to have both the advantage of a central collection and departmental ease of access by grouping its major collections around the central library. Virtually all institutions provided for some seminar collections in central library buildings erected between 1890 and 1930. And so it went, some one way, some another, with endless discussion in faculty library committees. A later chapter deals with the topic in detail.

With the creation of the American Library Association came not only steady consultation of librarians on professional problems, but cooperation in various important ways. The very first issue of the *Library Journal,* that of September 30, 1876, promotes "the lending of books to one another by libraries." This gradually grew into the practice of interlibrary loan which now involves literally millions of transactions annually by academic and public libraries. Also from the 1870s date the first attempts of major libraries in urban settings to reach agreements on purchasing policy so as not to compete, particularly in acquiring expensive materials. Harvard reached such understandings with the Boston Public Library, Columbia with the Astor and Lenox libraries; there were many others. Later the practice became regional, as witness agreements by the University of Texas with Louisiana State University, Baylor, and Tulane. Finally, of course, such cooperation became national with the Farmington Plan of the late 1940s.

Well before World War I university administrators came to recognize the need for professional leadership for academic libraries. In *Scholar's Workshop,* which focused principally on Chicago, Columbia, Harvard, and Yale, Kenneth Brough states:

> By the turn of the century it had become obvious that the chief librarian of a great university must possess an unusual combination of abilities in order to meet the responsibilities of his position successfully. He must have a wide knowledge of books, and he must also understand their worth and effective use in the program of instruction and research. He must have a grasp of established principles of library management and at the same time be able to stimulate and direct innovations to meet new demands. He must combine the predilections of the scholar with the competencies of the administrator and the businessman. He must be a promoter skilful in furthering his plans for the advancement of library service . . .[4]

Few if any universities could claim success in meeting the above requirement for selection of librarians; necessarily, emphasis was placed either on proven scholarship or professional background. The latter generally meant a degree or certificate from a library school in addition to the undergraduate degree. As noted, Dewey had established the first library school at Columbia in 1887 and moved it two years later to the New York State Library. This was followed by the school at Pratt in 1890, then Drexel, Armour (soon to move to the University of Illinois) in 1892, and others.

At some universities principal importance was attached to strictly professional background in the selection of the library director. This was the case at Texas, Indiana, Illinois, and California at Berkeley. At other institutions, notably Chicago and Columbia, the emphasis was on scholarship, on solid achievement in a subject field. However, not all the administrators with basically "professional" background had library school degrees. As late as November, 1945, I was present at an incident which bore witness to this. Seated at a table were the library directors of Princeton, M.I.T., the University of Pennsylvania, Rutgers, Rice Institute, and one or two other leading institutions. Along came Gilbert Doane, director of the University of Wisconsin Library. Said he, with a smile, "May a mere professional librarian sit with you distinguished gentlemen?" There was hearty laughter for, indeed, none at the table had library school degrees although all were highly respected by the library world as well as in scholarly circles generally.

The secondary roles were largely in the hands of women. There was acceptance of the importance of special training for librarianship—and *training* was emphasized at the expense of theory far too long—coinciding with some lowering of the bars prejudicial to the higher education of women and their employment in academic roles other than the traditional one as wielder of the ferrule in rural schools. Some of these women made notable contributions as heads of library schools through publication and committee work. Others, less known to fame, gave their working lives to emerging university libraries and, as directors, set them well on their way to becoming respectable research libraries. A very few of these people received local recognition, among them Katharine Lucinda Sharp at Illinois, Olive Jones at Ohio State, and Eliza Skinner at West Virginia. At Oregon State University the students demanded that their long-time and beloved librarian, Ida Angeline Kidder, who died in February, 1920, lie in state in the new library building with honor guard. Classes were dismissed for three hours on the day of the funeral, and the casket was borne away, not in a hearse, but on the shoulders of grateful youngsters.

While a few women achieved recognition, the position of director was usually reserved for men. In these early days the outstanding contributions came principally from those whose names are closely associated with public library growth. A leader among these was, of course, Melvil Dewey, primarily an educator, whose many contributions are noted elsewhere in this work. Others of nearly equal status in library leadership during the last decades of the nineteenth century are Richard Rogers Bowker, Charles Ammi Cutter, and William Frederick Poole, whose great index to periodical literature was begun while he was a student librarian at Yale. There were a number of leaders in library education besides Dewey; of them Katharine Sharp, founder of the school at Armour, is most closely connected with university developments. The most notable leader of a university library was Justin Winsor, librarian of Harvard from 1877 to 1897—scholar, innovator, national leader in professional concerns, and builder of that university library. Similar contributions were made by Reuben Guild, librarian of Brown from 1848 to 1893, a leader in organizing the 1853 conference, active in that of 1876, and a member of the council at the first International Conference of Librarians held in London in 1877. His biographical sketch in the *Dictionary of American Library Biography* ends: "Reuben A. Guild's accomplishments were many and substantial, although no single thing he did constitutes a monumental achievement. He was instrumental in early library cooperative efforts, he was active and influential in community affairs, he wrote and edited many useful works, and he helped to build and organize the Library of one of America's leading universities during a critical time in its growth."

Even the largest libraries of the early twentieth century were relatively simple organizations of a few departments, supervised in most, if not all, respects by a chief librarian who had despotic powers, whether or not exercised in autocratic fashion. There were relatively modern card catalogs which utilized printed cards. The books were classified, mostly by Dewey. Stack access was liberally granted only to the smaller collections; it was strictly limited to faculty, or to graduate students and faculty, at the largest libraries. Mutilation and theft or unauthorized borrowing were problems but not recognized as sufficiently serious to require guards. With few exceptions buildings were simple affairs consisting of a main reading room which housed the ready-reference collection, multiple-tier book stack, one or two supplementary reading rooms for reserves and for periodicals, staff work areas, and the space necessary for card catalog, delivery desk, and similar minor essentials. There were generally a few seminar rooms and faculty studies but no rare book rooms. Most but not all libraries provided modern reference service, often a printed guide to use of the library for free distribution, and usually a course in the use of the library or some orientation lecture arrangements for incoming students. The buildings were open until relatively late in the evening, during the day on Saturdays, and frequently at some time on Sunday afternoon. One reflects with nostalgia on its simplicity. Yet the hours of staff labor were long, the pay pitiful for all except the boss, the responsibilities just as real and pressing as fifty years later. Certainly the university library of that day, however ivy covered, was no Eden for the staff.

A precise picture of the turn-of-the-century university library is given by the University of Illinois's 1907 *Handbook of the Library,* one of the early student guides. According to it, the library contained 87,136 bound volumes and 11,421 pamphlets. Hours were 7:50 A.M. to 10 P.M., Sunday 2–6. Summer session was shorter, 8–12; 1:30–4; 7–9. There were fifteen departmental collections. Home loans were for two weeks and fines two cents a day. There were special collections of reference works and books on reserve; the latter circulated only during periods when the library was closed.

The book stack was open to faculty, graduate students, and seniors. Others had access if sponsored by a faculty member. There was a two-credit course on the use of the library. An effort was made to encourage noncurricular reading by providing a table of books "covering a variety of interesting and popular subjects," also a new-book shelf. And note this: "Interesting articles in current periodicals are called to the attention of readers by noting them on the blackboard in the east reading room." The *Handbook* is noteworthy for a number of other features such as the history of the library, the classification scheme, lists of periodicals, principal reference books, description of other local libraries, and other information useful for a conscientious student. Here indeed was a library well organized for service although lacking the depth of a research collection. Much of the credit for the Illinois scene goes to Katharine L. Sharp, who became librarian in 1897. Her program of modernization was not as dramatic as that of Dewey at Columbia, but it was nearly as complete.

In 1876 only two institutions had libraries of more than fifty thousand volumes; by 1900 Harvard had more than doubled its collection and reported 560,000; Yale, as usual in the number two spot, had grown from 114,000 to 360,500 in the same period. As the new century dawned, Chicago had passed the three hundred-thousand-volume figure, and Columbia was about to achieve it; five other universities had libraries with more than one hundred thousand volumes.

All these figures, including that of Harvard, are pitifully small in comparison with university library requirements of a century later. But the growth by 1900 indicates serious attention had been given to library development by at least a few emerging universities; by 1920 the picture had brightened considerably. Harvard then reported more than two million volumes, Yale well over a million. Of the other institutions founded by the close of the Civil War, only Columbia and Cornell had more than a half million, but Princeton, Michigan, and California at Berkeley were pushing that mark. Authorities differ on the size of the Pennsylvania and Illinois collections; both were either slightly above or slightly below the half-million figure. Of the newer institutions, only Chicago had more than half a million. It was after 1930 that great library growth came to Indiana University, Wisconsin, Duke, Northwestern, and a number of other leading research libraries of the later twentieth century.

The universities of this period had very limited horizons and the book collections reflected that fact. The world of interest was basically western Europe and North America. The amount of publication of research interest was very limited. It was entirely different in 1976 when a library limited to two hundred thousand volumes was considered rather minimal for the needs of a liberal arts college and a million volumes by no means generous for a complex university. But around the turn of the century, collections of one hundred thousand volumes or more were very respectable for research needs. It was only after that time that the library became generally established in university planning as a major department, absolutely essential to graduate work and faculty research, which must have important budgetary support.

While student bodies increased in size gradually throughout the latter nineteenth century, they remained very small by modern standards. For the year 1900, among the largest were Michigan with 3,303, Columbia with 3,933, California at Berkeley with 2,001, and Yale with 2,517. Consider the following figures for the same year: North Carolina had 497, Oregon 200, Rutgers 194, and Iowa State 620.

By 1920 enrollments had increased dramatically. The percentage of college-age youth attending universities was on the rise and was to increase steadily until the present time. The largest state universities now had enrollments approaching ten thousand. Figures for graduate students, still small, were growing. Columbia led the nation in the production of doctors of philosophy with sixty-nine for 1920; in 1900 the figure had been twenty-one. Chicago came second with sixty-five; twenty years earlier it produced forty-three. Harvard was third with forty-nine Ph.Ds; in 1900 there were thirty-five. The 1920 production of doctors of philosophy drops from that point—Cornell had forty-five, Hopkins had thirty-one, Illinois twenty-nine, Yale twenty-eight, California at Berkeley twenty-three, Pennsylvania twenty-one, Michigan fourteen. Only a handful of other universities were producing graduates at the doctoral level.

As these universities grew in size, and in depth and range of studies, their libraries, though of very modest dimensions, were organized into departments that provided the basic services that we know today. Ahead lay a whole catalog of problems and responsibilities undreamed of at the time: knowledge stored in strange forms, responsibilities for literature in strange languages from remote lands recording advances in utterly new fields of investigation, problems of preservation of material, to name a few. Administrative problems that lay in wait included government reports, recognition of minorities, labor unions, program planning, budgeting, deterioration of paper, mutilation and theft of material on a large scale, even sabotage of catalogs and collections by dissident students. It is doubtful if a librarian of the twenties, translated suddenly to the professional literature of the seventies, would be able to read with comprehension one-half the literature or have any grasp of most of the topics. Certainly the early twenties were the dawn of a new era for the profession, an era fraught with problems but bringing great progress.

CHAPTER 4

Between Two Wars, 1920–1946

The years from 1920 to the end of World War II brought moderate growth and expansion of programs to universities and their libraries. The first decade was one of general economic growth, closing with a great boom, and institutions blossomed in this favorable climate. The next decade, famous for the Great Depression which followed the stock market crash of late 1929, was exactly the opposite. It was a bleak winter during which every major university and library suffered severe cutbacks. The country had barely recovered from this when the threat of war, then war itself, stopped virtually all forward movement in higher education.

Bleak though it was, in some respects the decade of the thirties brought to full bud a professionalism, a spirit for joint action, a sense of responsibility that blossomed into great progress when the war ended and sizable funds were in hand. If the year 1876 was the annus mirabilis for the profession as a whole, the decade of the thirties was to a degree also "mirabilis" for research librarians. It was not as spectacular, there was no instant action, but there was a fine budding and blooming as with nature in the month of May. The period saw the birth of three influential professional journals, the *Library Quarterly* (1931), the *Journal of Documentary Reproduction* (1938), and *College and Research Libraries* (1939); with these came an extraordinary flood of publication on professional problems where previously there had been only a mere trickle through the *Library Journal.* In this decade the Association of Research Libraries (1932) and the Association of College and Reference Libraries (1938) were founded. Microforms suddenly assumed their role as a major resource for scholars. Were there no other advances, these alone would mark the decade a remarkable one. As for the twenties, the period was one of physical growth but only minor professional advances.

Consider first the growth of the parent institutions: the universities emerging in the late decades of the nineteenth century, led by Gilman, Harper, Eliot, and others, had established aims for both instruction and faculty research of a practical nature to meet the needs of national and community life. But tradition was strong, particularly in the private institutions. Approved subjects such as history were gradually broadened to include eastern Europe and Asia, but largely ignored Africa, Australia, and North and South America except for the United States. Aspects of history, other than strictly political and economic, received scant attention. Graduate studies in business came to be accepted, grudgingly, in the late twenties and thirties. The state universities of the Middle West and West were becoming targets of eastern criticism for offering credit and promoting research in areas of activity which were considered demeaning to the dignity of academe.

Research and the movement into doctoral level work were slow to gain recognition. One authority held that there were only about twenty-two major universities in the United States in the period 1926–47. The definition of "major" rested on the record of turning out more than 1 percent of the nation's Ph.D's.[1]

The research interests of these institutions are naturally reflected in the support of their libraries. Expenditure figures for an earlier age lose much of their significance because of the drastic change in actual value of currency, fluctuations in foreign exchange, and other factors. However, comparisons are often illuminating. A 1944 study by Ralph Ellsworth showed that among fifty-three leading institutions, the average expenditure for books went from approximately thirty thousand dollars in 1920 to approximately seventy thousand in 1931. That was the peak year. There was then a decline to less than forty thousand dollars in 1934, rising slowly to about sixty-five thousand in 1941. Twenty of the largest universities were spending well above one hundred thousand dollars in 1929–32 (average figure) declining to approximately eighty thousand in 1935, then reaching about one hundred thousand for 1937–41. Ellsworth then summarized the expenditure situation:

> During the 1920s funds for books seemed almost unlimited, and universities acquired collections of books and journal files at an astonishing rate. But with the depression years faculties and administrators quite inevitably began to consider the results of their twenty years buying spree. If it could be said that the 1920s represented a decade of rapid and more or less unplanned (at least as far as inter-institutional programs are concerned) acquisition and that the 1930s represented a decade of more intensive evaluations, then surely the 1940s will represent a decade of tentative evaluations plus vigorous attempts to use the evaluations as a basis for defining proper acquisition policies, both for individual institutions and for groups of libraries.[2]

The pattern for library growth for the twenty-six-year period ending in 1946 is indeed curious. Appendix 2 shows that some of the presently largest libraries had barely begun to recognize the importance of collections (see the University of Washington, Ohio State, Wisconsin, Texas, and Indiana). Duke and UCLA were relative infants, but beginning to put on weight. The larger, established libraries more than doubled in size, and several tripled, give or take a few thousand volumes (Michigan, California at Berkeley), and Illinois increased fivefold. It was only as this period was drawing to a close that Fremont Rider, in his *Scholar and the Future of the Research Library* (1944), startled the profession with his prophecies, in the tradition of Jeremiah, of the results, generations hence, of such growth. His tables showed that even the largest libraries approximately doubled in size every sixteen years and his graphs portraying the results of such increase over several generations were indeed sobering. But these problems were easy to shrug off in the wartime days of lean support.

However, statistics are wearisome and paint only part of the picture. Let me put them aside and speak from my own experience as a student assistant, then a staff member of the Harvard College Library, 1931–38.

Quite bluntly, there was very little sign of administration. Alfred Potter, the librarian, with whom I worked closely for four years, devoted virtually all of his time to selection from catalogs of secondhand books and in examination of incoming material. Under him were four assistant librarians, none of whom I ever saw together as a group, and very, very seldom did any two confer. Thomas Franklin Currier, a gifted cataloger, ran that department. Walter Briggs presided over circulation and the stacks, doubled as reference librarian, and always had time after lunch for more than an hour with the *Boston Evening Transcript.* George Parker Winship, in charge of rare books, was most conspicuous by virtually complete absence. Clarence Walton, young and aggressive, was apparently in some disfavor or disgrace, and relegated to running the university archives. Finally there was Robert Blake, part-time director, part-time professor of Byzantine history, who occasionally conferred with Potter but spent most of his time on teaching and research. When I achieved some minor administrative responsibility and permission or funds were needed I would approach Mr. Potter for approval. The invariable response was, "It's all right with me but what does Robert say?" Trot, trot down the corridor to Mr. Blake. Query: "Arthur, have you spoken to Alfred?" Reply: "Yes, and he says it's all right with him if it's all right with you." I do not recall ever having been turned down. That was administration in the leading university library in the 1930s.

Harvard was at that time unusually fortunate in having a great building adequate for all needs, a considerable endowment in book funds, and a well-organized, competent staff, the legacy of William Coolidge Lane and Archibald Cary Coolidge, librarian and director respectively, both of whom had retired in 1928. It was running partly on momentum. This is not to say that problems had not accumulated for Keyes Metcalf's talents to solve when he became director in 1937.

Indicative of the attitude toward the library of at least a few universities is the record at Tulane, which had had a graduate school a good many years prior to 1937. At that time, according to the university's historian, "The libraries were weak and fragmented" and organized in six major units. "These had a total of some 239,000 volumes excluding pamphlets. This fragmentation was administratively indefensible, but before it could be corrected there had to be constructed a central building large enough to accommodate the proposed united libraries."[3] Constructive action began in 1938 when a university committee on libraries was appointed. The budgets for libraries were consolidated into one. There was agreement on the amalgamation of the Newcomb and Tilton libraries. The Howard Memorial Library, an independent reference library, agreed to merge its excellent reference collections if an adequate building were erected. With its holdings would also come the annual endowment income of twenty-five thousand dollars. The new building was planned and erected by 1941, in the nick of time, just before defense restrictions were instituted.

By the early thirties most of the major universities had built large central libraries, some of which still serve that function, but with additions. Complete administrative responsibility rested with the director, whose organization was separate departments for ordering or acquisitions, cataloging, and circulation-reference (sometimes together, sometimes separate). Staff for rare book collections was slow in coming, a few in the late thirties, more after 1945. The director usually had a principal assistant, seldom honored with the title of assistant or associate librarian. Governance was autocratic, usually benevolent, possibly harsh in some cases. Book selection came principally from the faculty. There were few if any procedure manuals or statements of policy except with regard to cataloging. Service to students and faculty was largely passive, though some libraries had aggressive reference departments. Budgeting was a simple matter of applying for a few new positions, more book funds, and similar needs, but all was done on a few forms with none of the complexity that was to come later, unless state authority was involved. It was a pleasant world in which virtually all real progress depended on the imagination, talent, and force of the director.

The large universities were beginning to acquire browsing rooms to encourage extracurricular reading interests. A few had their own binderies, photostat services, and so forth. All had a minor staff member in charge of reserve book operations, run mostly with student help. It was a simple existence untroubled by staff classification and pay plans, zero budgeting, technical apparatus more complicated than typewriters and microfilm readers, worries about deterioration of materials, and a host of other problems that were to crop up in the next two decades.

A more authoritative critic of the period than the writer is Louis Round Wilson, dean of Chicago's Graduate Library School and recognized unofficially as one of the two or three leaders in the research library field. In his summary of major developments in the university library field in the 1930s, he says nothing about its being a pleasant world, but to him it was a productive period:

> In spite of the fact that the period was one of profound financial depression, of slashed maintenance budgets, and of painful readjustments, it was none the less one in which the erection of library buildings, the provision of gifts for library purposes, and the development of the Friends of the Library movement were unusually noteworthy.[4]

Wilson went on to list some notable university library buildings. There were quite a number in the two-decade period, such as Michigan (1920), Minnesota (1924), Washington (1926), Duke (1927), Illinois and North Carolina (1929), Cincinnati (1930), Yale and Rochester (1932), Columbia (1934) and Oregon (1937). Design was standardized, treatment determined by the campus style.

From the vantage of the seventies the designs seem sterile, all following the same questionable pattern and varying only as campus architectural style required variety of exterior treatment. And despite the enthusiasm of Wilson's statement not a few large universities stumbled through these decades with buildings grossly inadequate either to house their book collections or to seat their students. Depression, then war dictated postponement until the late forties.

Wilson was particularly pleased with "the considerable extension of the Friends of the Library movement begun at Harvard, Yale, and Columbia in the 1920s. Chicago, Princeton, North Carolina, Duke, New York University, Johns Hopkins. . . . and other universities and colleges increased the total organization of this character from three to fifty during the ten year period. Their development is significant not only on account of the contributions which they have already made to the libraries concerned, but because of the recognition which they give to the functions of the library in the field of higher education."

A third development of special interest to Wilson was that of library surveys, but these were just beginning, under his leadership, in the period before the war and belong properly to the next chapter.

Another topic of importance in his eyes was library cooperation. He was justly proud of what had been accomplished in North Carolina by Harvie Branscomb, director of the Duke Library, and Robert Downs, director at the University of North Carolina, a post Wilson held for many years before going to Chicago. It was during this period that the several colleges in Nashville joined forces to build the Joint Universities Library. Another type of cooperation was that imposed by law in Oregon and Georgia, merging the libraries of the various state institutions of higher education in one system of library administration. Among other types of cooperation discussed at length in the Wilson survey are document centers (of slight interest today), union catalogs (a notable movement discussed in a later chapter), cooperative cataloging, and the publication of a number of union lists (serials, newspapers, manuscripts, etc. which demanded unselfish labor in hundreds of depositories). To quote him once more, "Possibly the most rapid and spectacular development of the decade took place in the field of the photographic reproduction of library materials, especially reproduction on film." This was indeed "spectacular." The birth and rapid acceptance of microforms were to revolutionize the building of library collections in the fifties and sixties.

One more area of major advance was the professional organizations. The Association of Research Libraries brought together the leaders of the two-score largest research libraries, and the Association of College and Reference Libraries attracted the talent of a large membership. Both got off to a slow start. One might say that their infant years were unproductive but twenty years of growth for them, as for members of the human race, brought great strength. The decade also saw the birth of the three library journals previously mentioned. Wilson closed his summary with paragraphs on the Library of Congress and other federal agencies, and with some prospects for other developments in the years ahead.

What Wilson did not cover, for obvious reasons, was the leadership that emerged in the period between the wars. There were giants. Wilson himself, of course, the builder of the library of the University of North Carolina, the great dean of Chicago's Graduate Library School, influential in all scholarly and philanthropic circles, a productive innovator, a wise counselor whose guidance was sought by many institutions.

Probably senior to all in the esteem of most librarians of that period was William Warner Bishop, director of the University of Michigan Library from 1915 to 1941. He was a prolific author, greatly respected by educational leaders, extremely influential in foundation circles, and more active than any other librarian in international professional developments. He was indeed "our first international librarian."

While Bishop suggested the elegance of a Victorian gentleman, his contemporary, Charles Harvey Brown, tall, rangy, forthright to a fault, typified his adopted state where he was the director of the Iowa State University Library. Probably more than anyone else of this period, Brown was the leader in sundry professional circles, local, state, and national. He was a founder of the Association of Research Libraries and of the Association of College and Reference Libraries, a president of ALA, an inspiring teacher, and, like Wilson and Bishop, much sought out by other institutions as a consultant.

Among other leaders of notable accomplishment are James Thayer Gerould, librarian of Princeton from 1920 to 1938 and particularly distinguished for his contributions to bibliography, and Theodore W. Koch, librarian of Northwestern from 1919 to 1941, author, translator, leader in book-collecting circles, and, like Bishop, a senior figure in European library circles. Frank K. Walter, librarian of the University of Minnesota from 1921 to 1943, is best known for his several books on bibliography, but his great accomplishment was the extraordinary building of his library from insignificance to national stature. Frederick Kuhlman, who launched the unique Joint Universities Library in Nashville, a bit dour, a perennial critic, was another creative leader in professional circles.

To the list of university librarians should be added a brief note of recognition of a few who, though possibly less notable on the national scene, were outstanding builders and leaders of the important libraries entrusted to their care. Among these special recognition should be given Phineas Windsor for his contributions to several university libraries, but especially the University of Illinois, to Donald Bean Gilchrist, librarian of the University of Rochester for twenty years from 1919 and a founding father of the Association of Research Libraries, to Earl Manchester, librarian of Ohio State from 1928 to 1952, to Henry B. Van Hoesen of Brown (1930–50), a farsighted innovator and authority on bibliography as well as shrewd builder of the collections, to John Edward Goodwin of UCLA (1928–43), and finally to Archibald Cary Coolidge, director of the Harvard Libraries from 1910 to 1928, a scholar brought into librarianship who contributed as much or more to the growth of that great library as did any of his distinguished predecessors.

The record would not be complete without a word about the libraries during the wartime period that closes this chapter. A summary made by Luther Evans, librarian of Congress,[5] stresses the reference services that were of importance to so many areas of national need: on the production end, for strategic intelligence; or to provide information for actual combat use, as for example in landing operations. One of the most vital needs was for maps, for which the newly created Army Map Service scoured the country. University libraries served the specialized training programs which were farmed out to virtually every major campus. There was a natural reduction in graduate study and a dropping off of normal faculty research. The need for books and journals from Europe was of great concern and a Joint Committee on Importation of seven national library associations was effective in providing the "muscle" to release much material intercepted "in the national interest" by censors based in Bermuda. A number of major research libraries sent their rare materials to rural locations or other housing considered safer from bomb attack. Otherwise, it was a case of mark time, make do with less, be patient and plan, plan, plan. Much of the revolution in several areas of library operations which followed the peace must have germinated in the impatient marking of time of the late war years. At least 1946 brought a new day, a renewal of life, to the university library.

CHAPTER 5

Expansion in the Generation Since World War II

It was the best of times, it was the worst of times for university libraries, these thirty-five years from the Fall of 1945. Never had there been expansion of such magnitude, never had funds flowed so freely, never had technology had so much to offer the profession, never had the library had such opportunity to serve advanced study and research. Yet never had there been so much ground to cover, so many users, such criticism as demands were not fully met, such threats to the very security of collections, catalogs, and building, such widespread student rebellion, such general complexity of operations.

To quote Richard de Gennaro writing in 1975, "During the last two decades academic libraries, in parallel with their parent institutions, experienced the greatest period of growth and affluence that they have ever known. The watchword was 'more'—more money, more books and journals, more staff, more space, and more technology . . . Although libraries got more of everything during those years, they still could not keep pace with the growth of new fields of research, new doctoral programs, and the increasing production of books and journals. Two decades of affluence not only failed to help solve the many problems that were brought on by the exponential growth—they exacerbated them"[1]

It was indeed a time of unparalleled growth, enormous in all respects, growth in students and faculty to be served, growth in research interests to be supported, growth in budgets, growth in administration, growth in problems and perplexities, and of course growth in sheer size. Both the university president and the library director of the prewar era would be aghast at the operations of the seventies, the tens of thousands of students, including thousands at the graduate level, the instruction given at great distances from the main campus, the plethora of new subjects taught, the complexities of employment practice, the restrictions in matters of student discipline, the governmental regulation, and the responsibilities for security. The director of that day would also be appalled at the outpouring of half a million volumes annually from the world's presses, the importance of collecting in Slavic dialects and African documents, union negotiations, staff involvement in policy determination, the increase in mutilation and theft of library collections, the difficulty of communication with senior university administrators, the strange new machines. It was indeed an entirely new ball game which left no time for reading secondhand catalogs and inspecting incoming books and journals, except as snatched during evening and weekend hours.

War is a great leveler, a disturber of the old order; its aftermath brings challenges in virtually all aspects of life, and nowhere more so than in education. In July, 1952, Ralph Ellsworth wrote:

> The modern university feels a new kind of responsibility to the social order which leads it to spread the benefits of teaching and research over every recognizable phase of the citizen's life. The university is close to the current scene and is very sensitive to it. Witness the presence of institutes and workshops for lawyers, teachers, plumbers, hotel managers, farmers, and those in other vocations in the normal life of the university, particularly those in large urban cities, or in state supported universities.[2]

With all this went considerable fragmentation of knowledge, partly because of size of student and faculty bodies, principally because advances in knowledge almost forced division; so psychology split off from philosophy, chemical engineering from chemistry, and so forth. And, virtually unheard of before 1940, there came the area studies, complete programs devoted to Russia, the Middle East, Africa, and Southeast Asia, to name only four of some prominence. Much of this growth was fueled by federal grants. For at least a brief period, organized research in universities reached an annual expenditure of approximately a billion dollars, of which over half involved contracts with the government.

Consider the enrollment picture. As shown in Appendix 5 the nearly one and a half million students in college in 1939–40 had increased to nearly ten million in 1975–76; even more dramatic is the increase in enrollment for graduate study, ten times that of the earlier date.

Several universities had become truly gargantuan: Minnesota and Ohio State both had more than fifty thousand students in the 1970s; few, however, had more than twenty thousand on a single campus. These enrollment figures should not be confused with figures for university systems with a number of campuses. For example, the University of North Carolina recently claimed an enrollment of 79,682, of which only 20,162 were studying at the main, Chapel Hill, location. Note that universities often report enrollment to include all who registered for study at any time in the fiscal year. With these figures went a similar growth in courses offered, in the research interests of the faculty, and in expansion of published research.

The growth in enrollments and interests brought changes other than making the institution larger. State legislatures, foundations, the federal government, and other sources of support and power exerted influence on university administrators. Much of this was critical. The complexities of modern life, the closer regulation, the enforcement of standards, required a host of new administrative positions and expenses. There was a general breakdown of student discipline, not just the alarming protest violence of the late sixties, but legal action of sundry kinds, for example against instructors over poor grades, suits in response to disciplinary action, or for failure to admit to study programs. Whole new departments, often headed by a vice-president, were required for personnel matters, public relations, physical plant, computer services, research and development, security, extension programs, financial development, affirmative action, and minority-handicapped special needs, as well as the traditional roles of academic dean, financial or business vice-president, counseling or personnel dean. It was not unusual for a university to have eight or ten full vice-presidents and thirty or forty associate and assistant vice-presidents, a far cry from the days when the senior administration consisted of the president, a business-financial officer, librarian, a physical plant boss, a director of athletics, and two or three personnel deans who handled admissions, discipline, and student affairs!

All this had the effect of interposing layers of administrative officers between the president and the library director. In fact at some large universities there was no contact at all, year in and year out, and it was a constant battle to keep in any sort of touch even with the academic vice-president or provost.

Along with the dramatic increase in enrollment, especially at the graduate level, went a similarly extraordinary increase in the number of research-oriented institutions. Many had been basically four-year colleges, as UCLA, Wayne State, Duke, the University of Massachusetts, and Dartmouth. Consider, for example, the extraordinary transition of the University of California at Santa Barbara. In 1944 it was made a college of the university and it remained basically a college with only a moderate library program, having a collection of 40,500 volumes (1944), until 1958 when it became a general campus of the university, a change more in name and size than in functions and graduate degrees, but only for a few years. So the library building which had been erected in 1954 when the collection numbered some eighty-five thousand volumes, had to be enlarged eight years later. Aggressive purchasing as well as swollen enrollments filled these two units and a third, a high rise, was completed in 1967. The fourth and last addition was built in 1978. As indicated by this building program, there had been liberal funding to build the collection to 1,275,000 volumes by 1978. To summarize, in less than twenty years, collections had been brought together to support a wide program of doctoral study and research.

At the same time, research institutions were being created out of whole cloth. California produced a master plan in the early sixties which called for unparalleled expansion not only of existing campuses, but also the building of two new research institutions. It was a heady experience to stand on an open plain at Irvine, California, with the only building an architect's shed, and have pointed out the locations of all the academic buildings that were soon erected. The same happened in other states. New York built a huge college and university system, some of it brand new, some of it by taking over and expanding existing private institutions. This was also happening in Texas, Illinois, Wisconsin, and elsewhere.

As universities grew in size and complexity, so was increasing attention given to mission. This led to reaching out, often hundreds of miles, to offer instruction at off-campus locations. The university extension movement actually dates from 1906 at the University of Wisconsin. It was followed in 1912 by the University of North Carolina, where the program was initiated largely through the leadership of Louis Round Wilson. The universities of North Carolina and Wisconsin did notable work from that period onward in taking university facilities, including a measure of library service, to all manner of citizen organizations; they also offered various, usually short-term, instruction in towns and villages around the state. Extension service "caught on" elsewhere, especially in the thirties, and expanded enormously after 1946. It then became the rule, rather than the exception, for major universities to be offering courses for credit at the undergraduate and often also graduate levels, at a dozen or more locations far from the central campus. The need of these centers for library service was slow in gaining recognition in budget allocations. On the one hand top administrators and faculty stoutly maintained that the off-campus instruction was every whit as good as that on campus; and almost with the same breath it was said that not so much could be expected from students in these more remote centers.

The programs were generally acclaimed as financially very successful, but many quietly judged them to be academic fraud because of their lack of basic facilities, including minimal library service. Universities such as Pennsylvania State, Indiana, Purdue, and Kentucky were responsive to needs and set up respectable library facilities at the principal centers. Some of these matured later into full-time branches of the state university. But little book service could be offered at the centers in high schools or other public buildings around the state, where instruction moved from place to place as consumer demand ebbed and flowed, characterized by one extension director "like a floating crap game." This type of instruction was strictly of "Mark Hopkins and student on a log" category, only there were two-score students on the log and few instructors of the Mark Hopkins caliber.

As a result, probably hundreds of thousands of students receive first degrees each year without exposure to real library facilities and many thousands are awarded master's degrees, particularly in business and education, with virtually no use of a research library. This is the picture at too many institutions, at least in the last thirty years.

The late thirties and early forties brought to the fore a new group of directors, a few standing head and shoulders above their colleagues, as the problems of the war years and those immediately following demanded solutions. Historical record demands at least brief recognition.

Keyes D. Metcalf dominated the leadership for much of the time and has been generally recognized as the dean of university librarians in his many years of active work following his retirement from Harvard in 1955. He was equally effective with educational and financial figures outside the library field as he was with those inside; he led in a number of bold enterprises, notably the Farmington Plan; he came to be regarded as the great authority on library buildings and as a consultant he served literally hundreds of institutions; his leadership at Harvard was bold and generally successful.

Of a different mold is Robert B. Downs, for many years the director of the University of Illinois library and dean of its library school. He is preeminently the leading scholar-administrator, equally effective and equally productive in both fields. His published studies on research collections are a principal monument, as is his leadership in academic recognition of librarians.

Innovations and boldness of leadership characterize Ralph Ellsworth of Iowa and Colorado. Like Metcalf he was much in demand as a building consultant and was as effective a spokesman outside as inside the profession. His numerous experiments with service patterns were always interesting, usually successful, sometimes not. For a period he was hated by catalogers for his strictures on traditions in that field; he was equally loved by most for his humanity and his warm personality.

The expansion and complexities of the postwar years helped to bring into prominence a score or more of leaders in university librarianship worthy to stand with Metcalf, Downs, and Ellsworth. UCLA claims two such, Lawrence Clark Powell and Robert G. Vosper, curiously similar in respect to their talent in staff leadership, collection building, and influence in the wide world of collectors and academe. Vosper became the principal American figure in international library circles. At Chicago it was Herman Fussler who as a young man became the authority on most matters involving photographic reproduction and later led in the application of automation to library operations. At Wayne State it was G. Flint Purdy, the builder of that fine library from its infancy, the national authority on library statistics and standards. At Cornell it was Stephen McCarthy, reorganizer and rebuilder of that library empire, consultant extraordinaire, and later leader in research library development as the head of the Association of Research Libraries. At Princeton it was Julian Boyd and William Dix. The former is best known as the leader of the revolution in library building planning, and as the great Jefferson authority; he was influential in many other areas of university leadership. Dix, his successor, became a principal spokesman for libraries before Congress.

Technically outside the university picture but a major contributor to its progress was Verner Clapp, deputy librarian of Congress for many years, then president of the Council on Library Resources.

Among the most distinguished leaders of the 1960–75 period are Douglas Bryant of Harvard, Richard Logsdon of Columbia, Gordon Williams of the Center for Research Libraries, Frederick Kilgour of the Ohio College Library Center and Benjamin Powell of Duke.

These are a few of the men who led as the pressures of enrollment, burgeoning book collections, and sophistication of services demanded larger libraries designed for the new age. The building boom began in the late forties and continued into the fifties; it was to reach its climax in the sixties. Listen to Jerrold Orne, the authority on library building across the land, writing in the December 1, 1971, *Library Journal:* *

> A billion dollars in five years! How many academic librarians five years ago would have believed it possible that nearly a billion dollars would be spent on academic libraries in the next five years? Incredible as it may seem, we now know it . . . Our returns indicate a grand total expenditure in library projects for the five years, beginning January 1, 1967, of $984,919,814. . . . Five years ago American academic libraries experienced the first flush of a great change in building experience. The primary impetus was the booming population expansion in colleges and universities, and the secondary, but directly related influence, was the infusion of generous federal funding specifically for construction.

It was indeed federal money which spurred the boom. The principal flow came with the Higher Education Facilities Act of 1963 which granted one-third, later 50 percent, of the construction costs of approved projects. There was also provision for loans. The grants were discontinued in 1969. Six hundred and five separate library buildings at colleges and universities were aided by the program. Other assistance to libraries was received by federal programs limited to scientific and medical developments. A few of the largest buildings erected in this period: Chicago (1970, cost $20,000,000), New York University (1970, cost $20,000,000), Indiana (1969, cost $14,900,000), Pittsburgh (1967, cost $13,400,000), Northwestern (1970, cost $12,322,000); others include Kent State, California at San Diego, Emory, Utah, Pennsylvania State, Tulane, and Georgetown, all costing over six million dollars, all erected in the five-year period.

These were central libraries. The complexities of the years brought other needs, especially to seat and to service the large undergraduate bodies. Harvard led the way with the first building designed to serve undergraduate library needs with its Lamont Library (1949). Michigan followed with its undergraduate library, unique for the flexibility of the interior, in 1958. Others were built, notably at Texas, South Carolina, Stanford, and Illinois. On two campuses, UCLA and Cornell, an old central library was adapted for principally undergraduate service when the new, great research libraries were completed.

*This is a five-year review "covering all college and university libraries completed and occupied from January 1, 1967 to December, 1971." Over 400 library building projects are listed; of these 257 are "completely new General Academic library buildings."

The demands of size, the emphasis on special services, and in some cases the requirements of donors, promoted the concept of large, special libraries. Thus, Harvard built Houghton adjacent to the main library to house its rare books. Years later, Indiana followed suit with the Lilly Library and Yale with the Beinicke. Growth of collections also brought increasing interest in combining small departmental libraries into larger units. This was particularly true of the sciences. One such notable consolidation was made at Brown, whose science library, completed in 1976, brought together two major libraries (Physical Sciences and Biological Sciences) which had years before themselves been formed of separate collections serving Mathematics, Astronomy, Physics, Chemistry, Engineering, Geology, Biology, Botany, and Psychology.

This was recognition that interdisciplinary developments in many areas of learning, but particularly in science and technology, are poorly served by scattered libraries organized according to university departments of instruction. To quote Robert Vosper, "The whole new development in the direction of the automated library systems, which arises because of the proliferation of scientific literature and the difficulties of controlling it, urges a more centralized library pattern." Judicious consolidation also makes possible better staff services, longer hours of opening, and other benefits.

Not every institution could afford such expensive buildings, and the ingenuity of library administrations was often taxed by lack of shelving on which to put the growing collections. One solution, with a number of variations, was compact storage. The standard book stack is laid out with aisles three feet wide. Reduce that to eighteen inches and store more books. Or eliminate 90 percent of the aisles altogether by putting shelving on wheels, running on a track. The range of shelving is moved by motor in some installations, by a good firm shove in others. Other compact shelving provided for books in long drawers, much like a file cabinet. Still another type, used in the Center for Research Libraries, made provision for each three-foot section of shelving to have, on either side, two eighteen-inch sections arranged on pivots so that, in effect, each aisle provided access to four normal sections.

At one time or another, many large libraries simply ran out of shelf space and had to withdraw segments of their collections, tagged as "little used," to go into compact storage, possibly in the basement of another building, sometimes in a structure erected for that purpose, on a relatively cheap site and of economical construction. Daily delivery service met the needs of the readers. The division of the book collection involved raised major problems, as did the few attempts at a comprehensive weeding of a research collection. There was no easy answer to the inevitable query, "Will it ever be needed?"

There were important shortages of more than shelving. Until the early 1970s there was an acute lack of professional librarians. The number needed was commonly placed in the tens of thousands until, all at once, it was realized that there was a surplus. Over the two decades a number of new library schools had been born. The salary picture had been a national disgrace until the late forties, but this improved greatly as the new leadership recognized its responsibility to its staff and as competition for qualified staff inevitably brought improvement. This in turn stimulated interest in the profession.

The shortage of library school graduates became a surplus as the budget stringencies of the early 1970s in all types of libraries brought an end to expansion of staff, then curtailments.

With the change in the salary picture, library staffs developed a different attitude toward their work and the governance of the library. Over the two decades from 1950, a great many staff achieved faculty rank and status, and immediately assumed a role in policy determination. Where such status was not achieved, there was often recognition of the library staff as an academic body. Virtually all university libraries had some type of collegial body by the early 1970s. This was in addition to the traditional "staff association" which included all workers in the library, and whose activity was traditionally social and recreational. The collegial body elected officers and created committees to investigate and recommend on matters of importance. On occasion it might take the director by the ear over some conflict. It demanded a role in the selection of top library administration, and in a very few cases such bodies apparently forced the resignation of the director. Such actions were unheard of before the war.

A radical departure from tradition was the growth of staff unions. These first appeared in janitorial and building maintenance work. Then clerical staffs began to gain union status. As this is written, a relatively few large professional staffs are unionized, but the trend seems to be in that direction. Unionization is sometimes as a part of the faculty, sometimes as a separate group.

Still another change in library staff is the recent recognition of the importance of the specialist in a related discipline, whether it be an expert in reprography, a bibliographer, budget expert, automation engineer, or whatever. The complexities of the modern library require many new skills.

And finally, as an adjunct to the staff, came the computer! This often maddening, sometimes miraculous machine brings grief and joy to all concerned as it performs, or utterly hashes, the duties it is given. Certainly it did not turn out to bring the easy solutions to most information storage and retrieval needs that were predicted by scientists shortly after the war. It has, however, begun to provide critical services in cataloging, in some aspects of bibliographical control, and in reference services, as is discussed in a later chapter.

And as though an independent-minded staff and an unpredictable new technology were not enough to disturb a director's sleep, there was the additional burden of a new threat to the very preservation of the collection. Enter the Vandals, not from without, but from within the sacred ivied walls of academe.

Vandalism and theft undoubtedly occurred early in university library history, but there is no evidence that they were major problems until the thirties. The name of Klas Linderfelt, librarian of the Milwaukee Public Library, elected president of the American Library Association in 1891, will not be found in the official role of presidents. He was arrested for embezzling library funds in April, 1892, and steps were taken at once by the executive board to cover so far as humanly possible. There have been isolated cases of malfeasance in the university picture, as in all walks of life, but the one which had a profound influence on library operations occurred at Harvard in 1931. There the disappearance of most material in one branch of history led to an investigation and the discovery of several thousand purloined volumes in the apartment of a junior faculty member. Restored to their proper shelves, each of the books bore, and bears to this day, a new bookplate stating: "This book was stolen from the Harvard College Library. It was later recovered. The thief was sentenced to two years at hard labor. 1932." Shortly thereafter, the marble vestibule of the Widener Library was fenced, decorously of course, so as to require everyone leaving to pass an inspection desk, where briefcases were opened and all books inspected to make sure they had been properly charged. This was the beginning of the inspection practice which spread gradually to virtually all university libraries in the late forties. To be effective, it had to involve every user, regardless of rank; many a professor fought it as demeaning but library administrators generally held the line and the practice came to be accepted as normal.

Inspection was naturally only a deterrent. And with this measure to stop large-scale theft came a distressing increase in mutilation, particularly of journals. To the unprincipled, it was a simple matter to cut or tear out the pages wanted, whether as a convenience to read at home, or to quote, or to have in one's file. Malefactors were seldom caught. Those who were so unfortunate were disciplined severely in the thirties and forties, but not after the late fifties when the whole climate of university authority changed dramatically. It became clear that the crimes of stealing, mutilating, and defacing library books, which carry fines and short prison terms in most states, are not limited to students and the young, for faculty and administrators were found equally guilty.

While sensor devices, discussed later, have been used successfully in recent years to curtail book theft, no important deterrent for mutilation has been discovered. Libraries often fall back on microfilm to preserve the text of journals which have been badly cut up. Few libraries would be so naive as to put bound copies of *Playboy* on the open shelf.

Yet another danger appeared in the seventies when prices being paid for illustrations by a certain artist in several nineteenth-century journals commonly kept on open shelves were published. As a result, thieves went, razor blades in hand, to a large number of libraries to pick up the specified illustrations. The damage was done before the alarm was broadcast.

The capstone of this distressing topic is the vandalism of the late sixties. The wave of student protest at that time took the form, on many campuses, of destruction of books and card catalogs, of arson and bombing of libraries. It was fire at Wayne State, Indiana University, New York University, California (Berkeley), SUNY at Buffalo, and Yale. It was destruction of the card catalog at Queens and the University of Illinois. It was bombing at the University of Washington and Columbia. Specialized libraries were virtually destroyed at Cornell and Stanford. Elsewhere there was defacement of the book collection, smashing of windows and of equipment, stink bombing, and sundry other destructive tactics. Fortunately, the wave was only one wave and the peril short-lived. In the whole history of culture, there are few movements to equal the shame of this senseless, wanton destruction.

As college and university librarians came to see more of each other in professional meetings, there was natural exchange of views on all manner of topics. This led to an interest in the library survey, namely a thorough examination of a library's operation by experienced colleagues from other institutions. This interest led to an offer by the American Library Association to survey university libraries officially for a fee (1936). A manual for college surveys was projected at that time but never completed.

The first university library to undergo a thorough evaluation by outside experts under ALA contract was Georgia, in 1938. Two years later, it was Indiana University, then the universities of Mississippi and of Florida. Many others followed suit, particularly in the two decades after 1950, some under ALA contract, most without that stamp of approval. Among librarians in demand because of standing in the field and quality of previous surveys were Robert Downs of Illinois, Maurice Tauber of Columbia's School of Library Service, Stephen McCarthy of Cornell and Raynard Swank of Stanford.

A principal objective of the complete survey was to describe and evaluate collections, staffs, services, and procedures, then recommend measures for improvement. Most but not all surveys were published. From the general recognition of the effectiveness of the survey there came to be increasing use of the outside expert, usually the director or principal officer of a library, to spend a few days as a consultant on a particular problem. By far the greatest use of the consultant was for building plans, but many were used for problems of collection building, cataloging, acquisition processes, automation, circulation systems, and the like.

Outside experts could help with most matters, but not with that ever-present worry, financial support. With finances, as with other aspects, the period was the best or the worst of times, depending on one's point of view. Budgets received unprecedented increases. For 1946–47, the first full year of post-hostilities operations, only a few of the largest libraries spent more than two hundred thousand dollars for library materials, including the cost of binding (see Appendix 4). Compare that with figures for 1977–78, as reported by the Association of Research Libraries, when twenty-five ARL member libraries each spent in excess of two million dollars for the same purpose!

The record shows that these libraries increased their growth dramatically; with the later budgets, however, the increase is drastically reduced by inflation, and by devaluation of the dollar in world markets. The data given in Appendix 4 are not valid for average costs because other major factors are included. However, they do indicate that the average addition in 1977–78 cost slightly less than four times as much as in 1946–47.

The cost of living index rose relatively slowly for twenty years after the war, then rapidly increased. The average price of U.S. periodicals rose from $8.66 in 1967–69 to $24.59 in 1977. The increase for U.S. trade and technical books for the same period is from $8.77 to $18.03.[3]

The postwar library director matched his predecessors in zeal for building greater and bigger collections, faced as he was by expansion of scholarly interests and publication; on the other hand he was increasingly concerned with the problems of uncontrolled growth. The publication of Fremont Rider's *The Scholar and the Future of the Research Library* pointed up dramatically what everyone knew but did not care to think about, that libraries, large and small, doubled in size in a relatively short span of time. Rider showed that span to be sixteen years. According to his formula, if the Harvard Library were to continue its past rate of growth, its 4,609,000 volumes owned in 1944 would grow to about 19,000,000 by 1977. As Appendix 3 shows, growth was somewhat less than half that figure, but even so Harvard was adding a hefty 200,000 volumes (net) annually.

The problem of growth is treated in some detail in Chapter 6. Suffice it to say that the subject dominated the thinking of this period, but it was not exactly a dark cloud. Mostly, as far as growth of collections is concerned, "this was the best of times."

Collections now included material in strange and wonderful new forms. Much of this so-called multimedia material was primarily for instructional purposes. Its importance and the problems of cataloging, storage, and care led to the development of a new specialist, the multimedia librarian, often the product of a college of education rather than of a library school. The collection and servicing are often the responsibility of a department with no administrative tie to the university library. To quote a 1977 finding of ARL, "There is general agreement that the majority of non-book media are produced for instructional purposes and do not directly support graduate and research programs."[4]

One of the new types of material, definitely part of the research collection, is oral history, a development that would have delighted John Langdon Sibley. This was indeed capturing for posterity the story of important events as seen by key participants. Oral history was the brain child of Allan Nevins and dates from 1948 when he launched the program at Columbia. It involved carefully planned tape-recorded interviews with people whose experience had bearing on some topic of importance which, it was felt, was insufficiently covered in publications. Usually the tapes were transcribed, sent to the person interviewed for editing, then retyped. Both tapes and final typed versions were retained. A little of this had been done as early as the mid-thirties when former slaves were interviewed under a federal Works Progress Administration grant. But it took a special bequest for Columbia to set the project really in motion. For well over a decade, Columbia was virtually the only institution doing systematic work in this strange new field. The importance of oral history was gradually recognized elsewhere and funds found for special investigations. A 1965 report lists eighty-nine projects, many of them minor. In 1966 an Oral History Association was formed. It had arrived! A few years later, a number of collections were made available on microfilm and microfiche, despite the very real problem of copyright, normally held by the interviewee. With this action, oral history records became widely available to scholars.

The sixties also brought into use "dial access" by which a student at any one of a score or more of locations around a campus could dial in for a particular audio program, perhaps to hear a repeat of a lecture, a symphony for a music course, or some practice in a foreign language. Later, this graduated to an audiovisual facility whereby a television-type screen would show a program, such as a dissection for biology or an experiment in physics. One of the earliest and most advanced installations was put into operation at Ohio State in 1960, which initially had 150 student listening-posts with access to eleven programs. By 1970 there were over four hundred student booths in thirty-seven different locations operational ninety-five hours per week. Successful as dial access has been on some campuses, it has been ignored by most.

Under the leadership of Metcalf, Downs, Boyd, and other leaders of the forties, a score of bold cooperative programs were planned and put into operation. The war in the West was hardly over before American research libraries were scouring Europe under official auspices for the scholarship they had been unable to get during hostilities. Several years later the Farmington Plan began to bring to one or another of the several score cooperating libraries virtually everything of reseach value published in western Europe. Other principal developments of a similar nature are the Public Law 480 program for the procurement of material principally in the Middle East, the Documents Expediting Project to improve receipt of government documents and the Universal Serials and

Book Exchange. These, along with the many projects organized in the Center for Research Libraries, are discussed in Chapter 12.

If growth was the outstanding feature of the period, networking ran it a close second. There were few if any university libraries which did not belong to four or five networks. The trend of the future was toward cooperation in all operations, but principally collection building, bibliographical control, and cataloging. There were the major, national networks and the local, working agreements. But with all this there continued to be recognition that pacts and treaties to collect and loan had their limitations. Listen to Gordon Ray, speaking at Dartmouth College in 1978:

> As collections become unmanageably large, arguments for cooperation grow stronger, but arguments for a great measure of self-sufficiency remain formidable. It has not yet been demonstrated that major reliance on interlibrary cooperative arrangements with respect to collections will save money, nor in most instances has the individual user been brought to regard large-scale interlibrary loans as anything better than an exasperating substitute for having the materials he needs immediately available for consultation on his institution's shelves.[5]

So the competition continued while cooperation flourished. And under the warm sun of greatly increased budgets, particularly in the late fifties and sixties, directors took bold steps. Thus Robert Vosper bought an entire Israeli bookstore of thirty-five thousand volumes to build up UCLA's Judaica and Hebraica. Such sweeping purchases were commonplace for the largest libraries, but not limited to them. The University of Baltimore bought the complete stock of ten thousand volumes of Peter Decker, a leading dealer in Americana, and, in 1968, Kent State swallowed with one transaction the two hundred and fifty thousand-volume holdings of another dealer. In 1970, a single Pennsylvania State University purchase involved twice that many books. As Appendix 3 conclusively shows, most libraries were by no means dependent on their neighbors' collections. The cooperation was fine, but at the same time the competition was keen.

To those of us who were young as the war ended, but old enough to hold responsible positions, the late forties were indeed years to be alive. The old rules no longer held, experimentation and change were in vogue. At the University of Pennsylvania there was a new administrative team. Violent hands were laid on traditional procedures. The book stack was opened to all students, a revolutionary action at that time for a large university in an urban setting. Dirty plaster statuary of Greek philosophers was deposited in the trash despite a contrary edict from the executive vice-president. A blazing fire was lighted in a fireplace that was still virgin at age sixty-five (it smoked badly, but the students loved it), bright paint was first applied to equally virgin walls. Nothing was sacred. The only question asked was, "Will it work?"

To those of us who are now finishing our careers as these lines are written, the scene appears to be quite different. Is this a matter of age, or are there really clouds ahead? There are those who hold that the new technology will make libraries obsolete. There are enormous obstacles to action from governmental regulation and from labor union restrictions, to name only two sources of irritation. There is no time to spend on books as such, only time it seems to plug holes, fill gaps, to administer in a sterile fashion. The best of times, the worst of times. It may indeed be, to the new leaders, as bright and challenging, for all its problems, as were the postwar years to their elders.

Part II
Aspects of Librarianship

CHAPTER 6

Building the Collection

The beginning of research collections in the United States was, historically, the "prity library" of Harvard, mentioned but not described early
in 1638, shortly before the famous bequest of his library of over four
hundred volumes by John Harvard. This was a gentleman's library, catholic in scope and distinctly modern, since over 25 percent of the books had
been published after 1630.

The history of academic book collections for the first two hundred
years is largely a dull record of all too few donations of private libraries
and of destructive fires. Libraries were not troubled with budgets, for
they had virtually no regular income, nor with acquisition policies, for
they took whatever was offered. With distressing regularity collections
were wiped out by fire.

For Harvard the principal donors of the colonial period were members of the Hollis family, Englishmen who never crossed the Atlantic but
whose interest in the Harvard Library and benefactions to it continued
throughout the seventeenth and eighteenth centuries. For Yale it was
Jeremiah Dummer, who sent more than eight hundred volumes from
London in 1714. Many were his personal gifts; others he had collected
from friends and acquaintances. These were by no means the castoffs that
characterize many modern donations, but were solid material covering
numerous fields. Dummer is credited with interesting the colonial governor, Elihu Yale, in donating a large box of books.

Of Jeremy Belcher it is often said that he did for Princeton what John
Harvard did for Harvard; he left it a valuable library of nearly five hundred volumes in 1755, only nine years after its founding. Similarly Columbia received a library of considerable importance in 1754, the year of
its charter. This gift from Joseph Murray was of his estate and library,
valued at £8,000.

There were of course other important donations to the early institu-
tions. To the College of Rhode Island, soon to change its name to Brown
University, came important gifts from John Brown in 1783 and Nicholas
Brown a decade later. William and Mary received several significant gifts

of libraries and funds for books early in its history from Henry Compton, from Gilbert Burnet, from Robert Boyle, and from Francis Nicholson. Both the books and the records of the gifts were lost in the two fires that destroyed the library in 1705 and 1859.

The list of early benefactions would not be complete without mention of the enormous contribution of Thomas Jefferson to the University of Virginia. No scene in early library history is quite so touching as the picture of that wise and good man devoting himself ceaselessly to the needs of the library, a labor which most unfortunately was partly lost when he died.

With few exceptions, collections developed very slowly for nearly a century following independence. The academic institutions of the country were still basically "undergraduate" in nature and had few pretensions to research. They continued to be satisfied with libraries formed from private donations plus a few hundred dollars assigned to book purchases, when available. Subscriptions to journals were rare. Fortunately, literary societies were active on virtually all campuses and formation of libraries of current literature had high priority with society funds and interest. As these libraries were turned over to the parent institutions in the 1880s and 1890s, they greatly strengthened the central libraries.

Occasionally an institution sought to improve its library with a buying trip abroad. President Tappan of Michigan took such a journey in 1853 and bought nearly a thousand volumes with the fifteen hundred dollars he had personally raised for the library. It is noteworthy that in his inaugural address of the previous year he had said, "We have erected vast dormitories for the night's sleep instead of creating libraries and laboratories for the day's work." President Tappan was one of the few early college presidents who insisted that there be an annual appropriation for books. Fifteen years before, Michigan had sent Asa Gray to Europe on a buying expedition. Gray had been instructed by an unusually enlightened board of trustees to emphasize "standard English works in history, biography, voyages and travels, poetry, statistics, and science." Gray was primarily interested in advancing his own knowledge of botany, certainly a worthy objective in light of his later fame in that field. So while he selected much of the science material, he left the remainder largely in the hands of George P. Putnam of the publishing firm of Wiley and Putnam. Both Gray and Putnam were in their twenties. With the five thousand dollars provided by the trustees, 3,401 volumes were purchased. Over forty-four percent of the books were history, biography, and travel. Very little of a classical nature was chosen; in fact the collection included only forty-four titles in foreign languages.

An outstanding foreign purchase was that made for the University of Vermont in 1834 by Joseph Torrey. His $8,750.00 was an amazing sum for that institution at that time. With it he bought some seven thousand volumes. Other nineteenth-century college presidents who went abroad to buy for their libraries were Joseph Caldwell for the University of North Carolina in 1824 and Andrew White of Cornell in 1868, just months before that institution opened its doors to its first students.

The Yale Library profited from two buying expeditions in Europe in the early nineteenth century, those of Benjamin Silliman in 1805 with nine thousand dollars for books and instruments, and of James Luce Kingsley in 1845 with a roughly similar sum with which "he bought about six to seven thousand volumes at an average price of less than a dollar and a half, including all shipping costs and insurance."

The year 1841 is of special significance in research library development for it was then that John Langdon Sibley was appointed assistant librarian at Harvard. Sibley soon took off on a revolutionary tack by raising the banner for collecting anything and everything that was printed as suitable for a research library. To quote his own words from an 1879 address:

> I began to beg for the Library. Appeals were made to authors for their books and pamphlets. I asked people to send whatever they had printed, whether they considered it good for anything or not. "Clear out your garrets and closets, send me their contents." And with such earnestness did I plead, that I literally had boxes and barrels sent to me, and once I received a butter-firkin. Almost always I got something precious which I had for years been trying to obtain. Even the butter-firkin contained an unexpected treasure.[1]

Sibley took justifiable pride in the fact that the Harvard Library had grown in volumes from 41,000 to 164,000 and in funds from $5,000.00 to $170,000.00 during his thirty-six years of service to it as assistant librarian and librarian. Much of this growth came from his solicitations. "I acquired the name of being a sturdy beggar," he once remarked.

Sibley held to his conviction that any record was grist for the scholar. In 1865 the Harvard Overseers proposed weeding the collection, but "found the Librarian prepared to die on that particular barricade." It was only much later that directors of other research libraries came to share his views. The concept was modified still later as the sheer volume of printing around the world forced librarians to become selective in many fields and depend more and more on cooperative collecting.

In 1850 only Harvard and Yale had book collections of more than fifty thousand volumes. The great majority of small collections, formed largely from gifts, were not tailored to the needs of the institution. However, the society libraries of the students were built to meet the reading and intellectual interests of the members and therefore contained much of the best modern literature. As these collections were gradually absorbed by the institutions in the later decades of the nineteenth century, the college library collections were immensely strengthened.

Growth continued to be slow for several decades. By 1876 only one other institution had passed the fifty thousand volume mark, even with the society libraries included in the count, and a scant thirty-four other colleges reported more than fifteen thousand, a total considered hardly exceptional for a high school library today. Collections of a few hundred unsuitable volumes were by no means unusual. But it was about this time that one institution after another faced up to the library responsibilities required of the new curricula and their emphasis on research; because of this, dramatic growth began slowly to take place.

Of the institutions claiming origins on or before 1865 and which are today distinguished for the size and value of their collections, only seven appear to have emphasized library development before 1900: Harvard and Yale of course; Columbia was, as noted, stirred to belated collection building by President Barnard and, led first by Melvil Dewey, then by George Hall Baker with the support of President Seth Low, the number of volumes in the library was increased ninefold by 1900. Particularly dramatic is the increase in acquisitions from 411 in 1883, the year that Dewey arrived at Columbia, to the 25,404 volumes added in 1899.

Michigan had had a strong start in library building from the two European buying expeditions of President Tappan and Professor Asa Gray. Support then languished despite presidential interest. In 1871 a collection of nearly ten thousand books, journals, and pamphlets, the library of Professor C. H. Rau of Heidelberg, was purchased. Even with this addition the university could report total holdings of only 27,500 volumes in 1876. Support was then regularized and increased gradually over the next twenty-five years. As the new century dawned, Michigan first officially recognized its role as a university not only to teach what was known but to expand knowledge through research. Raymond C. Davis retired in 1905 after twenty-eight years as librarian and was succeeded by Theodore C. Koch, an able leader.

Cornell, which opened its doors in 1868, emphasized library development from the beginning. It received an extraordinary gift of twenty thousand volumes from President Andrew White in 1887. To Cornell, along with Pennsylvania, goes considerable credit for erecting a large building designed for research use. This was the gift, in 1891, of Henry W. Sage along with three hundred thousand dollars for library endowment. The collection grew from 39,000 volumes to 225,000 in the twenty-four years from 1876.

At Princeton the increase was from 29,500 to 152,000 in 1900. Ernest Cushing Richardson came as librarian in 1890; his great leadership in all aspects of the library's development attracted gifts and was instrumental in winning larger appropriations.

While Pennsylvania claimed a total collection of 23,500 volumes in 1876, the nucleus was kept, eighteenth-century fashion, in locked cases in College Hall. A professor doubled as librarian and handled the circulation chores a few hours a week. Finally, in 1884, a trained, full-time librarian was employed in the person of J. G. Barnwell. An important step forward was the erection of the library building, designed for a large collection and scholarly uses, in 1891. With minor additions this was to serve the university for seventy years. Under these circumstances there was a natural increase of interest in building the book and journal holdings. By 1900 Pennsylvania had a respectable collection of 183,000 volumes.

At the dawn of the new century only one other university could claim a library of research pretensions—the newly organized University of Chicago. Official statistics show a total library of 330,000 volumes; however, this figure is based on the purchase of an entire bookstore in Berlin by President Harper in 1891, the date of founding. At the time the collection was supposed to comprise 280,000 volumes and nearly half as many pamphlets. The figures are challenged by Haynes McMullen, the historian of the library, whose research indicates that the actual receipts from the purchase were probably sixty thousand books and thirty-nine thousand dissertations. In addition Chicago had the small library of the Baptist Union Theological Seminary, which became part of the new university. During the 1890s and early 1900s the university appropriation for books varied from slightly more than ten thousand dollars to twice that sum. Growth was undoubtedly restricted by the fact that the head of the library for twenty years was given the title and authority only of associate librarian. Zella Allen Dixson was a graduate of the New York Library School and undoubtedly competent, but she suffered the handicap of that era, the wrong sex.

Two perceptive critics characterized the general situation in 1910 as follows:

> University library collections by 1910 consisted of miscellaneous gifts, books bought in support of classroom teaching, collections of research materials, and special collections. The difference in quality between the libraries was, of course, determined by the mixture of these elements. The universities with the strongest graduate programs had developed the strongest libraries, and that early start has kept almost all of those libraries ranked among the best in the country.[2]

The number of universities with major collections of research potential increased rapidly after 1900. By 1920 eleven claimed collections of a quarter million or more; by 1940 sixteen university libraries were over the half-million mark and by 1960 twenty-six had a million or more volumes. For the year 1975 no less than twenty-five had in excess of two million and seventy-seven institutions reported more than a million volumes.

At this point a word on these "volume" statistics. "Volume" has been variously interpreted at different times in history but a normal definition is that of a printed, typed, or processed work in separate covers that has been cataloged or otherwise fully prepared for use. The definition is often interpreted to exclude unbound pamphlets; it generally excludes microforms, of which today's major libraries have literally hundreds of thousands of "volumes." Further, neither the author nor many of his colleagues who are directors of libraries would claim that their figures were other than approximations. Actual count is usually based on work done many years before, possibly carelessly. Year by year the known withdrawals are subtracted and the new additions are added. Errors occur. Once in a while someone, overanxious for standing, may inflate the picture. Then there is the question of what units are involved. Consider Princeton and Rutgers, two great institutions less than twenty miles apart and close cooperators in all library matters. Princeton's library is all on one campus and largely concentrated in its central Firestone building. On the other hand Rutgers has six major campuses with large collections serving each. From the Newark campus to the Camden campus is a distance of nearly a hundred miles. Both Newark and Camden have departmental as well as central libraries. It is clear that in effectiveness for research purposes the total of 1,829,000 volumes Rutgers had in 1975 does not compare with the contents of Princeton's Firestone Library (2,715,000 including branch collections) or with the 1,847,000 volumes then held by the highly centralized library of the University of Southern Illinois. The same dispersal of collections that exists at Rutgers is true of a number of other state universities. And what libraries are counted? For example the Office of Education reported that the University of Wisconsin had over half a million volumes in 1922. Another reliable statistical source reported 304,000 for that library. A check with Wisconsin reveals that the lower figure was indeed correct, that the larger figure probably included the collection of the Wisconsin State Historical Library, housed in the university library building at that time. An extreme example of conflicting report is that of the Bureau of Educations's annual report for 1876 which lists Columbia as having only half the number of volumes reported owned in the same Bureau's 1876 report, *Public Libraries in the USA.*

In the same vein there is the question of quantity versus quality. Is the million-volume collection twice as valuable as one half its size? Here the many factors involved boggle the mind. Much depends on just the location. A library that is situated in a great center of research libraries such as Boston, New York, or Philadelphia need not contain as much as would be required in Lincoln, Nebraska or Austin, Texas. And is the focus of the library the same as the focus of the university that it serves? Bryn Mawr's library, a fine research collection, would imperfectly serve the needs of Rice University, and vice versa. Was the University of Cincinnati Library greatly improved in the 1960s when the legal relationship of the Cincinnati General Hospital was altered slightly so that its large library of old medical journals became part of the university library, even though they remained in the same dirty old basement?

Despite all this, there is a general relationship between quantity and quality. Much in the libraries of Harvard or Yale would be considered junk, but, as Harvard's Sibley wrote in 1857,

> The library . . . is a reservoir from which all minds . . . are . . . to be supplied. No limits can be set on its wants. . . . The field of intellectual labor is now so broad, and so carefully and extensively cultivated, that applications are made . . . for books, pamphlets, and papers which by a superficial, one-sided inquirer would be considered worthless.[3]

A Melville writes *Moby Dick* and it is dismissed as trivia. The whole field of science-fiction writing was in equally low regard until recently. An Emerson might appreciate a young Walt Whitman, but few others did. And so it goes. In general with libraries it is true that the more widely the net is cast, the greater the useful haul.

In later years a very few libraries followed Sibley's philosophy of collecting virtually anything on any subject. They were, of course, limited by tight budgets, but almost any item received by gift or exchange went up on the shelf. This policy was firmly extinguished in the late 1930s, not only by the enormous increases in the output of the printing presses, but also by restrictions of space and budget.

It was, however, only with the establishment of graduate instruction and emphasis on faculty research that libraries had begun consciously to collect materials other than the monographic works of individual authors. Scholars had to turn more and more to original sources, and this meant an emphasis on official documents of governments and other bodies, on yearbooks, on handbooks, on transactions, on proceedings of learned societies, and on reference works. Curiously, even journal literature had been slighted. Libraries were slow in subscribing to any; the subscriptions of the student literary societies must have had some influence in lowering the bars. As late as the early 1900s a few libraries were regularly discarding back numbers of journals, which they would later have to replace at great cost. In 1897 the importance of journal literature was minimized even by A.C. Potter, later librarian of Harvard College, and at that time in charge of all its ordering of material:

> The demands of the professors [for periodicals] are almost insatiable. In order to keep abreast of any science it is necessary to have costly and constantly increasing periodical literature of that science. The aggregate expense of providing these indispensable tools of the professor's trade is enormous, and the value of them is often in the main temporary, for the most important results are sure to appear sooner or later in the form of monographs, and the original tentative form will retain mainly an historical interest. Every periodical subscribed to constitutes a permanent liability against our funds, and cripples the library's purchasing power in other and more lasting directions.[4]

While Harvard was still digging in against faculty demand for journals, the University of Illinois was heading in the opposite direction. In addition to journals, it recognized a special responsibility to collect state newspapers as a resource for the study of contemporary Illinois history. Starting with 1910 issues, the files of over two hundred Illinois newspapers were acquired and bound. Fifteen years later the library was receiving regularly no less than 554 newspapers, of which approximately one-half were out-of-state. Government documents were likewise sought, not just those of state and nation, but of municipalities. By 1932 the library had over thirty thousand documents of varying nature, from over three thousand American and three hundred foreign units of local government. Behind this drive for any material of potential research value lay the strong interest of Edmund James, president of the university from 1905 to 1920, and the leadership of Phineas Windsor, director of libraries from 1909 to 1940. In 1912 the university had approved a faculty library committee resolution that the collection, then numbering slightly more than two hundred thousand volumes, be built up to a million within the decade. In actuality nearly three decades were to pass before that goal was reached.

To quote an authority on the library of the University of Illinois:

> In a brief span of years from 1900 to 1930, this library moved from an inconspicuous place among American university libraries to a position of national importance among research libraries. By 1930 its reputation rested on an extensive collection of the basic literatures of all subjects, comprehensive and notable collections in several distinct subjects, unique holdings and special collections for advanced study, highly developed bibliographical services, and deliberate specialization in its acquisition policy.[5]

The type of emphasis given at the University of Illinois and at some other leading American institutions was a considerable departure from the traditional patterns of collection building in Europe. Except for the German universities there just was not the emphasis on original sources, nor was there general interest in such topics as the history of science or science fiction, or in current popular literature even by the foremost authors. As American universities matured in the twentieth century their students and faculties made daily use of large masses of such material, virtually ignored by most European libraries.

The relationship between quality of the library and quality of research and graduate instruction gained limited recognition after 1900. In the recruitment of senior faculty the quality of the book collection was recognized as a principal factor, along with salary, teaching load, and provision for retirement. By 1940 this applied no longer to just a half-dozen leading institutions, but to the rank and file. "Good libraries attract good scholars" became an accepted maxim. Two studies of quality of graduate programs done in the period from 1925 to 1965 show the close correlation of quality with size of library collection (exceptions: the Massachusetts Institute of Technology and the California Institute of Technology because of their obvious specialization). In the humanities and social sciences at least, the quality of advanced work done at any institution generally bears a direct relationship to the size of the library collections. And size to a large extent determines the quality of the collection. Of course other factors are involved, such as availability of research materials in neighboring libraries. To quote two critics:

> Good scholars need good libraries, and good libraries attract good scholars. This interaction is the dominant theme in the story of American university libraries. With very few exceptions the prominent graduate programs at the turn of the century created the outstanding library collections of that time. . . . The collections of American university libraries have been built with vision, ambition, knowledge, dedication, and large amounts of money. The influence of pacesetters has been great, yet each university library reflects very much the particular academic history of its institution and especially the influence of a relatively small number of scholars and librarians. On balance, it has always been the scholar who provided the impetus; the librarian has made it possible.[6]

Of greatest importance always has been the control of acquisition policy. President Butler wrote of the pre-Civil War era at Columbia:

> In those days the trustees really administered the College in all its details, leaving practically no authority or initiative to the faculty, and to the president only such as he could acquire and command by reason of his personality and arguments. The trustees had formed the unfortunate habit of interfering with every detail of college administration, no matter how small.[7]

What was true of Columbia was true elsewhere. The selection of material to be bought for the library was often directly in the hands of the trustees, but only in the nineteenth century or earlier, and generally for only the first few years of later institutions. The task soon devolved on the faculty and until the present century few librarians had any direct responsibility in the matter. Powell's study of the librarians of southern state university libraries comments:

The selection and purchase of books was therefore no heavy task for either librarian or faculty member. It became a faculty responsibility soon after the universities opened and remained so almost without interruption until after the turn of the century. At that time the universities adopted the practice of placing a small amount of the regular appropriation under the direction of the librarian to be spent for reference books and others of a general character.[8]

The president was often involved, but only as a professor or a member of the committee on selection. Although the faculty took the initiative in book selection, trustee committees were often appointed to approve use of book funds, and this involved scrutiny of lists, usually annual lists, of material recommended for purchase. This trustee committee would normally recommend a sum for acquisitions for the next budget.

Mildred Lowell, historian of the Indiana University Library, comments as follows regarding early practices there:

> Books for the collection were selected both by the Board of Trustees and by the faculty members. The Board of Trustees, representing the pressures of the general public for more "practical" collegiate education, selected titles of contemporary works in literature, travel, biography and history which they believed should be read by students. Faculty members seem to have selected titles which had closer relevance to the curriculum and which represented the classical-education point of view. Considerable dependence on the private collections of faculty members for curricular use was evident until late in the nineteenth century; apparently the library did not adequately meet the needs of the instructional program and it probably was not expected to. In fact, the lack of pressure on the part of the faculty members for the acquisition of these materials in the University Library may reflect their philosophy about the relation of the library to instruction.[9]

Selection remained largely a faculty responsibility for a long time; change came gradually with the increase in funds, in publishing output, and in competent library staff. I was a staff member of Harvard's Widener Library Order Department in the early 1930s. Here recommendations for purchase were received daily from faculty and duly processed; only a very few of that library staff took any interest in collection building. There were no bibliographers, with the possible exception of staff who handled the ordering and processing of material in Slavic, Oriental, Hebrew, and other non-Roman alphabets. While the task of a young assistant like myself was to verify and complete bibliographical information and determine lack of ownership, he might also be involved in selection. At one time, while barely of voting age, I was doing the principal book selection in modern poetry and the labor movement as well as books reviewed each week in the *New York Times,* mostly as an after-hours activity, and without academic background in either poetry or labor. An informal, relaxed group of six people plus student help handled some of the selection and all of the ordering in western European languages for Harvard's principal library when accessions averaged, along with the important flow to departmental libraries, about one hundred thousand volumes annually.

As a larger proportion of annual book budgets was assigned to library directors, funds were applied first to purchases of journals and reference books, and only later to wider use. The director in turn depended more and more on his staff, but only after World War II did it become common practice to have librarians who devoted full time to collection building. This change was gradual, brought on as much by changes in the faculty role as by increased competence and acceptance of the library staff. Faculty became more mobile, less tied to a single institution and therefore less devoted to one book collection as growth in their personal reputations brought offers from other campuses. Careers were built more and more in a field of study at more than one location. The considerable increase in the pace of research and in the extension of knowledge and publication in narrow fields absorbed increasing amounts of the scholar's time and energy. The rapid growth in graduate studies meant a heavier burden for the faculty. Finally, there was pressure on the library to acquire quickly the increasing volume of publication and to have it on the shelves as soon as scholars were likely to learn of it through reviews. So there came into being a new type of librarian, commonly called bibliographers. They select material within assigned fields by bringing to the task a knowledge of the book trade, of bibliography, and of library functions. Of equal importance are subject knowledge and linguistic competence. Bibliographers must have close liaison with their faculty clientele and keep currently informed on needs for teaching and research within their assigned fields. A commentator of the early seventies wrote:

> To one degree or another most of the larger academic libraries in the country have pieced together a cadre of such specialists during the past ten to fifteen years, and the tide of book selection has pretty much ebbed away from the faculty, generally, it might be said, to the pleasure of the faculty.

Many libraries still follow the once universal practice of budgeting book funds by subjects, if not by allocations to academic departments. Traditionally, these assignments are at least scrutinized by the faculty library committee, which may alter sums. For years librarians have sought a magic formula for the division of the book fund by department of instruction. Many mathematical formulae have been devised, some seemingly too complicated for comprehension by anyone other than the creator. Occasionally a faculty committee, deadlocked, has thrown up its hands and decided to divide the pie evenly, whereby subjects with very modest book needs like home economics and physical education rank equally, or nearly so, with history and English literature. Usually, though, common sense and mutual respect prevail; if the library director has the confidence of the committee its approval of his recommendations becomes an annual formality.

A principal problem is the determination of an acquisition policy to govern library development. In theory this should be relatively stable over a number of years, yet have sufficient elasticity to allow for unforeseen needs. And, again in theory,

> The university administration, following consultation with, and advice from, appropriate academic groups, should provide the library with an official statement of policy, in some detail, as to the institution's present and probably future program of teaching and research.[10]

Unfortunately such statements of policy have been few and far between and, even when prepared, have had little validity for the future. Faculty interests and graduate study emphasis veer this way and that with changes of staff and the emergence of new national and international problems. Good fortune may present to the library a unique opportunity to acquire an important collection on a subject not emphasized in the policy statement. So the library director of the fifties and sixties more and more had to depend on judgment in guiding the policy of collection development. He really needed the sixth sense of a sailor steering a craft through shoal waters in a fog. As a distinguished California librarian wrote in a different metaphor,

> There is the matter of new territory to be covered. Here the evidence is dim and we must hark to the twittering of birds and observe the pattern of tea leaves in order to identify subjects of investigation new to us, so that a reasonable amount of anticipatory collecting can be

done. In this, as a Columbia professor recently remarked, "prevision and enterprise are indispensable."[11]

In recent years some of the largest research libraries have given up the traditional budgeting by subject and have assigned funds instead by bibliographer. Thus one staff member covering perhaps several large subjects would count on a specific sum and use his discretion in its distribution. Faculty input continues, of course, but only as individual members are moved to request items; this is sometimes done by professors deeply concerned with building up the library; more commonly they are motivated only as their work requires consultation of particular books and journals.

The great increase in scholarly publication coupled with the availability of funds in recent years has led the largest libraries to use blanket orders. At first these were simple agreements with certain presses, usually university presses, to take all current output on approval, except for certain subjects or certain forms, such as juvenilia or reprints. Finally, in the 1960s, a number of research libraries contracted with booksellers to send any publication judged of research value but reserved the privilege of returning any for credit. Such agreements always have restrictions as to language, country of origin, subject, and form. They are carefully framed, and are altered in the light of experience. For success they depend largely on the judgment of the supplier's bibliographers, who are, or should be, mature scholars. In this way libraries were relieved of much of the burden of placing tens of thousands of orders. The element of judgment as to what to accept and what to return remains, as does the burden of ordering what the bookseller has missed.

In the early 1900s most research libraries utilized to some degree the device of interlibrary exchange of publications, a matter of "send us what you publish, or have in duplicate, and we'll do the same." The practice is still quite common, but it is expensive in staff time and there is always the open question as to the value of the receipts.

California at Berkeley had one of the earlier and more successful exchange operations. This began in 1884 when Joseph C. Rowell, the librarian, sent out ninety-eight letters to learned societies and universities all over the world, proposing exchange relationships.

> Only thirty-five favorable replies were received. Rowell was not discouraged, but continued to pursue efforts in this direction. In 1893 the University's first two series publications appeared. . . . These

helped considerably. . . . In 1909–10, 2,008 volumes were received by exchange; at that time University publications were being sent to 932 other institutions.[12]

Part of the success of California's program was apparently due to faculty participation through personal contact with scholars elsewhere. During the depression of the 1930s Indiana University used personnel made available by federal work programs to push exchange, not only of Indiana publications, but also of library duplicates. Similar practices were common after 1900.

In foreign universities where the institute or seminar collection was the principal research instrument, much emphasis was placed on acquisition by exchange. The "ordinarius" or professor holding the principal chair in a subject was normally in contact with colleagues at other universities on other matters, and arrangements for the informal exchange of all publications followed almost without official request. In some instances the same practice was followed in the United States but generally proved impractical as administrative responsibility for libraries was centralized.

In the late 1950s and 1960s some libraries built up exchange relations with Soviet libraries, principally to acquire current Russian press output. The Russian libraries usually specified just what publications they needed. These were then bought and sent by the American institution. It is an expensive, time-consuming procedure, but many libraries found it a better way than that of reliance on Russian bookstores.

The development of cooperative collection policy with local libraries received early attention. In his report for 1888 as librarian of Columbia Melvil Dewey wrote:

> It is hoped to arrive at an understanding with other great libraries in the city by which each library will undertake to keep certain subjects fully up-to-date, thus making it unnecessary for the others to buy largely in these directions. In such a division of subjects the special field of our library will be determined by the wants of the various schools.[13]

Dewey drew up a detailed statement of what Columbia should collect with the implication that other subjects would be handled elsewhere, as, to quote him again, "completeness in Theology we can wisely leave to the libraries of the two great seminaries near us." However, Dewey's career at Columbia came to an abrupt close and it was some years later when

George Hall Baker reached an agreement for Columbia with the New York Public Library as to fields of primary interest. Columbia took more formal action in 1931, when the librarian's report included this statement:

> Resolved, That the University librarian be requested to investigate the relations between the libraries of Columbia University and other libraries of the city, particularly with a view to ascertaining in what departments of learning the University may wisely augment its collections in the interest of both the community and the University . . .[14]

Columbia's interest was by no means the first. Harvard's understanding with the Boston Public Library antedates it. In 1895 the principal libraries of Chicago reached agreement on cooperative collection building. Other early examples are: California at Berkeley with Stanford, and later with other nearby libraries; Michigan with the public libraries of Detroit and Cleveland; Minnesota with the state historical society library, the Minneapolis Public and the Hill Reference libraries.

Of the scores of such understandings among research libraries probably best known and furthest developed is the cooperation of the University of North Carolina with Duke University at nearby Durham, and, to a lesser extent with Tulane in by-no-means nearby New Orleans. Aside from the detailed agreements as to which library would specialize in what subjects, Duke and North Carolina have furnished each other with complete author catalogs. Graduate students may borrow freely from either library. A bus totes books back and forth. The pact has attracted foundation money. In various smaller ways the two campuses, fierce rivals in some other respects, work together in warmest harmony for the common good.

Despite exchange of publication agreements, cooperation in collection building, and similar economies, throughout the twentieth century there has been pressure for increasing the pace of acquisitions. Of the college age population of the country, 4 percent attended college in 1900; it was 7.2 percent in 1920, 15.4 percent in 1940, 28.4 percent in 1950. The U.S. Office of Education estimated that 60 percent of high school graduates would be enrolled in college by 1975 and that the figure might later go as high as 75 percent. By 1964–65 the figure for students winning bachelor degrees was 501,248 and seven years later it had increased 75 percent to 887,273. Doctoral degrees, excluding the first professional, rose from 9,829 in 1959–60 to 34,064 in 1975–76. Meanwhile enrollment in graduate schools, excluding first professional, rose from 242,000 in 1955 to 582,000 in 1965, and nearly doubled to reach 1,030,007 in 1975.[15]

While the burden of such increases in numbers and in depth of studies can well be imagined, additional pressure came from the growing realization that excellence in teaching and research was tied to excellence in library holdings. This was realized as far back as 1816 by a few, as witness a much quoted letter of that year by George Ticknor, then at the University of Göttingen.

> One very important and principal cause of the difference between our University [Harvard] and the one here is the different value we affix to a good library, and the different ideas we have of what a good library is. . . . We found new professorships and build new colleges in abundance, but we buy no books; and yet it is to me the most obvious thing in the world that it would promote the cause of learning and the reputation of the University ten times more to give six thousand dollars a year to the Library than to found three professorships, and that it would have been wiser to have spent the whole sum that the new chapel had cost on books than on a fine suite of halls. . . . I cannot better explain to you the difference between our University in Cambridge and the one here than by telling you that here I hardly say too much when I say that it *consists* in the Library, and that in Cambridge the Library is one of the last things thought and talked about,—that here they have forty professors and more than two hundred thousand volumes to instruct them, and in Cambridge twenty professors and less than twenty thousand volumes . . . we are mortified and exasperated because we have no learned men, and yet make it *physically* impossible for our scholars to become such, and that to escape from this reproach we appoint a multitude of professors, but give them a library from which hardly one and *not* one of them can qualify himself to execute the duties of his office. You will, perhaps, say that these professors do not complain. I can only answer that you find the blind are often as gay and happy as those who are blessed with sight . . .[16]

There was pressure on libraries from other points. The research activity which results from such emphasis increased enormously the volume of publication until 1972 and the world output was estimated at 520,000 volumes. But books are only a fraction of the store libraries must collect. There are fifty thousand or more journals judged to be of research value by the British Library Lending Division; there are also the microforms, manuscripts, government documents, maps, music, recordings, slides, film, etc. that must receive attention. Academic interests which had been limited to relatively few major areas of the sciences and humanities are now moving in a hundred directions undreamed of in the early 1900s. There has been an explosion of interest in area studies—all parts of Africa, Eastern Europe, and the Orient—following World War II. At least a few universities were offering instruction, formal or informal, in as many as seventy languages, and books in twice as many tongues were regularly received by them. These and related pressures brought about a flow of annual acquisitions topping the two hundred thousand mark for several libraries in 1975. Most librarians of a previous generation would have considered such a figure impossible and indeed ridiculous.

Yet there had been such predictions. In 1944 Fremont Rider stirred the research libraries of the country with his book, *The Scholar and the Future of the Research Library*. His thesis was concerned with the problems that lay ahead if growth of collections continued as in the past.

There was nothing essentially new in this work, as the facts of growth were well known, but by dramatizing the matter, Rider focused the interest of the library world on this most important topic. It was clear that research libraries had been doubling in size, on the average, every sixteen years; from this the author drew the questionable inference that growth would continue indefinitely at the same rate. Thus, a century hence, the Yale Library would contain two hundred million books and its card catalog alone require eight acres of floor space! The author justified these predictions with the telling observation that the picture, if seemingly preposterous, was no more so than the actual 1944 figures for the Yale Library would have been to the Yale librarian of a century earlier. Rider then went on to offer his solution: great dependence on photographic miniaturization, principally by microprint. The computer had not then entered the picture.

No author, no matter how perceptive, could have foreseen the degree of growth in all aspects of higher education and especially in graduate study and faculty research that came in the thirty years following World War II. It is extremely unlikely that the decades ahead will bring any corresponding increase in funds although student bodies may grow moderately in numbers.

During the thirty-five years following 1940 research libraries should have grown at least fourfold, according to Rider's formula. Most of them did. However, growth was notably slower for the largest libraries of the 1940s. In that period there was unparalleled university growth in funds, students, and programs, all incentives to rapid library expansion. Yet Harvard grew to only slightly more than twice its size and Yale tripled. Of the twelve libraries with collections of over seven hundred thousand volumes in 1940, aside from the two above, five approximately tripled in size, three met the norm by quadrupling, and two increased fivefold. To the above approximate percentages must be added figures for a number of other libraries which, small at the time of World War II, grew enormously in the favorable postwar climate. At least fifteen libraries with collections in 1975 of more than a million volumes had grown tenfold or better in the thirty-five years since 1940. Three of these are University of California campuses (Los Angeles, Santa Barbara, and San Diego) which had recently come to full graduate and research programs. Four are southern institutions (Florida State, Universities of Florida, Georgia and Miami), the one of recent origin, the other three recent in emphasis on research. The others are Kent State, SUNY at Albany, Wayne State, Massachusetts, Maryland, Indiana, Southern Illinois, and Pittsburgh.

Unique in library history is the building of the collection of rare, principally twentieth century literature at the University of Texas in the 1950s and 1960s. This was estimated to have cost fifty million dollars, of which more than half came from gifts and about sixteen million in special appropriations from the Board of Regents. It focused on manuscripts and author's archives in French, English, and American literature, and in a relatively short span made Austin the single most important center for the study of many of the senior writers and of literary movements of the century. This development has undoubtedly assisted other important but less spectacular collection building at Texas, notably in Latin-American materials and southwestern history.

Such movements require the drive and genius of a leader. In the case of Texas the leadership came not from within the library staff but from Harry Ransom, professor, vice-president and provost, president, and finally chancellor of the University of Texas system.

Less spectacular but of comparable importance were the accomplishments in building collections of rare books and manuscripts by William Jackson, director of Harvard's Houghton Library. A legion of bibliographiles devoted themselves to one institution or another, as C. Waller Barrett to Virginia, James Buell Munn to Harvard, Wilmarth Lewis to Yale and DeCoursey Fales to New York University.

An interesting vignette on collection building at Yale comes from James T. Babb, then director of its library:

> In the nineteenth century most of the Yale faculty lived well. They had large homes, built up private libraries adequate for their teaching and research, and only used the Library for the odd book. There were few exceptions—men who were constantly in the Library and helping the librarians to strengthen our collections. . . . My predecessor but one as Librarian, Andrew Keogh, often jokingly said that the Yale professor in the nineteenth century married for money and spent his salary on books. Most of these fine and scholarly collections were willed to the Library and helped to round out our holdings in many fields. This is no longer true.[17]

Of the score or more of bibliophiles in American intellectual history who brought together the greatest collections, several established and endowed separate reference libraries. Examples are the Henry Huntington Library in San Marino, California, the Folger in Washington, and the Morgan Library in New York. Several others took similar action by attaching their libraries to universities. The William L. Clements Library was given to the University of Michigan in 1922. It is separately housed and independent of the university library, but supported by the university and administered by a committee of which the university president is chairman. The Clements Library is extraordinarily rich in early Americana, particularly the settlement of the New World, Indian relations, the Revolution and beginnings of self-government.

Somewhat similar in collection emphasis and comparable in importance is the John Carter Brown Library of source materials relating to the Americas printed in the Colonial period. Like the Clements, the university president is ex officio chairman of the board and the library is administered separately from other libraries of the university.

Still another great collection which is located adjacent to a university campus and administered separately by the institution is the William Andrews Clark Memorial Library of the University of California at Los Angeles. The Clark's fame rests on its rare books and manuscripts concentrating on English culture of the seventeenth to nineteenth centuries.

A number of collections of international fame are located in buildings named for the bibliophile and housing his collection, but usually including other material. Noteworthy among these are the Lilly Library at Indiana University, the Beinecke at Yale, the Houghton at Harvard. Still other great donated collections are incorporated in a main building, as for example the University of Minnesota's James Ford Bell Library on the early history of world commerce. Virtually every large university library has a rare book or special collections area named in honor of a prominent collector-donor.

There have also been mergers of libraries, as of institutions. In rare instances, one library swallows another, cannibal fashion, to its great advantage. An outstanding case is the absorption of the library of the American Geographical Society in New York by the University of Wisconsin at Milwaukee in 1978. The University Library is of recent origin, had standing as a research collection for scarcely more than a decade when it put its sheltering arms and roof over the greatest special collection on geography in the country, some 220,000 volumes and 600,000 items. Included were rare maps and publications of the greatest value. The arrangements for the move across six states involved safety precautions and police protection so elaborate that the description reads like a James Bond story.

The rise of the great library now serving the University of California at Los Angeles is typical of, but outstanding among, the considerable group of complex universities which have come to maturity in the post-World War II period. UCLA was basically a normal school until 1919, when it became the Southern Branch of the University of California. Five years after that transformation it had the good fortune to obtain as librarian John E. Goodwin, who scotched the idea that the sole research collection should be located at Berkeley or that UCLA could depend on the Huntington Library, and proceeded to build the collection up from the thirty-nine thousand volumes on hand when he arrived. Graduate study was undertaken in 1933; doctoral programs date from 1936. The collection numbered some 462,000 volumes in 1944, when Goodwin was succeeded by Lawrence Clark Powell, a man slight in body but great in energy, in influence, and in knowledge of the book world. Under Powell the collection grew to 1,568,000 volumes by the time of his retirement in 1961. It was then that Franklin Murphy, a confirmed library builder, came as chancellor and brought with him Robert Vosper, as talented as Powell in leadership qualities and possessed of a particular genius for collection building. This team preached equality with Berkeley, which meant top claim on book fund dollars from the university regents for some time. In the twelve years before 1973, when Vosper retired, the library was more than doubled in size to 3,284,000 volumes, and well housed and well served by a superior staff. Somewhat similar is the recency of the University of California campuses at Santa Barbara and San Diego, where great research collections have been built up since 1945.

Comparable, but less spectacular, has been the growth of the libraries serving the major campuses of the State University of New York. Several of the southern states, notably North Carolina, South Carolina, Georgia and Florida, have provided the funds for enormous growth of their university libraries in the years since 1945.

While most of the modern mass acquisition of books and journals comes straight from the bookseller, this was not the case in an earlier period. Much of the collection building came about through the purchase or donation of private libraries, and this meant a distinct flow of books from the old world to the new, slow before 1900, greatly accelerated thereafter by the double impetus of great wealth in the United States and the loss of fortunes abroad, occasioned by World War I. The movement of important books took two main channels, either into the hands of an increasing number of American bibliophiles and by gift or purchase from there to libraries, or direct to libraries by purchase from European owners. Most large research libraries have scores or more of collections formed by individuals which are relatively exhaustive for research. Some collector-formed donations were broad in nature, like Harvard's Amy Lowell collection emphasizing, but not limited to, selected authors in English and American literature, or the Kilgore collection of Russian literature; others were sharply focused, for instance the John Carter Brown library at Brown University, dealing with the exploration and first settlement of America, and the Bancroft (Western Americana) at Berkeley. Illustrative of collections dealing with particular authors are the Milton collection at Illinois and the Petrarch collection at Cornell. Occasionally a collection is built around a type of publication, such as political tracts of a given period, the output of private presses, or types of illustration. These are formed by individuals and passed on to libraries either by gift or purchase.

Robert Vosper commented on this acquisition of entire collections as follows:

> A variety of urgent methods and tactics have been applied in this undertaking, over and beyond the essential, but slow and less colorful task of diligently searching out individual books. Each of these successful American libraries, and this is equally true of the private as it is of the state universities, is studded with those rich plums, the

en bloc collections that had already been carefully constructed by scholars or private collectors prior to being brought into the institutional library holdings. The librarian, working against time, against many other demands on his budget, and against the competition of his eager colleagues, but urged on and abetted by his faculty and often his administrative officers, has sought out these private libraries in the world's book market. Against equal competition he has sought them out as gifts in the homes of their collectors and in meetings of bibliophilic societies.[18]

At times this westward flow has created ill feeling, and this was particularly the case when one institution or another made several major forays. In recent years there has been some traffic in both directions. For example a few important private collections have been shipped from the United States to London for auction.

History is concerned with the past, not the future. However historians may speculate, one thing is certain. As long as universities continue to be instruments of research, to extend man's knowledge, their libraries will grow in size. Means will be found, possibly not to house tens and hundreds of millions of books in their present form, but certainly to preserve the findings, the talent, the wit and wisdom, and the records of the future. There is no going back, no solution of the storage problem by wholesale withdrawal of material now accumulated. And while microforms, computers, and other creations of modern technology are increasingly useful in recording for present use and for posterity, as this is written the book in its present codex form remains the most practical device for most scholarly purposes.

CHAPTER 7

Governance and Leadership

While our libraries in their early years lacked all else, they were amply furnished with detailed statutes covering virtually all contingencies of operation known to man. The emphasis was predictably on the prohibitions. Thus Harvard adopted in 1667 a long statement of "Library Rules for the Library Keeper." Like most similar documents issued over the next two hundred years it detailed just who could use books, penalties for misuse, what books could not circulate, circulation records, hours of opening, etc. Also it laid down the law for the "Library Keeper" as to the records he must keep, who was to have a key to the library, his responsibility for damage and loss of books, maintenance of a catalog, sale of duplicates, and so forth. For example, in the language of the day,

> The Library keeper shall write or cause to be fairly written in a book (to be payd for by the Treasurer) the names of all the Books belonging to the Library. First in the order as they are placed and disposed according to the affixed catalogue. Secondly, In one continued Alphabet setting down the Authors name and what of his works are in the Library and where. Thirdly The names of the severall Donours of the Books with the Books given by them. . . .
> The Library Records and other manuscripts and what else shall be judged expedient shall be kept in a chest in the Library under Lock and Key to be kept by the Library keeper.[1]

As the Harvard Library grew in size so too, it seems, was the growth in regulation. As previously noted, the 1854 edition of *Statutes and Laws of Harvard College* devote 73 of its 208 numbered paragraphs to library controls and operations. Similar rule and regulation were standard practice until the late nineteenth century. It is occasionally found much later at institutions in their infancy. But maturity brought to nearly all institutions reliance on broad statements of policy from the trustees. Typical of the best of such statements is the one, previously quoted, that was established in 1895 by the University of Illinois Board of Trustees. This laid down the fundamental policies as to objectives, composition of the university library, and responsibility for proper operations, in six concise paragraphs. And it also took exactly six concise paragraphs for the Regents of the University of Texas in 1891 to lay out the regulations for its university library.

> All books, pamphlets, maps, etc. (other than account books and books of record) purchased with funds of the University, shall be deemed to belong to the University Library.
> All parts of the Library shall be in the custody of the Librarian, who shall be responsible for the condition of the same.
> All reference books and current periodicals, magazines and newspapers, shall be made as easy of access as practicable to all patrons of the Library, and no limitations not necessary to their preservation shall be placed upon their free use.
> All other books, except such as are referred to in the next paragraph, shall be delivered for use by the Librarian or his assistants only, upon a proper call.
> Books which are purely technical and relate to the work of a single School or Department only may be taken out by that School or Department under such regulations and for such times as the Librarian may determine; but the Librarian shall not thereby cease to be responsible for their safe keeping and proper use.
> The Librarian may make and enforce such rules for the government of the Library as are approved by the President.[2]

In formative years it was customary for boards of trustees to have committees on the library. At the University of California (Berkeley) close supervision of library matters by the board of regents existed for only thirty years. It was relaxed in 1898 when a faculty Advisory Committee on the Library was created. The regents continued to have committees concerned with library operations but these were not generally active. In summary, while the regents exercised direct authority on library matters until nearly 1900, after that time their role was mainly concern regarding finances and the routine confirmation of appointments.

C. H. McMullen, the historian of the University of Chicago Library, summarized the role of the trustees there as follows:

> There were several individuals and groups of individuals outside of the Librarians themselves who influenced growth. The most powerful of these was the Board of Trustees. In the beginning it occasionally made decisions on minor matters as well as on major problems, but after the first few years it concerned itself with only the more important items of policy.[3]

At Columbia the trustees continued to exercise considerable direct control until the twentieth century. Previous mention has been made of the pique of Nicholas Murray Butler over their "unfortunate habit of interfering with every detail of college administration, no matter how small."

In reference to the respective roles of the university president and his board of trustees, the historian of Indiana University Library has written:

> Surviving evidence indicates that the Board of Trustees was the most important single force in the development of the library from 1829 to 1874. It was the Board which directed the first president to select the original collection, provided housing for the collection, drew up the library rules, designated which faculty member should serve as librarian, selected some of the book collection, appropriated the money to be spent for the library, and ordered a library catalog to be compiled and printed. It is possible that Board members did some of these things not on their own initiative but rather as the result of prodding from other people or social pressure. In the next period of the library's history, the presidents became the dominating force in the shaping of the library.[4]

The above should be qualified for many institutions because there is so little evidence of any "dominating force in the shaping of the library." Of course this was true only before these collegiate institutions blossomed into true university status and achieved the full-time leadership of competent, professional librarians. The president of the institution, as its chief officer, had the power of major control over all aspects of library operation; whether or not he exercised that control to any considerable degree depended on factors of personality and interest. In the nineteenth century relatively few chief officers took considerable personal interest in the growth of collections, in the physical provisions, or even in library use. From the first days to the present the president has played a key role in determination of library support, but a relatively lesser one in the broad area of library governance. Some made the building up of the library a major objective of their administration, but the majority neglected it entirely. President Folwell of Minnesota (1869–84) was so concerned for the library that he added the title and duties of librarian to his other responsibilities and served the library faithfully for fifteen years; he continued his interest and support as a faculty member until his death in 1929. In contrast it is told that a later president of

Minnesota, when presented with a detailed report on the needs of the library, called the librarian in for discussion. To quote the university history:

> James Thayer Gerould, the Librarian, was amazed at the thought of getting action so prompt. Northrop enveloped him in an atmosphere of soothing benignity and they talked of many things. Presently with an air of fastidious and tolerant distaste Northrop leaned forward and picked up the corpulent document. "My boy," he asked, "did you send me this?" Gerould admitted that he had. Northrop put a benevolent hand on the librarian's knee. "In the future if you have anything to say to me, just feel free to come in here and say it," he commented encouragingly. The hand that held the report groped toward the wastebasket and let the report drop into it.[5]

Many a library director of the mid-twentieth century could vouch for encounters of a similar nature, if so fortunate as to have been received in the presidential presence. Other directors have close and warm presidential contact, full cooperation and wise counsel every step of the way. This was so of "Curly" Byrd, one-time football coach and president of the University of Maryland from 1935; also of Franklin Murphy, president of the University of Kansas and later of UCLA.

History is full of incidents illustrating too great a presidential interest in library matters. An amusing case of this was the concern of W. T. Thompson, president of Ohio State, regarding the proposed appointment of Paul North Rice to a junior post. Rice, who later became a distinguished leader in research library circles, had just graduated from Wesleyan University in Connecticut, where, according to the president, "conditions have been so bad and where the young men have called down the adverse criticism of all intelligent people for their thoroughly bad attitude. I have a sincere doubt in my mind whether any graduate of that university within the past five years is sound ethically. . . ." However, Rice got his appointment, probably because Olive Jones, the OSU librarian, was so highly respected. President Enoch A. Byron of Washington State (1893–1915) ordered books regularly for the library, and his successor, Ernest O. Holland, is reported to have been positively addicted to the joys of buying scholarly sets of books for the library while traveling in Europe. Presidents Gilman of Hopkins and Harper of Chicago were responsible for the decisions regarding decentralization of collections at their respective institutions in the late nineteenth century. The decisions were of the greatest importance to library development for several generations. In both cases the faculty members approved of decentralization; they were men who enjoyed the convenience of small collections and felt no need for a broad collection and professional library service. The successors to both Gilman and Harper apparently left library operations largely to their head librarians. And at Columbia it was President Barnard's great concern for the library that brought Melvil Dewey in 1883 and supported the revolution he wrought in that library's operation in a few short years.

It is curious that presidents seem either to have understood completely the role of the library as indeed the heart of the academic program and done their best to further it, or else they have lacked any appreciation of the library's role, evinced no personal interest, and given as little support as politically expedient. In other words, there are few instances of a middle course.

If the president all too often assumed that all was well with the library, this was not the case with the faculty, upon whose collective shoulders fell the general role of advisor and critic and, especially in the earlier period, of advice with the firm overtones of command. In writing of the history of southern university libraries, Benjamin Powell stated:

> The Faculty library committee achieved permanent status in most institutions soon after the turn of the century. It became a standing body about the time the trustees committee ceased functioning as a supervisory body. The duties it assumed in the beginning were similar to those the trustees had relinquished. As librarians attained more stature and became permanent officers, however, they accepted more and more responsibility, leaving the committee to serve in an advisory capacity. Theoretically, the role of the committees in recent years has been that of an advisory body, but its authority has increased or decreased to correspond to the resourcefulness and leadership of the librarian.[6]

At both Columbia and Chicago, committees of the faculty played dominant roles in much library policy determination in the early 1900s. James H. Canfield of Columbia is believed to have opposed the function of the committee; he is also credited with the conviction, shared by many another library director, that often such a committee can be very useful to a strong director and a considerable source of trouble to a weak one.

With the passage of time these committees came to be generally recognized as constructively advisory to the director on matters of broad policy. In theory they were also a channel of communication to the faculty, served as spokesmen for the library at faculty meetings, and, as necessary, urged support for the library to the university administration. Until very recent years the committees were consulted on the division of the book budget by subject or academic department. Committees frequently offer guidance in matters of collection building, periods of loan, hours of opening, restrictions on the use of collections, and similar matters which affect them directly. They often advise on staff appointments; most other administrative matters are either left alone or raised only for information.

This relationship is characteristic only of the typical committee of the 1960s and 1970s. Before that time there was often direct conflict. This resulted either in a period of faculty committee administrative control, through its chairman, of virtually all aspects of operation or, with a headstrong director, open clash with no holds barred.

There was frequently an intermediate step in the transfer of library responsibility from trustees to faculty. At Ohio State a library council was composed of the president, librarian, and one faculty member from each of the four schools then in existence. This was to take over the reins of library policy from the trustees. The committee was to make rules and control funds, while the librarian had "the care and custody of the library." About the same time, around the turn of the century, Syracuse University had a similar mixture of representation on the library committee: the chancellor, the librarian, deans of the colleges, two trustees, and representatives of the faculties.

At the University of California (Berkeley) the regents invited faculty to serve on its Standing Committee on the Library as early as 1875; it was not until 1898 that the university had a library committee composed exclusively of teaching personnel. It is noteworthy that the trustees framed the basic document regarding library responsibilities and role at the University of Illinois in 1895 but it was the faculty who revised that statement in 1915, apparently on its own authority.

As libraries grew in book collections, size of staff, and complexity of operations, they required full-time administrative talent. Governance then centered in the director's office. In only isolated cases was such leadership exercised in the nineteenth century, notably by Sibley and Winsor at Harvard, Dewey briefly at Columbia, and Rowell at Berkeley.

The new leaders, men like Wilson at North Carolina, Windsor of Texas and Illinois, Bishop of Michigan, Manchester of Ohio State, were generally active until World War II yet were, many of them, founders in the sense of being the first to establish true research collections and sophisticated library operations. There were, after all, only a score of mature universities with well-established doctoral programs by the mid-twenties. So, in one sense, the real rise of the research library in America with few exceptions, has taken place in the lifetime of your chronicler.

The majority of these directors of large university libraries prior to 1950 exercised diplomacy in dealings with top administration and faculty committees but were autocratic in their direction of operations and in personnel matters. They were the bosses. They knew it and the staff knew it. Wilhelm Munthe commented in 1939 "We (Europeans) would never think of delegating to the chief librarian the authority that he has in America, where his power frequently reminds us of that of the administrative director of a corporation."[7] Typical of many was Harold Leupp, director of the California (Berkeley) libraries from 1919 to 1945, and in some respects the chief administrator as associate director from 1910. Leupp is credited with kindness and sympathy in much staff contact; on the other hand "he had a very stern and harsh side to his personality . . . he was a perfectionist and had an astonishing memory for details. He strove for efficiency in getting work accomplished quickly and accurately. He became impatient and on occasion gave vent to outbursts of temper when he came upon situations which, by his standards, revealed inefficiency . . . He always kept in close touch with all that was going on in the library. . . . He once wrote, 'the days are few and far between when I am not in every department at least once, and for a long enough time to make my own observations.' He possessed a Puritan-like belief in the virtues of hard work and strict discipline."[8] Leupp's control extended over such matters as dress and grooming, as did the control of most directors of that day.

Not all heads of libraries were such tight administrators. Many had warm sides to their natures. But there was a single-mindedness and a devotion to duty, a driving force to collect greater resources, improve control over them, build new buildings, and generally facilitate research, that verged on the fanatical and that, on reflection, seems regrettable because it was highly competitive; the era of cooperation among libraries was not to come until the late forties.

With dawning recognition of the importance of the library by the research-oriented faculty, there also came serious questions about the qualifications of the director. In brief, should he be essentially a scholar, alive to the needs of scholars and therefore, by assumption, alert and proficient in meeting them, or should he be basically a librarian, know-ledgeable in library techniques and, it was assumed, relatively ignorant of scholarship? At a number of leading institutions, particularly Chicago, Columbia, Harvard, and Pennsylvania, the faculties viewed the professional librarian with distrust and for considerable periods turned library operations over to scholars with little background in library operations. In certain cases this worked well as the directors set aside their various interests and immersed themselves in building their libraries; but when scholarly activity continued to take important time the library suffered relative stagnation. The great state universities almost without exception sought leadership from librarians of proven competence. Thus it was Koch and Bishop who created the great library at the University of Michigan, Windsor and Downs at Illinois, Manchester and Branscomb at Ohio State, Rowell, Leupp, and Coney at California (Berkeley), Goodwin, Powell, and Vosper at UCLA, Miller at Indiana, Gerould, Walter, McDiarmid, and Stanford at Minnesota. The majority of these directors were also productive scholars. The publishing record of a Downs, a Bishop, a Walter, or a Justin Winsor is equalled by few professors. Others, notably Louis Round Wilson of the University of North Carolina, were educational statesmen as well as library directors and widely recognized as such. Still, many of the leaders of major university libraries went through exhaustive examinations from investigatory committees. Despite the fine backgrounds and accomplishments of many directors, they were viewed with suspicion simply because they were librarians and therefore basically administrators, ergo bureaucrats. To the scholar the perfect library is the one that puts his wants and needs first. Richard Logsdon, university dean for libraries at Columbia for many years, quotes one of his law faculty: "It's all very simple—have the titles I need, when I need them, and of course where I need them. Be sure they go to the Law Library."[9]

The directors just named are all men, yet librarianship is commonly considered to be a woman's profession. The blunt truth is that strong prejudice against women as administrators existed until the 1970s. While administration was considered definitely a male prerogative, some women did rise to senior positions in less advanced research libraries and made remarkable contributions. Mention has been made of the imaginative leadership of Katharine Sharp at Illinois; similarly at the University of West Virginia the library was transformed by Eliza J. Skinner, who took over in 1897. She emphasized student use, opened the library from 7:45 A.M. to 10 P.M. daily, gave full access to the shelves, brought together into a central collection nearly all the small, untended departmental book collections, and was instrumental in getting the library recognized by the state legislature as a major department of the university. Unfortunately for the university she accepted a position at the Library of Congress in 1902.

The extraordinary honor paid by Oregon State to Ida Kidder on her death is believed to be primarily a tribute to her personality. However, the record shows that in only twelve years she set the library well on its way to becoming a mature support of research. She planned and built a fine new building; she introduced professional standards for cataloging and classification; she began a highly successful course in the use of the library; she gave students personal guidance in their cultural reading; and she increased the size of the collection eightfold. Few librarians have equaled her success in promotion of a library with the university administration and the state legislature, as well as the student body.

Of equal interest and little known is the contribution of Olive Jones, for many years from the turn of the century librarian of Ohio State. James Skipper's dissertation on the history of that library states flatly: "Olive Branch Jones was the most influential personality in the development of the library." In like vein the Brigham Young University Library history states that Professor Alice Louise Reynolds "probably did more to promote and build the Brigham Young University collections than any other person."

The libraries ran on "woman power" largely because salaries did not attract men, and the salaries remained low because they were paid to women. An important factor was the large percentage of graduates of women's colleges between 1880 and 1900 who did not marry, but pursued independent careers. Teaching and librarianship were the two professions most open to them. And then there were the strange misconceptions of most men. Herbert Putnam, Librarian of Congress, had the effrontery to tell the graduating class of women at Simmons in 1912: "Your fair chance [for employment] . . . seems limited by some prejudice in favor of the other sex . . . Upon what superior traits of men, in business or in office, is it based? The first is manliness [sic] . . . The second characteristic distinction is a trait—it is a sense of proportion." He goes on to elaborate "the failure of women as a sex to develop, except within narrow areas, the inventive faculty; or in music and the arts, the creative faculty; or in administrative work, to show what is called initiative." And after narrating the virtues of women he concludes "They [the virtues] have a substantial market value; and they have also a tremendous social value. If they do not make for progress, they assure stability. If in business or office they do not lead to promotion they at least assure preference in the positions which are subordinate."[10]

The Harvard College Library was probably the first to employ a woman (1858). Dewey shocked the Columbian environment in 1883 by hiring not one but six, all from Wellesley. One of them wrote many years later, "At that time Columbia College was almost as hermetically sealed to women as is a monastery." Their starting annual salary was five hundred dollars, a modest but fair sum for untrained assistants.

The winning of academic recognition on a par with that of the teaching faculty has been a long, hard struggle, by no means won as this is written. The early head librarians had academic respectability because their primary duties were in the classroom, and the library responsibility was considered to be secondary. But as the full-time, professional librarian evolved, he received no such recognition. A survey of a number of leading universities in 1870 showed that none gave their chief librarians academic titles, unless they were members of the teaching faculty.[11] Many were listed as members of the faculty, but following the main roll. They were lumped with registrars and other miscellaneous officers. From the middle of the nineteenth century on, there was some recognition of the librarian as no longer the clerk, hoarding the precious trove, but as the learned and kindly savant, knowledgeable of every tome and eager to guide and lead the student in his reading. Ralph Waldo Emerson was probably the first to promote the importance of a "Professorship of Books," basically a librarian's role, and it was used by others for several decades, but neither the title not the role won recognition.

By 1900 quite a few of the leading universities listed the head librarian with officers of administration in one way or another; most if not all are assumed to have been members of the faculty but apparently none had professorial titles by virtue of their library duties. Very few library staff junior to the head had any faculty or administrative recognition in the college catalogs of 1900.

Columbia blazed a trail for others to follow when, in 1911, the trustees voted "The librarian shall have the rank of professor, the assistant librarian that of associate professor and the supervisors shall rank as assistant professors and bibliographers as instructors."

During the first decades of the twentieth century, the quest for status received increasing attention in library literature but made little progress.

The subject was investigated in 1939 in a study of practice in 129 institutions. In these, ninety-eight chief librarians had faculty status, thirty-one did not; of the assistant and associate librarians, thirty had faculty status and forty did not; departmental heads had faculty status in twenty-seven libraries and no academic rank in four; professional assistants held faculty status in twenty libraries, but not in thirty others. The study adds that "in each of the four categories the status was frequently nominal."

In 1944 the University of Illinois achieved full faculty status and rank for all of its professional staff. It was the first major university to take the step. Others followed with partial or complete recognition in the 1950s and sixties. By the early seventies the majority of universities has swung over to recognition of most, if not all, of the professional staff as members of the faculty, often with faculty rank and titles.

A partial explanation for the delay in recognition of librarians as academicians lies in the old-fashioned, generally erroneous public concept of the librarian as the housekeeper in the store of books. Some dullards of yesteryear possibly were little more than that, but the profession for nearly a hundred years has exercised leadership in providing imaginative service to students, which led soon after to equal leadership in building collections for research, in facilitating faculty research, and in actual teaching, usually in the library, often in the classroom. Factors against recognition have been the often disgraceful prejudice toward women as academic equals, the jealousy of the institutional faculty to hold the line against any type of instruction other than that of formal credits via the classroom, the plain ignorance of many administrators of the learning process that proceeds daily and hourly in every research library, and finally, in some instances, the incompetence of library staff.

In recent years it became evident that the position of library director was fully as insecure as that of the university president. In 1971–72 seven directors of the Big Ten university libraries plus the University of Chicago resigned, only one of them because of age. There is patently relative insecurity in a post where previously stability up to honorable retirement age was assumed. The reasons cited are various. Pressures from the president's office contribute, but a new element is the rising emphasis on participative management and the critical assessment of the library staff. The day of benevolent autocracy is long gone, the difficulties of the post are greatly increased, and, obviously, in library as in other operations, the chief officer is the scapegoat for dissatisfaction. As previously noted, the larger staffs are now virtually all organized as faculties or as collegial assemblies. Consultation is the order of the day but the director still is entirely responsible to his president and trustees for the effectiveness of library operations though the decision making is shared with the professional staff.

CHAPTER 8

Financial Support

It was late in the nineteenth century before academic libraries had any need of funds for purposes other than the purchase of books. Staff consisted of a faculty member assigned to the library as extra duty. In most instances, at least until mid-century, there was no bill for light or heat because there was no artificial light and seldom any means of heating in those few colleges which had separate library buildings. Periodical and newspaper subscriptions were unheard of until late in the nineteenth century. So, as we have seen, books were acquired through occasional gifts or bequests of private libraries; more rarely as an individual, usually the institution's president, ran a fund drive for the library.

In the late eighteenth century several colleges began to charge students library fees, and this practice spread in the following decades. Usually it was a dollar or two a year. Several based the fee on the use of books, charging for each volume withdrawn on a sliding scale, dependent on its size (folio, quarto, octavo, etc.).

The fee system could not support any library with pretensions to serving research but it did provide enough to sustain life and some growth toward the twentieth century at a number of institutions, principally state universities, which developed important graduate programs in later years. As might be suspected, these steady library fees attracted covetous eyes. In writing of the southern universities, Powell comments: "In some of the institutions, the library fees were placed in the general funds of the university and spent for other purposes. None exceeded ten dollars per student, and the average was about two dollars. Had the libraries received all the income from fees, their income would still have remained too small for the demands of the period. Only Virginia and North Carolina were aided substantially by endowments, and these came after 1900."[1]

No library in the South or elsewhere received regular, annual appropriations for books until 1838, when this began at South Carolina College. On the other hand, no institution was then as fortunate as South Carolina College in having regular appropriations from the state legislature! Several of the Ivy League institutions, notably Harvard, Yale, and Brown, were building book funds by the 1830s, and these provided a gradually increasing annual income. However, few libraries had important endowment income until the twentieth century.

Undoubtedly unique among methods of supporting libraries was the 1869 action by the Delaware legislature; this provided a fine for selling "spirituous, vinous or fermented liquors" within two miles of the college or "procuring the same" for any student. One half the fine was to go "to the college for the use of the library." Recent visits to the campus would indicate that the act has since been repealed.

In isolated instances departments of instruction would quietly, informally, and quite illegally extract library fees from their students for departmental use. This was true of several departments at the University of California at Berkeley in the 1920s. As late as the 1950s the School of Nursing at the University of Cincinnati was charging a library fee without the knowledge of the central administration. Need was the justification. Historically there was precedent for this in the long-established practice of the German institute, which supported its special research library with such fees. Judgment in this matter was considered within the proper jurisdiction of the professor heading the institute, who collected the money and governed its use.

So the general state of library finance at mid-nineteenth century was at best a few hundred dollars annually from a combination of fees and minor gifts. The data in Appendix I show that in 1849 only Harvard, Yale, Brown, and South Carolina averaged over a thousand dollars annually for library purposes. A number of libraries had no annual support of any kind.

By the time of the 1876 report on public libraries of the commissioner of education the picture had not improved in any important respect. Of the thirty institutions listed in the 1849 table, only twelve reported anything at all as "total yearly income from all sources," or as endowment. Of these, only seven had an annual income in excess of one thousand dollars.

A new element had entered the picture of institutional support in the form of the Morrill Act signed by President Lincoln in July, 1862. This provided funds for the support of a college in each state "where the leading subject would be branches of learning related to agriculture and the mechanic arts." It assigned to each state thirty thousand acres of public land, or the equivalent in land scrip, for each senator and representative of that state then in Congress. The emphasis on agriculture and the "mechanic arts" was a dramatic departure from the traditional classroom curriculum. The initial support was reinforced by various legislation in later years. Most important were the 1887 authorization of agricultural experiment stations at the land grant institutions and the 1890 Second Morrill Land Grant College Act which provided further endowment for existing institutions and the establishment of duplicate colleges for students "in those states or territories where a distinction of race and color is made in the admission of students."

The federal lands were in some instances disposed of with ruinous haste at fire-sale prices, partly because of the great need for some hard cash, partly because of the salesmanship and cupidity of smart speculators. But some of the federal funds from the original and subsequent acts did provide for book purchases. The greater value of the legislation was, of course, the impetus given to the founding of universities.

State legislatures were extremely slow in recognizing a responsibility for the annual support of state colleges and universities. In nearly all states there was some minor initial support for a building and for the expenses of the first year; further support was only occasional and for a special need, or in response to some particularly astute political pressure. The badly needed annual support became the rule rather than the exception only late in the nineteenth century. Benjamin Powell's study of southern university libraries states that "regular financial support from the states was not available to all of the universities until about 1900. The coming of regular support for the libraries coincided with the state appropriations to the universities."[2] The University of Texas received its first legislative appropriation in 1888. Indiana was assisted as early as 1867. Ohio State University, which was founded in 1870, received only a few thousands a year for many years. In Minnesota the legislature voted some land, authorized bond issues, and so forth before, in the words of James Gray, the university historian, "it had accepted its destiny as provider of the purse" and voted a tiny tax levy for the university in 1878.

There are few reliable statistics on library budgets at the turn of the century. At that time the handful of universities with research programs had departmental libraries that were, in nearly all cases, separately administered and separately supported. There was no collection of data by the library director, no reporting to a professional association, the state capitol, or Washington. However, by this time the leading institutions were budgeting funds annually for their central libraries, with specific provision for staff and equipment expenses as well as for books and journals.

A study of university library problems by George Works, financed by the Carnegie Corporation and published in 1927, used data supplied by eighteen institutions "believed to be broadly representative of the principal types of large colleges and universities, and of conditions prevailing in the various geographical areas of the United States." This study shows that, for the period 1900–25, the increase in financial support of libraries compared favorably with the growth in university expenditure for teaching salaries. In a few cases the percentage increase in funds for the library was dramatic, but this was true only when the base was very low. For example at Tulane the base for library support was $600.00 (1900), contrasted with $42,725 for faculty salaries; at North Carolina the base for library expenditures (1904) was $3,879.00; at Cincinnati (1900) it was $2,140.[3]

By 1920 a few leading universities had annual library expenditures for all purposes of over one hundred thousand dollars, as indicated by data in Appendix 4. These and other financial figures, although roughly valid, must, however, be used with caution. For example, a number of institutions could not provide figures for several or all of the university's departmental libraries for 1920; this was occasionally true for later dates. By 1960, however, the figures supplied to the U.S. Office of Education and the Association of Research Libraries, reproduced in Appendix 4, are believed to have been reasonably accurate.

There was a dip in budgets at most institutions in the early 1930s, due to the Great Depression, but by 1940 the parent institutions were far stronger, and support of their libraries vastly improved. By 1938 at least nineteen libraries had annual budgets of more than one hundred thousand dollars and several close to, or more than, five hundred thousand.

By 1960 most budgets were for a million or more and by 1976 they were all well above that, indeed the median of the twenty largest was approximately $7,700,000.00. For all ninety-three university libraries reporting to the Association of Research Libraries, including seven Canadian members, the median expenditure for the 1977–78 budget year was $4,468,000 and the average $5,201,910.

The funding of university libraries received increasingly critical attention as the profession developed more competent administrator-scholars and as the expanding research needs of the universities required more and more of their libraries. A study of the period 1921–41 revealed that "it is clear that since 1933 the universities have allowed their library expenditures to fall behind in relation to their total educational expenditures. The average university spent more for educational purposes in 1941 than it did in 1932, whereas it spent less for books in 1941 than in 1932."[4] The study shows a more favorable picture for the whole twenty-year period. There was a tremendous increase in expenditure for books between 1921 and 1931, then a moderate dip under pressure of the Great Depression of the thirties, then a rise nearly to the 1929–32 average in the late thirties.

The issue of relative importance of the library to the mature university came to a head in the early 1950s. Was the library truly the "heart of the university," the principal organ in the educational-research function and so recognized in administrative councils and financial support, or was the "heart of the university" merely to be accorded lip service along with motherhood, God, and country, but otherwise largely left to fend for itself?

To the 1950 Commission on Financing Higher Education of the Association of American Universities the library presented principally a problem of growth, not indeed a cancerous growth, but more akin to the growth of weeds in a garden. A principal finding of its cursory treatment of libraries stated: "If this [growth] were to continue unchecked, and if much more income is not provided universities, they will soon be in the position of having to drop one or two professors each year in order to keep up the library. This is an obvious absurdity."[5]

The commission's study took for granted that an increased proportion of university funds would inevitably be required for library support because of assumptions made by library leaders, chief among them Keyes Metcalf, director of the Harvard University Library. In 1951 he stated:

> So long as a library grows more rapidly than the rest of the university to which it is attached. . . . the library will tend each year to take a larger percentage of the total resources of the university. It will mean taking money from another part of the university and giving it to the library.

This thesis, which Metcalf expanded in various publications, was based on (1) the cost of storage space as collections grow, (2) the increased unit cost of cataloging with increase in size, (3) increased cost of service both from increase in size and improvement of service, and (4) the expansion of research interest into new fields of study and previously ignored areas of the globe. To continue the quotation,

I think it fair to say that one of the greatest handicaps that librarians face today is the fact that they have the reputation for using more than their share of university appropriations. They are accused of being magpies who collect anything and everything, not because the things will be used, but simply because they are magpies. The library is considered a rathole down which any amount of money may be poured without, alas, drowning the rat.[6]

Metcalf then offered such solutions as restrictions in collecting, reductions in service, dropping professorships annually in order to transfer funds to the library(!), annual elimination of material from the collections, greater efficiency in operation, fund raising by librarians, greater cooperation among librarians in such areas as cataloging, collection building, and finally storage of lesser-used material.

As might be expected the "rathole" metaphor was picked up in unfriendly quarters, and faculty circles resented the suggestion that some of their members should be sacrificed annually to the benefit of the library, a modern version of the ancient Athenian tribute of its young to the Cretan minotaur.

As predicted, research libraries did grow increasingly expensive under the pressures of new academic programs, growth in the volume of publication, gradual inflation, and similar factors. At the same time support for their parent institutions increased dramatically. The key factor was the percentage of funds available to the institution for its educational and administrative program which could or would be assigned to library support.

It is not entirely clear whether university libraries in the seventies were taking a larger or smaller percentage of the "academic and general" funds. The best evidence indicates a slight decline. A scholarly investigation based on data from twenty major universities shows that for the period from 1939 to 1949, there was a decline in library support at sixteen of the twenty and an increase of less than a percentage point at three. There was wide variation for both years. In 1939 three institutions budgeted less than 2 percent and six less than 3 percent as contrasted with three that budgeted 7 percent or better and eight at 5 percent or better. Ten years later, five budgeted less than 2 percent, eleven less than 3 percent, and five 5 percent or better.

A more recent, equally scholarly study of available data concludes:

The average large and medium large research library, contrary to some impressions, does not seem to be taking an ever larger percentage of its parent institution's current expenditures. Furthermore, the average library's percentage of total institutional expenditures for educational and general purposes seems to be relatively small.[7]

Data from twenty-four large and medium-large university libraries covering the years 1945–46 to 1969–70 show that the median percentage of funds applied to library purposes went down from 3.9 percent to 3.35 percent; the mean for the twenty-four went down from 4.1 percent to 3.7 percent. Fussler, the compiler of the above data then comments:

> It is recognized that the general and educational expenditures of a university will include research grants, fellowship support, and other expenditures that may seem to have little effect upon the needs for library services. In fact, some programs funded in this manner quite often make extraordinarily large demands upon the library and its resources, without commensurate funding or support.

While librarians must always look to the parent institution for their principal nourishment, many have had great successes in enlisting supporters who not only gave collections, but also regular donations of money. At first this was done by the director, by such "sturdy beggars" as Sibley of Harvard and Foote of Washington State. But the organized, continuing fund-raising activities of libraries may be dated from 1925 when the organization of Friends of the Library was established at Harvard. This started off with nineteen charter members under a chairman but with most of the "push" coming from the director's office. The practice spread rapidly through the Ivy League institutions and to the large state universities. Yale and Columbia were similarly organized in 1928 and were followed by Princeton and Hopkins in 1930. At Berkeley the establishment of a "Friends" group in 1931 had some influence on the segregation of the more valuable books in a separate "Treasure Room."

In reality Ohio State can claim a "first" with its University Library Association dating from 1897, or even its German Library Association of 1888. Archibald Cary Coolidge was well acquainted with *La Société des Amis de la Bibliothèque Nationale et les Grandes Bibliothèques de France,* a truly magnificent title! It was probably this example that led to the Harvard action. The principal object in 1925 was to have a group to which to turn when special collections came on the market. This continues to be important to Friends groups, but all were soon charging annual dues, sometimes payable in books.

A related development was the appointment of honorary curators, either of a subject, as early English novels, or of a type of publication, as theater playbills. In most cases curators are selected for their interest in, and knowledge of, the assignment, as well as for having resources to make sizable gifts to the collection. Relatively few libraries have made more than an occasional appointment of this nature.

The development of both "Friends" and "Curators" owes much to the imagination, zeal, and organizational ability of Archibald Cary Coolidge, director of libraries at Harvard from 1910 until his death in 1928. This success in attracting gifts of books and money for the library really dates back to the 1850s when Sibley was in charge. Harvard's success has been at least equaled in modern times by such leaders as Knollenberg and Babb of Yale, and Powell and Vosper of UCLA.

While the Carnegie Foundation and other philanthropic bodies responded with grants to support particular projects of all types of libraries, none were interested in regular, continuing general support for collection building or staffing of university libraries. The administration of the university should know best how funds for normal budget needs should be apportioned; grants to a branch of university operation were therefore inappropriate.

As a result there was no recognition of the all too general tendency on the part of university administrations to support libraries only after all other needs were met, until 1955 when the U.S. Steel Foundation began its grants to the Association of College and Reference Libraries for distribution to college libraries. These annual grants from U.S. Steel were continued until 1970. It was thought that the U.S. Steel initiative would attract the support of other foundations, and a few such did indeed assign money to the ACRL grants program in the early years, but the activity suffered from its designation as a U.S. Steel project and from a reluctance on the part of foundations generally to be drawn into activities which continue year after year.

The American Library Association first sought federal support of public libraries in 1946 but it was a decade before the Library Services Act (principally to improve rural library service) was passed. The first appropriation of slightly more than two million dollars was increased to five million in 1958 and six million in 1959. Authorizations later peaked at two hundred and twenty million dollars; appropriations at eighty million under the Library Services and Construction Act, legislation which was much broader in support of public libraries of all types.

Direct federal support of university libraries began with the Depos-

itory Library Act of 1962 which nearly doubled the number of depositories and greatly increased the range of material supplied without
charge. This was followed by the Academic Facilities Act of 1963 which
provided grants for buildings, including libraries, and was of the greatest importance in making possible the new library facilities required by
growth in collections, student bodies, and in complexity of operations.
Next came the Higher Education Act of 1965 providing major grants
for a number of needs, including the strengthening of collections. The
annual appropriations for 1967 through 1969 were twenty-five million
dollars; after 1972 they were greatly reduced and made available, in
sums of under five thousand dollars, to virtually all colleges that applied. Later, specific, large-scale assistance to a very few jury-selected
research libraries was provided by Title IIC of the Higher Education
Act of 1965. Funds for university libraries also came from the government through other channels, principally legislation in support of medical and scientific facilities.

It has been noted that in the infancy of libraries, funds were required
only for books; indeed, a very small sum would have been assigned to
"salaries" had the cost of the librarian-professor been divided in accord-
ance with the division of duties. But as university libraries acquired standing, they also acquired staff and budgets, not only for salaries, for books,
journals, and binding, but also for such other expenses as travel, equipment, and supplies. Costs of light, heat, janitorial care, and building
maintenance are normally assigned elsewhere.

In the years of adolescence, or development, of libraries, staffs were
small and salary costs quite minor, but by 1920 a number of university
libraries had achieved their majority. An examination of the budgets of
the principal university libraries shows that many spent nearly as much
on collections (books, journals, and binding) as on staff. There is, however, considerable variation. By 1939 the proportion assigned to salaries
was greater, but in the majority of cases the expenditure for collections
was nearly two-thirds that for salaries and wages.

World War II and its aftermath brought an upturn in library staff
salaries and a change in budget structure. The norm for collection expenditure dropped to nearly one-third of total budget. A standard text
on university library administration published in 1971 suggested as normal 32 percent for books, 62 percent for salaries, and 6 percent for
supplies, travel, and miscellaneous. A check on the median figures for the
ninety-four university libraries belonging to the Association of Research

Libraries in 1976 shows that 36 percent went for collections, 55 percent for salaries and wages, and 9 percent for other expenditures.

Much of this change in percentages may be attributed to growth in services as libraries grew in size; another factor is the increase in personnel required by the very nature of the new material, in all languages, from all over the globe; increase in volume of expenditure entails complexities of orders, record keeping, etc. that run up the cost; and finally library salary scales began to be competitive with the commercial world.

In fact the salary policy of yesteryear at many institutions, particularly the private institutions of the east, is a blemish on an otherwise admirable record. In far too many cases library directors starved staff in their zeal to put as much as possible into collection building. Women were the basic work force until recent decades and women were exploited. This was the case throughout the profession. When Chancellor McLean of the University of Nebraska appointed Mary L. Jones acting librarian he told her "he should secure a man librarian as soon as the University could pay a fitting salary." It is a pleasure to report that she resigned after two years.

The distinguished library director and bibliographer, Margaret Stillwell, revered General Hawkins who formed the Annmary Brown Library over which she presided. However her hero worship was not entirely blind. "He sincerely believed I had the highest salary of any woman in the United States," she wrote in her autobiography. "He was wrong. He was subconsciously thinking in terms of the past, of my income as compared to that of the local seamstress in the Vermont village where he was born in 1831. He also told me that all I needed 'for maintenance and enjoyment' was rice pudding and just a little milk, three times a day. He was wrong on that count, too."[8] Many a library trustee and director apparently thought "rice pudding and just a little milk" sufficient for his faithful female staff and, unfortunately, most female staff accepted it, however resentful they might feel. It was only a few years ago that two superiors told me, "She doesn't need a raise. Why, her husband at ———university is a hot property!"

Men were also victims. A distinguished clergyman flushed with feeling as he told the writer of the two years he served his Ivy League alma mater in the 1930s at a salary of fifty dollars a month, barely enough for a rented room and three economical meals a day. In another case, also Ivy League, a long-time staff member with three children sought a raise from $75.00 a month from the newly appointed director who had been his immediate supervisor. The director was very sympathetic, put his work aside for nearly two hours, and showed exactly how one should budget to get along, all five of them, on the present salary. These cases are typical of much library leadership from 1900 to 1950. And not only the juniors suffered; the same treatment was accorded those with considerable responsibility, including assistant directors. It was not at all unusual for the second in command to be paid considerably less than one-half the salary of the chief. Highly competent professional librarians never in a lifetime acquired salaries adequate for anything more than the modest expense of a single person. This situation was clear to Wilhelm Munthe, the de Tocqueville of the library world, who commented in 1939:

> I leave it to the reader who is more conversant than I with living expenses in America to decide how many of the whole army of American library workers are paid more than a minimum required for a decent living by a single person with certain cultural interests. And how many are paid enough to support a family? I do not find it hard to believe that librarianship is actually "the worst paid profession in the United States." At any rate it seems to be based on the idea of celibacy.

He went on to comment that

> . . . an essential cause of the prevalent low salaries lies in the inconsiderate manner in which library boards have taken advantage of the oversupply of women workers. The library movement was just getting under way in the period when young women were more and more being forced out into the competition of the labor market.[9]

In retrospect it is clear that great wrongs were inflicted, great bitterness engendered in otherwise devoted, selfless, able staff. It is ironic that the worst offenders were some institutions which took great pride in the importance of their libraries, indeed considered them central to basic functions, and as policy paid top salaries to faculty.

Change came rapidly in the fifties because of the rapid expansion in the job market and consequent shortage of professionally qualified personnel. It was a case of pay or close shop.

As librarians achieved collegial assemblies and, in many cases, faculty status, they could speak with authority on salaries, as on other matters. And speak they did. A distressing situation which had endured for generations has at last been corrected.

As this is written, the future for the support of university libraries is indeed shrouded in mists. The cost of books and journals has been rising much more rapidly than the cost of living and the inflationary spiral shows no signs of abatement. Volume of scholarly publishing is still on the increase, as is the spread of research interests that libraries must support. Individual faculty will always be promoting new studies, demanding facilities for special interests, and the pressure from these bright, eager, often selfish scholars can be well-nigh irresistible. However, there will be economies of operation through technology, the very methods of much publication may change, cooperation will become more effective. Surely adjustments will be made, solutions found.

CHAPTER 9

The Pattern of Service to Students and Scholars

The restrictions on the use of libraries that prevailed in colleges until well into the nineteenth century seem utterly silly to the modern educator. Why were freshmen and sophomores barred from any use of the books? Why the limit of a volume or two a month? Why a fee for each and every book borrowed for home use? The reasons for these and other typical restrictions lie in a combination of factors: the nature of the educational processes of the day; the concept of the library as a treasury to be hoarded rather than to be used; the lack of staff; financial pressures, and probably a broad spectrum of sociological factors—the relationship of teacher to student, concern over what food was suitable for the young mind of the day, the lack of any tradition for the relatively free circulation of books to any segment of society. In short, one wonders if any serious thought was really given to the matter by most presidents and trustees. Tradition was the governing factor.

Despite all the restrictions, students did read. There was the almost daily activity centering around debate in the student literary societies and the sharp focus of the society libraries on these interests. And the truly motivated students used the college library as well. In the small, close circle of hardly more than a hundred boys and a handful of faculty, surely few professor-librarians could resist being moved by the evident interests and needs of the select few, highly motivated, bright teenagers. For example, Thoreau borrowed regularly from the Harvard College Library, only seven volumes in his first term (1833), but rising sharply to thirty in 1834, and continuing regularly thereafter, until two years before his death in 1862. At the same time he was taking books from the library of his debating society, the Institute of 1770. During his senior year, the total borrowed from the society was an amazing fifty-three volumes.

The Hawthornes, Emersons, and Thoreaus read widely at college, but they were the exceptions. Certainly the restrictions deterred all but the most eager students from the use of the college library. But as the nineteenth century wore on there were voices crying out against this attitude and advocating an entirely different approach. The most interesting and famous of these protests is that of Ralph Waldo Emerson, who published his essay "Books" in 1858:

> Meanwhile the colleges, while they provide us with libraries, furnish no professors of books; and I think no chair is so much wanted. In a library we are surrounded by many hundreds of dear friends, but they are imprisoned by an enchanter in these paper and leathern boxes; and though they know us . . . they must not speak until spoken to; and as the enchanter has dressed them, like battalions of infantry, in coat and jacket of one cut, by the thousand and ten thousand, your chance of hitting on the right one is to be computated by the arithmetical rule of Permutation and Combination—not a choice out of three caskets, but out of a half million caskets, all alike.[1]

The Emersonian concept is picked up and elaborated in several articles published in the 1876 *Public Libraries of the United States.* The theme throughout is one of the use of books, rather than their preservation, the importance of the post of librarian, the need of special background for the position. One chapter of the 1876 work is indeed entitled "Professorships of Books and Reading." In detailing, "what the new chair will teach":

> Not the history of literature, nor any one literature, nor any one department of literature, not the grammar of any language, nor any one language, nor language itself, nor any form of its use, nor even any particular form of thought. It is something higher than any of these; it is not any one subject, any one field of investigation, but it is a method for investigating any subject in the printed records of human thought. It might be compared with the calculus in applied mathematics; it is a means of following up swiftly and thoroughly the best researches in any direction and of then pushing them further; it seeks to give a last and highest training for enlarging any desired department of recorded human knowledge. It is the science and art of reading for a purpose; it is a calculus of applied literature.

And later, this modern touch:

> The matter of reading is at present in a wholly unorganized, unscientific, empirical condition, like navigation before the use of the compass and the application of scientific astronomy, or like mining before the introduction of scientific geological and mineralogical investigations and of scientific engineering. Every one digs wherever

he fancies; he may possibly find a deposit of gold, but he may find only mere barren rock or slag or dirt.

Cornell can claim the distinction of being the first university in the North to provide long hours (nine daily!) and to emphasize student use of books from the year it opened, 1868. But the first dramatic steps from the established universities came as Justin Winsor opened up the Harvard library, beginning in 1877, to be followed by even more dramatic steps at Columbia after the arrival of Melvil Dewey in 1883. Winsor and Dewey were the pacesetters, but acceptance of the new concepts came slowly elsewhere. The modern library, like the modern university, evolved gradually as funds became available, as book collections made research possible, as adequate buildings were built, as professionally competent staff came from the few library schools, and, of course, as faculty and administrative attitudes changed.

The first thing to change was, naturally, library hours. All libraries of institutions with pretensions to university status were open during daylight hours by the 1880s, many well before that date. However, it was only as the fear of fire was dispelled, and as funds could be found, that libraries had artificial light which in turn made evening service possible. Harvard's Gore Hall was one of the last to be so provided (1896).

As hours were extended, students were permitted access to the books. This was the obvious thing to do when the total collection was sufficiently small to be housed around a large room, possibly in alcoves. Problems arose as libraries were built with separate book stacks, as at Harvard, Pennsylvania, and Cornell. Winsor preached the gospel of open access but established the practice, followed at Harvard ever since, of access to faculty but student access limited to those doing graduate work and, as space permitted, to a relatively few undergraduates presenting recommendations from their professors.

The early book stacks made some limited provision for readers at tables. Soon the carrel was introduced and the faculty study. Beginning in the 1940s, greater emphasis was placed on making study areas attractive and comfortable. More attention was given to color throughout the building. Easy chairs were introduced. Book stacks were broken up with occasional table-chair accommodations as invitation to work right there on the spot. These breaks in the otherwise solid rows of shelving were termed "oases," surely with no wish to reflect on the nature of the material surrounding them!

Until the late forties, only a very few universities with somewhat smaller student bodies extended stack privileges to the body of undergraduates. It was felt that this open access, which was successful at Princeton and Brown, would result in disaster at other larger institutions such as Northwestern, Pennsylvania, or Michigan.

Indicative of the professional attitude to open stacks is the following, taken from the Office of Education study of library facilities in land grant institutions published in 1930:

> The opportunity afforded students actually to handle books has been recognized by modern libraries as an important factor in the use of books. However, as collections increase in size beyond 50,000 volumes, difficulties arise if stacks are opened to all undergraduates. To meet the need for examination of books and to give opportunity to students to "browse" among them, shelves have been placed in various public rooms of the library. In the larger libraries these shelves contain more volumes than were found in many libraries twenty-five years ago. The University of Illinois has 19,000 volumes in reading rooms open to all students; University of Minnesota, 13,000; Iowa State College 18,000; University of California 20,000, not including departmental or reserve reading rooms. The returns of the survey show that no complaint was made of closed stacks where 10,000 or more volumes were available in public reading rooms. The five institutions which noted student complaints of closed stacks were institutions whose total book collections available in public reading rooms numbered respectively, 4,998, 6,200, 1,100, 1,500, 1,420. All these institutions . . . also show loans per student that are below average.[2]

Attitudes changed after World War II, when most universities began to offer stack permits freely to undergraduates as well as to graduates and faculty. Some directors did so reluctantly. There were fears of hordes of students fighting their way through the packed aisles, wholesale mutilation of material, thefts, rape, and other terrible crimes. Crowds there were not; the attraction of the library simply was not sufficient. Misplacing of books was a serious problem and constant checking of shelves to restore order was necessary. There were occasional thefts of coats and purses, and very occasional cases of indecent exposure or worse. But the pluses outweighed the minuses. By the mid-fifties the open stack was considered so important to collegiate education at all levels that it was accepted as fundamental. Most central university library buildings erected since 1950 are so designed that closure of the stack area is a virtual impossibility. Only a handful of the largest libraries still retain restrictions because of special problems.

A very few universities with enlightened policies in most matters drew strange lines between permissions for male and female readers, ostensibly in fear lest the young ladies be embarrassed or molested. As late as 1925 at Indiana University freshmen women were shooed out of the library at 7:30 P.M. unless their work could not be otherwise arranged. Until very recent years, Harvard refused female readers entry to the main reading room; books were brought to them to use in a tiny room nearby, a space hardly suitable for more than four people. Access to the stacks was refused all women after dark, and this was a severe handicap to female graduate students and scholars. These quaint sexual restrictions were, naturally, intended for the benefit of the young, and not so young, women, but this concern was hardly appreciated.

To return in time to the revolution following the Civil War, the first important step to facilitate the use of books was the establishment of the reserve book collection, in other words to gather together special groups of material to meet the needs of particular courses. This practice dates from the 1870s, and is variously credited as a "first" to three professors of history, all named Adams: Charles Kendall Adams, later president of Cornell and Wisconsin, while professor of history at the University of Michigan from 1869; Henry Adams of *Mont St. Michel and Chartres* fame, professor of history at Harvard from 1870; and Herbert Baxter Adams, one of the "greats" of the original 1876 Johns Hopkins faculty. In each case, books were withdrawn from the general collection and made noncirculating to insure availability. They were put on special shelves, in alcoves, or in seminar rooms. As the practice grew, reserves were put behind counters and produced on request, or shelved in a reading room devoted entirely to reserved books.

It is from this same period that the seminar collection and seminar room came into vogue, following the model of the German university. The library buildings erected after 1880 generally had a few such rooms designed to serve graduate study in a particular discipline. The seminar arrangements continued to be regarded as fundamental until the 1940s. While modern library buildings normally contain seminar rooms, they seldom provide for seminar collections. In actual practice it was found that the segregation of a small group of books for the special benefit of a few advanced students was a luxury; it was also a question whether or not the existence of the collection might lessen knowledge of, and use of, the broader literature in the general book stack.

Other devices were tried. Rental collections, sometimes of textbooks, sometimes of titles on reserve and sometimes of current and popular literature, had a vogue in the 1920s and 1930s. Chicago had one as early as 1898, run by an alumnae club and later taken over and expanded under library auspices. It grew in size and in receipts until absorbed by the university bookstore in 1928. The University of California at Berkeley began its rental service in 1929, and phased it out in 1943, again because it was shifted to the bookstore. Both operations relieved the heavy pressures on the reserve book service.

Another device to increase student use of books was the "browsing room," later to go under various other names such as "leisure reading." The first of these with quarters of its own, with an attendant selected for knowledge of literature and rapport with students, with comfortable chairs and pleasant decor, was the Farnsworth Room in the Widener Library at Harvard, established in 1916. The success of this collection led to incorporation of similar rooms or reading areas and collections in virtually all university libraries.

Unlike the Farnsworth Room, the Bull's Head Bookshop, established in the University of North Carolina library building somewhat later, did not start a trend; it performed similar notable service to the intellectual climate by serving as a meeting place, by providing a book service that minimized the commercial, and by arranging book talks and author readings. Such activity in the library was eyed with suspicion by the typical university bookstore, dedicated principally to the sale of texts, sweat shirts, and drinking glasses, and hungry to turn a profit.

The growth of universities and their libraries, in numbers of students and faculty, in breadth and depth of research interests, in size of library collections, in sheer distance between academic buildings and, of course, in financial support, all combined to put pressure on libraries to find organizational patterns suited to meet these changing conditions. An obvious development was recognition of the need for departmental libraries and the effort was to keep them from careless proliferation and of a size to warrant professional staff and service.

Another major development of the late thirties was the divisional library. This new development was pioneered by Ralph Ellsworth at Colorado and Henry Bartlett Van Hoesen at Brown. The basic concept was to divide the central library into several major segments by subject, originally the humanities, the social sciences, science-technology, and, usually, education. Each unit had its own reading room stocked with major works on the subject, its own reference service provided by staff which had, or should have had, advanced degrees in pertinent subject fields, and its own catalog. In short, the division is basically a self-contained library within a library except for holdings in rare books and microfilm. In theory, and often in practice, it becomes the daily workshop for undergraduates, graduates, and faculty. It fosters a healthy feeling of common purpose, a student-teacher relationship. Divisional staff often have joint library-teaching appointments; they participate regularly in book selection and are sometimes assigned cataloging responsibility.

The divisional plan was picked up by a number of institutions such as Georgia, North Carolina, Louisiana State, Oregon, and Florida, but it did not become widespread. The emphasis on modular construction of the 1950s and 1960s militated against the separate reading rooms. The trend toward open stacks in most university libraries also worked against the divisional plan. And it was expensive in staff. Finally, there was the competing interest in the undergraduate library. Aspects of the divisional plan do survive, however, in the move toward separate science libraries, and in isolated cases in the arrangements for special reference service to certain disciplines, as education, business and classical studies, in the open stack library.

The emphasis on the university library of the present study precludes the mention of various other developments used to facilitate undergraduate use of books, but one of major importance to all levels of study is the undergraduate library. Historians trace the concept back to 1608, when it was broached at Oxford, and later to Harvard which, in 1765, set aside "a smaller library for the common use of the college." The case for separation of research and undergraduate materials and services was nicely stated as early as 1848 by President Edward Everett of Harvard, in his report for that year:

> A select library of works specially adapted for the wants of young men at college should be arranged, and its use granted gratuitously and on the most liberal terms to the students. This collection might be advantageously placed in a separate building. The proper care, preservation, and administration of a large, general library, intended to be a repository of the rarer works in every department of science and literature, require arrangements somewhat at variance with

those which belong to a select working collection for practical purposes in a place of education.[3]

Nearly a half-century later his successor to the presidency, Charles W. Eliot, spoke out in presidential agony over the cost of a great collection of books when a small collection would meet most student needs.

James H. Canfield, librarian at Columbia, was probably the first to establish an undergraduate library (1907). This consisted of six thousand volumes selected for suitability for undergraduate instruction. Brown followed the Columbia example in 1909 by setting up "a student library of some 15,000 volumes," which was placed on the main floor as an open-shelf library. The loan period was extended from two weeks to one month. As noted previously, many large universities had followed suit by 1930. Unfortunately, few provided staff knowledgeable about the collections and adequate to give reference service.

Therefore, the building of the Lamont Undergraduate Library at Harvard in 1949, a separate entity, was an event of major significance. It set the pattern for similar facilities provided soon afterward at Michigan, Chicago, Cornell, Stanford, South Carolina, Illinois, and Texas as well as many others. In general these emphasize: a book collection of sixty thousand to one hundred and fifty thousand volumes selected for undergraduate studies and interests; comfortable study environment in respect to heat, light, decor, seating; competent staff equipped to give good reference service; facilities and book stock arranged for ease of access; often special services and facilities such as listening rooms for music and poetry, exhibits, author talks, etc. In a number of cases the universities adapted the old central library building to undergraduate use when erecting a new, larger library, usually designated as the research library.

In the undergraduate library, considerable emphasis is placed on reference service—guidance in the use of catalogs, periodical indices, abstract journals and, indeed, the whole collection. But reference service has been slow in winning recognition on all American campuses. As late as the 1950s the head of a history department in a large university, a long-time member of the faculty library committee, opposed the appointment of a librarian to give reference service. In effect, said he, we don't need anyone to help us use the library. Let students find their own way around. Of course the professor himself was notorious for seeking personal assistance from the director and the heads of departments in the library as he ran into problems.

Informal reference service of this type was certainly given before 1876, when Samuel Swett Green read a paper at the first ALA conference on "The Desirableness of Establishing Personal Intercourse and Relations Between Librarians and Readers in Popular Libraries." Green was sponsoring "not a new theory of library service but a new technique," as applicable to university personnel as to the general public. Professor Otis Robinson of the University of Rochester responded to Green by applying the proposal to college libraries:

> A librarian should be much more than a keeper of books; he should be an educator. . . . The relation which Mr. Green has presented ought especially to be established between a college librarian and the student readers. No such librarian is fit for his place unless he holds himself to some degree responsible for the library education of the students. . . . It is his province to direct very much of their general reading; and especially in their investigation of subjects, he should be their guide and friend.[4]

Green's paper is significant not so much for its influence as it is as a "first" in advocating direct reference assistance. This is a concept in line with Emerson's "Professorship of Books and Reading," but quite different because it emphasized informal guidance in the use of library facilities. Both stressed the educational role, but promoted different routes in effecting it.

Harvard under Winsor was the first major library to stress service and reader assistance. Winsor opened the book stack to the faculty and a limited number of students, in line with his guiding principle that nothing is "more important than the provision of large classes of books to which unrestricted access can be had." He fought the textbook system: "Who is bold enough to throw text-books to the dogs, and lead his class through the library?" Winsor inaugurated instruction in the use of the card catalog. He did not, however, contribute in any important way in either teaching the use of books and guidance in reading, as advocated by Emerson, or in what came to be recognized as reference assistance, "that branch of administration which deals with the assistance given to readers in their use of the resources of the library." In fact, Harvard was not to have reference service in its main library until Keyes Metcalf came as director in 1937. Winsor's only contribution was publicizing a service whereby questions could be posted in the library with invitation to some knowledgeable person to respond—an informal notes and queries operation.

It was Melvil Dewey, the trailblazer of the profession, who inaugurated reference service and gave it the form and direction it has retained ever since. On taking office at Columbia he at once announced that "the library offers students the best bibliographies, cyclopaedias, dictionaries, and other works of reference, and aims to induce [students] by example, by discriminating counsel, and by direct training, to know these books, to use them intelligently, and to acquire the habit of hunting down a needed fact. . . . What are the best books on the subject, in what order, and how to take them up, are points on which the undergraduate student most often needs light. . . . It is the first and paramount duty of the Reference Librarian to give such help." Dewey was not one to promote, then not follow through. His first annual report lists George Baker and William G. Baker as reference librarians. Later reports speak of the increasing work load and usefulness of this activity, with the comment, "we esteem this perhaps the most important single department."

Both the term "reference" and the function took root. Cornell had a reference librarian by 1891. Indiana added a reference librarian to its staff in 1897, but the position was allowed to lapse in a few years. Other libraries followed in the late 1890s and early twentieth century but not such major ones as Chicago, Yale, and Harvard. Regarding this period, Samuel Rothstein comments: "Interpreting the catalog and assisting undergraduate students were the chief responsibilities of the reference worker in the American college of the 1890s, with only an occasional hint as yet that such assistance might be pertinent to more advanced researches." A partial explanation for this limitation lies in the relative ease of using the collections and bibliographical apparatus of that day.

Reference as an organized, staff function was very slow in coming to a number of the major private university libraries. Some little help was available to the persistent, but it was help obtained from staff who were busy with other responsibilities.

The major state universities saw things differently and emphasized reference almost at once as their libraries developed regular budgetary support and skeleton staffs. They were prompt in setting up open-shelved collections of basically reference books and staff to assist with the use of the catalog and the entire book collection. This generally involved some organized instruction in the use of the library. The University of Illinois created its reference department in 1897. The original staff of one had grown to three by 1913. While the largest and most progressive state universities recognized the vital need for librarians with specific reference functions, such recognition was slow in coming elsewhere. Of the forty-eight libraries covered by the 1930 Survey of Land Grant Colleges and Universities, only twenty-eight had reference librarians. One of the last major university libraries to appoint a reference librarian was Cincinnati, which did so in the early 1950s. This was the situation in the main or central libraries. Naturally even the largest departmental libraries, such as law and medicine, were much later in funding reference service.

Hand in hand with recognition of the importance of the reference function came an awareness of the need for formal instruction in bibliography and the use of libraries.

The first course in bibliography offered by an American university was an elective taught at Michigan in 1882. Columbia followed shortly after. Its President Barnard stated in his annual report for 1883, possibly with a nudge from the recently arrived Melvil Dewey:

> The average college student . . . is ignorant of the greater part of the bibliographical apparatus which the skilled librarian has in hourly use, to enable him to answer the thousand queries of the public. A little systematic instruction would so start our students in the right methods, that for the rest of their lives all their work in libraries would be more expeditiously accomplished. . . . In fact, it is hardly an exaggeration to say that now students often . . . spend half their time in the library finding out what they don't want to know, and the remaining half in getting confused notions of what they do want to know.[5]

Courses were taught before 1900 at a small number of other libraries, notably West Virginia, Illinois, Cornell, and Indiana. The need for such instruction was recognized and acted on gradually in the first decades of the twentieth century, particularly at the state universities of the Midwest and West. Formal instruction in either bibliography or the use of the library was very slow in gaining recognition at the large, privately supported universities of the East.

Few topics crop up as frequently in the professional literature since 1900 as library orientation and instruction in bibliography. Despite all the rhetoric, progress was scant, and the discussions of the forties and fifties resembled closely those of the turn of the century. A first development to win nearly universal acceptance was the "student guide to the use of the library." The first of these appeared shortly after 1900 at Illinois, Purdue, and West Virginia.

A second early development was the offering of tours of the building, conducted by reference librarians. The limitations of these were generally recognized, but they were continued as better than nothing. As enrollments swelled after 1945 tours were given up at many institutions because of the magnitude of the undertaking. Another "service" frequently offered was a lecture, usually by a librarian, and given in the library, to all sections of freshman English. This again became a problem too big for the library staff to handle at many institutions when the sections grew in number to one hundred or more.

Real progress dates from about 1960, as many reference departments came to recognize a responsibility for bibliographic instruction both in courses offered by the library and in lecturing to courses on research methods in given fields, or other instruction not under library control. And during these recent years came a proliferation of conferences, workshops, and meetings on local, regional, and national levels as well as a growth of publication of considerable merit. The American Library Association set up a Committee on Instruction in the Use of Libraries, in 1967. A few years later ACRL established a section on the subject and ALA approved a round table.

As this is written most universities have available a program to orient new students in the use of the library. These programs use either film, slides, or sophisticated audio equipment which enable the student to take his own tour, guided by instructions given through earphones. In such ways technology is now being tapped to introduce the student to his library in a reasonably effective manner. Libraries are making increasing use of self-paced study booklets, some of which are quite detailed, for completion of which course credit may be given. Notable examples are the courses developed at UCLA by Miriam Dudley and the University of Alaska by Millicent Hering. But the thrust of present interest is toward bibliographical instruction on a thoroughly scholarly level. Progress in stressing the importance of this on faculties and university administrators is distressingly slow. In the recent words of an authority:

> One looks almost in vain for serious recognition of bibliographic instruction by college and university teaching faculty and administrators. To be sure, lip service is paid in such comments as the library's being "the heart of the college," but except for librarians' publications there is scarcely any comment on the subject in the literature of higher education. . . . As for insuring their intelligent and effective use through bibliographic instruction, that's an idea hardly considered, much less accepted.[6]

For nearly a century librarians have been concerned about the educational function, as distinct from the research function, but the demands of the latter have generally been overriding. Librarians are well aware that there is no medicine quite as potent in creating library interest as a stimulating instructor in any subject, as effective in elementary physics and chemistry as in English and history. Unfortunately, few university instructors make the effort to awaken interests which are broadening and exploratory beyond the course outlines. And always there is the problem of sheer numbers in today's large university. What if three or four thousand freshmen were all to become eager to read widely beyond the requirements of the classroom, and to descend on the library en masse? There would be chaos. And so discussions continue, adjustments are made, but satisfactory solutions elude the profession.

CHAPTER 10

The Library Building

In one respect, the origins of library architecture resemble the origins of the book, in that one of the very earliest examples of building was, like the Gutenberg Bible, one of the finest. Architectural craftsmen of the present can benefit from reflection on the principles adopted by Michelangelo when he designed the Biblioteca Mediceo-Laurenziana in Florence for Clement VII in the early sixteenth century. Without any architectural experience at the time, Michelangelo created "the most important and influential Italian secular building of the sixteenth century" according to Rudolf Witthower, the distinguished critic. And an equally distinguished librarian, evaluating that library as a functional building, wrote "For the first time in the history of art, the inside of a library is conceived, not in terms of the requirements of religious architecture, but as a concept of its unique function." The design of Michelangelo was to create in his library an environment suitable for intellectual concentration. "Form follows function," which Michelangelo understood intuitively and executed with such amazing artistry, has been the rallying cry of enlightened librarians every since. Unfortunately, it has been accorded only lip service all too frequently by distinguished architects.

When books were produced only by hand at great labor they were few in number and greatly prized. Therefore they were chained to the reading desks or lecterns and stored flat immediately below. This system became obsolete after the invention of printing as greater numbers became available. Now books were placed upright on shelves, along the wall. But this still did not adequately provide for increasing numbers. Sir Christopher Wren is generally credited with the next step in storage provisions—the alcove library. In the Trinity College Library at Cambridge, built in 1675, he used alcoves with a table for consultation of material in the center of each. The alcove likewise provided natural division by subject. It reduced distraction, it facilitated record keeping and shelving, and it had aesthetic appeal. Small wonder that it is attractive to modern man.

The fledgling American libraries of a few hundred volumes had little

need for alcoves or for a "library architecture" until well into the nineteenth century. The initial requirements in nearly every case were a room,
if one could be afforded, some shelves, a table or two, and chairs. If no
room was available then cupboards that could be locked were used.
Security, not use, was the principal concern of the library, virtually the
only one.

The contact of the Bay Colony with Cambridge was close, and the
Trinity library well known. Yale arranged its library in six alcoves in its
very first collegiate building (1718). Likewise, Harvard used alcoves in its
library, rebuilt from the fire of 1764. The usual practice of the collegiate
institutions into the early decades of the nineteenth century was to locate
the library on the second floor of a three-to-four-floor multipurpose
building, which might in fact be "every purpose": dormitory, dining hall,
classrooms, even faculty housing! These buildings had to be heated and
had to have the illumination of candles and whale-oil lamps, both danger-
ous in the hands of irresponsible youth. Construction was mostly of
wood, and therefore the danger of fire was great. With few exceptions,
the alcove arrangement was utilized only as the collections grew to several thousand volumes.

A brief second stage in the development of physical facilities was the
placement of the library above the chapel. This was done at Yale in 1763,
Bowdoin in 1805, Wesleyan in 1824, and Brown in 1835. The room was
normally a rectangular one on the second floor, in alcove arrangement,
a window to each alcove. The chapel was safer than the all-purpose
academic building, but fire remained a constant fear.

The next step was, naturally, the separate building. The University
of Virginia could claim the distinction of primacy in 1825 but in theory
only, for the library was forthwith put to a variety of other uses. The
University of South Carolina built a library in 1840, Harvard in 1841, Yale
in 1843, Williams in 1847 and Amherst in 1853.

It is noteworthy that the first two collegiate library buildings were
erected in the South; even more noteworthy is the fact that the universities of Virginia and South Carolina both built libraries of distinguished
design. The University of Virginia building, famous for its rotunda, was
well planned for library purposes. Credit for a "first" must be assigned
to the University of South Carolina building, which has ever since its
completion served as the library and not for other major functions. It is
an unusually felicitous design, with a beautiful reading room which is a
nearly exact replica of Charles Bulfinch's original Library of Congress.

The deep alcoves have high arched windows for both ventilation and light. Walls are of brick. The library was spared by Sherman's troops and served a full century as the central library for the university; with the erection of the new library in 1940, the earlier building was redesignated the South Caroliniana Library and assigned the growing collection of local history.

The first two library buildings were in the South, but history must look to New England for the thread of development, for there library after library was built while southern institutions lay prostrate in Reconstruction poverty.

The first New England library buildings gave considerable attention to size—size to provide for future collection growth—but relatively little size for other vital functions. Put another way, the overriding goal was a large, safe storage edifice. Thinking did not go far beyond that. Alcoves were assumed, windows for natural light were a necessity. Virtually no provision was made for staff. Concern for reader occupancy was to develop only slowly as the nineteenth century drew to a close.

At this period when our forefathers did think of function, the major consideration was safety—from fire primarily, but also from water and theft, in short, preservation of the collection. The memory of disastrous fires was all too vivid. Books were precious. Use was hardly a consideration. The library was to be a storeroom. Safety dictated not only the construction of the building but its site, which was selected not for convenient access but for being a safe distance from other buildings that might burn. Fortunately, the campuses of these days were hardly so extensive that convenience was greatly sacrificed!

President Quincy, in writing of Harvard's first library, stated, "Harvard was determined at the outset, to use every precaution which the friends of the College would allow, to guard the library from destruction of fire. In every part of the structure, therefore, wood had been rejected, where its place could be supplied without a very great increase in cost in the construction, or inconvenience of some kind in the use, by stone, brick, or iron.[1] So the walls were of stone, the rafters and trusses of iron, the roof of slate. The university's decision to erect a separate library building was prompted as much by the fear of fire in Harvard Hall as by the need for more space.

Yale had experienced no fire but was equally conscious of the danger. The library had many moves—from the original collegiate building of 1718 to a chapel building in 1765, to a similar building in 1804, to another chapel in 1824 which had bedrooms on the third floor and therefore considerable danger of fire, and finally into a separate building, shared with the three literary society libraries, in 1846. This new building was of stone and brick in most parts, but floors, ceiling, doors, and window frames were wooden. However, its unusually talented architect, Henry Austin, used the major structural elements in such a way as to minimize the spread of flames within the building.

And so it went—Williams College built of brick with a metal roof, Amherst College used stone with not only a metal roof, but iron doors, galleries, and staircases. At Wesleyan it was brownstone. Only at Mount Holyoke, in this early period, was the library building attached to another building, but a fireproof door and a long corridor stood the college in good stead in 1896 when the main building burned, but the library was saved.

Certainly because of fire, possibly because they were so little used, most of these early libraries were built without any provision for heat. Harvard's Gore Hall did have a tiny furnace, but Yale, Williams, and Amherst all lacked any such facility. The New England winters soon forced reconsideration, and stoves, then furnaces, were added after some years; it was only after 1860 that heating was provided in original plans. With respect to artificial light, the record is better even though evening access was unheard of. Some provision was made from the fifties on and gas illumination was generally provided after the 1860s.

Library architecture emerged as a topic of discussion in the 1850s. It was emphasized in the first library conference held in 1853 in New York and was that same year featured in an article in *Norton's Literary Gazette and Publisher's Circular*.[2] American scholars and college presidents were generally familiar with the Bibliothèque Sainte Geneviève, completed in 1850, which had the first true library stack. There was also an emergent literature of European origin on the subject to which the few professional collegiate librarians of that day had access. And there was ever the debate over architectural style—Gothic-Italianate, Tudor, Romanesque, neo-Greek or whatever—for architects were then, as many continued to be over the decades, supremely confident of their ability to fit this or any other function into a predetermined shell.

Unlike many other institutions, Harvard had given students access to the shelves until the time the new library was built in 1841. The new building had essentially an alcove arrangement, but the "no admittance" signs remained up until the 1870s. Planning of the library was assigned to a committee of the faculty, headed by the president; Thadeus Harris, the longtime librarian, was not a member, nor is there evidence that he was consulted in any of the work. This was generally true of other New England libraries in the following decades.

The planning of Gore Hall, as Harvard's library came to be named, antedated that of South Carolina's building, but there was in any case no communication on such matters in that period. Therefore, there was no American prototype. Harvard took more than two years in developing its drawings for Gore Hall and even constructed a model. The result was a Gothic cathedral patterned after King's College Chapel, Cambridge, with alcove arrangements. Like many a later creator, President Quincy was inordinately proud of what was basically his creation. Later he wrote: "The appearance of the whole is imposing; hardly surpassed, in effect, by any room in this country . . . as none of the other halls of the University present any claims to excellence in architecture, the attention of strangers will probably be directed to Gore Hall . . . as the principal ornament of the College square."[3] The building probably did attract donations, as do most new libraries; the artistic judgment of the good president, however, was not shared by later critics. It came to be judged one of the least ornamental of all the Harvard buildings, in short, a veritable monstrosity.

While the architecture of Gore passed muster for some decades, there was a mounting protest against other shortcomings: dampness in the basement and in the single-thickness masonry walls; utter lack of any staff working space except in open corridors and alcoves; noise; lack of provision for expansion, lack of artificial lighting, and inadequate heating. Therefore, the building, planned to last until 1900, was less than two decades old before there was recognition of the need for either an important addition or an entirely new edifice.

Yale began giving serious thought to a library building in 1839; this was led by two professors who were generous contributors to the cost as well as to planning the shape it would take. Actual control was apparently assigned to a committee of the trustees.

Yale followed Harvard's example in building essentially a Gothic cathedral, but aesthetically one that was much superior. An innovation was provision for the libraries of the three literary societies, each with separate entrance. Arrangement was by alcoves. But there were the same problems that plagued Gore Hall and many others down to present times: dampness, inadequate light and heat, and lack of space. The Yale building was definitely an advance, not only in architecture and construction, but also in providing a reading room separate from the book storage, work space for the staff, movable shelving, and a measure of exit control.

Other New England colleges followed roughly the same pattern. In 1846 Williams built an octagonal library which, with additions, served its central collection until 1922. It was distinguished by careful planning for natural light, supervision from a centrally located librarian's desk, and good staff space. Amherst followed in 1853 with a building notable for complete lack of heat. This was remedied later by one stove in the basement which was credited with raising the temperature to 35° or even 40° on mild days in winter. Passage of time brought more wood stoves and the building served its original function until 1917.

This then, was the picture until the Civil War: most institutions, none of them universities in any modern sense, had small book collections stored in one room of a central building, usually in alcoves but frequently on any shelving arrangement which choice or whim provided. A very few institutions had separate buildings for their libraries. These were carefully located not for ease of access, but to be sufficiently removed from other buildings so as not to be endangered by fire. A major principle was separation of books from readers. Shelving was in alcoves, with galleries for expansion. Light and ventilation were provided by windows and skylights; gas lighting, which became normal in the latter half of the century, was provided only very slowly. There was little heat. Emphasis was on the protection, not the use, of books. A notable exception to nearly all the above and a shining example of enlightened librarianship was the University of South Carolina, but it was far from the mainstream and its example apparently had no influence on the important institutions of the North.

The three decades following the Civil War brought enormous expansion in higher education, as to many other aspects of American life. Student enrollment increased from 52,000 in 1870 to 232,000 in 1900. Led by Daniel Coit Gilman, first president of Johns Hopkins University and Charles W. Eliot, Harvard's vigorous young leader, the 1870s brought the emergence of true universities, bursting out like young chicks from the confines of the traditional collegiate shell. The principal prototypes were, of course, the German universities, notably Göttingen, where many Americans took graduate studies.

Most established American institutions, whether still collegiate or blossoming into graduate and professional studies, acquired separate library buildings during this period. And as these came under the direction of men who took librarianship for their profession, a number of principles developed in the eighties and nineties which were continued, with some refinements, until the mid 1940s.

First and foremost came general recognition for the principle of separation of book storage area from reading area. Behind this move was the need for a storage principle more compact than the alcove and concern for the safety of collections to which all and sundry had direct access. Until the seventies most institutions had opened their alcoves, and therefore their book collection, to students for a few hours weekly. Harvard was the principal exception in permitting no access.

A major factor in planning for function was the entirely unforeseen growth in the rate of acquisitions. This was true of virtually all libraries outside the South. For example, when Harvard's Gore Hall was built, the increase was, and indeed had been since the 1760's, approximately one thousand volumes annually. But with the new building it increased rapidly to well over six thousand volumes in the sixties, and the storage which was to have lasted comfortably for sixty years was filled in one-third of that time. Other institutions experienced the same acceleration in growth at a later date; it struck all with claims to university status well before 1900.

The solution to the problems of security and bulk was the multi-tier iron stack. This developed in Europe, first at the Bibliothèque Ste. Geneviève (1850) and later at the Bibliothèque Nationale and the British Museum. Its first American application was in the 1876 addition to Gore Hall. This was "a shell . . . built of masonry walls pierced by rows of small windows . . . Into this were packed book ranges, row on row, tier on tier . . . The aisles between the ranges were 28 inches wide and the tiers seven feet high . . . The stack was six tiers high, self-supporting throughout, and depended on the building only for protection. The vertical supports were of cast iron, the deck flooring of perforated cast iron slabs, and the shelves of wood, supported at the ends by light zinc Z bars fitting into the uprights."[4]

This iron stack was at once adopted as standard for university libraries. There were of course gradual refinements and improvements. The deck flooring soon became a wire-reinforced glass which theoretically permitted the passage of some light but still passed nineteenth century standards of modesty, despite the doubts of nervous women. Slabs were later often of marble, and still later, of concrete. Shelves of wood remained standard until the steel open-bar type was developed just prior to 1900. These wooden shelves were held in place by metal pins driven into each end; needless to say the shelves were prone to splintering, to the despair of stack attendants. These and other improvements in book storage were principally developed by Snead and Company of Jersey City which by virtue of its leadership had the lion's share of business in supplying shelving for large research libraries until the 1940s.

Readers' requests for books from the stack were initially serviced by attendants on foot, for with the principle of separation of book collection came restrictions on access to it. The pneumatic tube and an elementary book conveyor were first used in the new Boston Public Library building (1895). An essential for the movement of books in the larger stacks was an elevator; small libraries could get by with manually-operated dumbwaiters.

The provision of reading rooms for student use became standard with the adoption of the separate stack. This room provided some material for study and reference, books to which students needed ready access. The nineteenth century reading room often had alcoves, probably a hangover from the past, but also visually attractive, convenient for the separation of groups of material, and sufficiently removed from the large open area to aid concentration. And with the reading room came, late in the century, an essentially German transplant, the seminar collection. Both Cornell and Pennsylvania completed large libraries in 1891 and each provided a few seminar rooms as well as the large main reading rooms. By this time the reserve book function was established and required a separate reading area. Set off to the side or rear was the multi-tier book stack, with access limited to faculty and graduate students.

After the Civil War, recognition of staff needs for working space was universal. Offices were provided for one or several administrators as well as work areas for the various functions of ordering, cataloging, and circulation or service to readers. Likewise, most libraries now had some form of central heat and gas or electric light. This was, however, only for evening use; the provision of natural light for daytime work continued to be a major architectural consideration well into the twentieth century.

Until 1900 the reading room was usually found on the entrance level either directly on entrance or set slightly to one side. The stack was then either to the rear or placed at the other side of the main door, normally with some provision for a later addition. The University of Pennsylvania library had an entrance hall with stairs to an upstairs reading room. Straight ahead lay a circulation desk with catalog area and reference-reading room to the left, and book stack to the right. Principal workrooms were downstairs, at receiving-room (street) level. Stack lighting was electric, aided by a skylight. There was one elevator.

The Pennsylvania and Cornell buildings, like all late-nineteenth-century libraries, were aesthetically very heavy, almost like medieval fortresses, with thick brick walls, towers and protuberances. They were poorly lighted, noisy, gloomy, often drafty, and quite inflexible. Indeed, libraries large and small were to retain these characteristics for two generations despite changes in architectural styles. The Carnegie Corporation pled the case for simplicity and flexibility in libraries in its pamphlet "Notes on the Erection of Library Buildings" of 1911, but this was lost on the universities which tended to move in the opposite direction. Architectural treatment of the library was largely determined by the prevailing campus style, which was often the Gothic, so inadequate for library functions.

The heavy Romanesque influence of Henry Hobson Richardson, the leading architect of the post-Civil War decades, melted away after the completion of Boston's new library building of 1895, designed by Charles Folsom McKim. The great influence of this building on all American library architecture is, however, less a matter of design, which happened to be Italian Renaissance, than on interior arrangement, or functional plan. This provided a grand interior stair leading to one great reading room which stretched across the front of the building with thirteen high, arched windows, as much an aesthetic feature for the facade as for light and ventilation. Stack access and book delivery was on the same second-floor level, with stack tiers below and above. There were unfortunate features to the Boston stack and it had little or no influence on library design, but the basic plan of stairs, with a principal reading room across the front on the second floor, became virtually standard for university as well as large public libraries, until the post-World War II revolution in planning.

It was to the Library of Congress building of 1897 rather than the Boston Public Library, that librarians looked for leadership in stack plan and equipment. The genius behind this was Bernard Richardson Green, a civil and architectural engineer who collaborated with the Snead Company on much of the shelving development. Since there were nine tiers, steel columns were required in place of iron. Green studied the problems of fire, dust, weather, vermin, lighting, ventilation, conservation of material, ease of access, and economy of space. He designed a new bar-type shelf which was a great improvement for insertion and for support. Slits in the deck provided some light but were basically for circulation of air, an important factor for the control of dampness. Windows were sealed and air drawn by fans into the basement, filtered, heated as required, and allowed to rise, assisted by exhaust fans in the roof. The aisles were lighted with electricity. One critic sums up the contribution thus:

> The major characteristics of Green's design, then, were carefully made, rust-free, easily adjusted shelves, an effective communication and book conveying system, adequate artificial light, and a modern ventilation system that included sealed windows. With minor modifications this system is still in operation. It is easy to overlook the revolutionary character of these features in the building, and it explains why Metcalf was able to say 50 years later, "Modern bookstacks began with the Library of Congress".[5]

During the 1890s the forces which gave birth to large and complex library buildings to serve the emerging universities also fostered the cult of monumentalism, a disease to which university libraries are uniquely susceptible. Standard styles such as Gothic, Colonial, Southern Planter, Grecian, etc. were "bastardized in an attempt to contain vast study rooms, work areas and bookstacks within suitably impressive facades." If there was indeed a traditional style for the larger research libraries of the late nineteenth and early twentieth centuries, it was one emphasizing the monumental, splendid with towers, buttresses, domes, columns, etc. whether Grecian, Romanesque, Renaissance, or other style predominant on the campus. Some, as Columbia's Low Library, smacked of the temple; others, as at Northwestern, of the cathedral. Restraints entered the picture from about 1915 as simplicity was recognized not only as good taste, but also as a means of economy.

The buildings erected after 1910 generally adopted an innovation in stack planning by providing study space for readers. This usually consisted of small tables for individual use in perimeter areas with windows. Later on these became carrels equipped with individual light and a shelf or two. Use was limited to graduate students and faculty. And for a few very fortunate and very influential professors, the convenience of a separate study in the book stack might be provided. The stack was quickly recognized as an ideal place to study because of proximity to materials, seclusion from visual distraction, quiet, and protection from students, spouses, phone, and other interruptions—all mere harassments in the eyes of the scholar.

University library stacks were not normally as high as those of the

Library of Congress and it was standard to have a middle tier, level with the grand second-floor reading room, with several tiers above, and several below. There were many variations, as in the 1930 building of the University of Cincinnati, erected on a sharp slope. Here the entrance from campus is above six floors of stacks, and the main and highly ornamented reading room is up a full sixteen feet further. In such cases elevators and book conveyor system are essential.

Ease of student access to reading areas was not an important consideration, partly because library use was not generally recognized as central to the educational process until the thirties, and partly because the very idea of a mere flight of stairs as an obstacle to young people was decidedly ridiculous. There were no standards for size of reading rooms or number of seats in relation to student body. It was rule-of-thumb provision both for book storage and student accommodation.

This is not to say there were no principles. In 1891 C. C. Soule, a trustee of the Brookline (Mass.) Public Library, published in the *Library Journal* eleven points fundamental to library architecture. Among them were emphasis on function, design of the interior before consideration of the exterior style, simplicity of decoration, layout for economy of operation, ease of supervision and attention to natural light and ventilation. These points were applicable to all types of libraries and had considerable influence.

The larger university library buildings erected in the first decades of the twentieth century owe much to the pattern adopted by the University of California (Berkeley) library, completed in 1908. The single main entrance led directly to stairs and a large reading room across the entire front on the second floor, as at the Boston Public. Delivery desk, public catalog, and stack entrance were also on the second floor, thus making this the main service level. The general pattern was followed at Harvard (1914), Michigan (1920), Minnesota (1924), Cincinnati (1930), and elsewhere. The University of Illinois building of 1926 is unusual among those of the major universities because it permitted not one but a half-dozen additions to the book stack as the collections expanded. Either site or design made additions virtually impossible to such buildings as Columbia's Butler Library, Harvard's Widener, and Yale's Sterling. Unfortunately, in nearly all cases where stack addition could be made, the rest of the building is "frozen." Only in very recent years have some central libraries been successfully enlarged so as to provide the space needed for all major functions. An outstandingly successful example is the 1974 addition to the undergraduate library (1959) of the University of South Carolina.

So, as the country recovered from World War I and moved into the prosperous twenties, the typical established university operated with a central library with one or several reading rooms, a few offices and work area, and a book stack forbidden to undergraduates. There was little else. Electric lighting might deliver as much as fifteen footcandles at some points, but generally less. There was central heating but ventilation was a matter of opening a window, not only to admit air, but inevitably dust and other destructive elements. The most common building plan was adaption of that recommended for Carnegie buildings.

With few exceptions, library buildings designed for complex functions and book collections of several hundred thousand volumes began to be erected only in the twenties. The brief period of 1929–33 saw the completion of buildings designed to hold a half-million volumes or more by Yale, Duke, Rochester, Cincinnati, UCLA, Northwestern, and North Carolina. Other buildings erected in the same period were surprisingly small, when one considers later growth. For example, the University of Maryland provided for only 135,000 volumes, Tennessee 195,000, Florida State 195,000 and Southern California 371,000.

The thirties saw the erection of a number of buildings, more than would be expected in a period of acute economic depression. Among the larger ones were the Universities of Colorado, Missouri, Utah, Oregon, Virginia, Vanderbilt (Joint University Libraries), and Colorado State at Greeley. These buildings of the post-World War I period retained the huge, ornamental reading room but they added large but less conspicuous study areas for reserves, for periodicals, and occasionally for recent highly selective literature designed to build reading interests. There were carrels in the stacks and usually some faculty studies. Virtually all provided a few seminar rooms designed to hold books as well as for instruction. Generally some small provision was made for rare books, special collections, or archives.

Refreshing departures from the principles of the previous decades were adopted at Nebraska and Colorado. These two institutions created libraries in which broad areas of knowledge were handled as collections integral with basically all staff services. More precisely, the social sciences material, for example, was shelved in a separate stack under the care of staff with special expertise in the social sciences. Journals, reserves, reference books, all were at hand in that portion of the building. Book selection and sometimes even classification was in the hands of the divisional staff. Such an operation called for a very different interior. It was the first crack in the traditional concepts, a crack which was to become a yawning chasm as the young Turks who "went divisional" combined with others to create a revolution in concepts of function when the tempest of World War II had blown over and the world was ready to rebuild.

While library building was curtailed after the middle thirties because of the depression economy, the pressures of growing book collections and larger enrollments increased year by year. As the country moved gradually into a war economy, money became available, but not for library buildings. And when war was declared the campuses of the country were denuded of students, and library directors perforce turned their thoughts to the day when the soldiers would return with a consequent swelling of enrollment. Book collections virtually everywhere had outgrown physical facilities and new library facilities were given top priority for postwar building on scores of university campuses. As they bided their time, a good many directors of major university libraries were reconsidering basic principles of operation and dreaming of radical innovation and change.

When late in 1944 President Harold W. Dodds of Princeton invited some fifteen colleges and universities to form a committee on the planning of library buildings he could not have realized that he was setting in motion a revolution in building design that would drastically alter the operation of all types of academic libraries and have a profound influence on higher education. Naturally, he was only the unwitting agent. The prompting certainly came from Julian Boyd, Princeton's great librarian. The forces of which the revolution was formed were already at work. The requirements of the war effort had naturally put a stop to any and all building for higher education, and the enrollments, heavily affected by the military draft and industrial demands, had eased the pressure for more university construction. So for a number of younger and very able library leaders, it was half a decade of marking time and making do with the old, but it was also an opportunity to plan for the future. And planning for the future at a time of war, when important portions of the world are falling in ruins and change is everywhere in the air, is a time for thinking in revolutionary terms. The group of nine librarians who responded by meeting at Princeton on December 15th and 16th, 1944, formed the first of a long series of "library building institutes," which were held nearly every year into the seventies.

The minutes of the first meeting are a record of presentation, by each participant, of his building plans or expectations, followed by group discussion. There were no architectural plans. It was more a matter of financial hopes, site, size, emphasis, and special features which might be incorporated. There was little of a revolutionary nature until Ralph Ellsworth of the University of Iowa took the floor. He was, like Carl Sandburg, a fresh wind off the prairies, preaching eight foot, six inch ceiling height, modular construction, complete flexibility of interior space, groupings of faculty offices, seminars or classrooms, and books by broad subject to make the library truly a laboratory where students and faculty would live and work together in daily informal contact.

In more detail the minutes of the conference report Mr. Ellsworth as follows:

> We have tried to develop a library educational program, and we have tried to plan a building to serve this program. To deal with the building first: the difficulty is that library buildings go out of date too quickly and that they cost too much. We have tried to harden ourselves to do our library thinking in the same way that a chemist would think about the problem of building a laboratory. We are not interested in aesthetics. We have taken the old unit plan first proposed by Angus S. Macdonald and Alfred M. Githens in 1932; and we have experimented with it and developed it to a point where we think we will build our library that way—that is by an accumulation of modules 12 × 18 feet in the clear. That module will have four corners and there will be hundreds in the building. We hope the four corners will be hollow steel columns. They will also have facilities to carry wiring. The columns will suspend the floor plans. They will include lighting fixtures; in fact the ceiling will be lighting fixtures. The floor plans will include acoustical treatment. We hope the construction will be "dry," all pre-fabricated and fitted on the job. The library will be arranged on the interior by hanging partitions between columns at any place . . . Free standing bookcases between columns may also serve as partitions. Every module will be so treated in terms of lighting and air-conditioning that it can be used for any purpose. Once the structure is up, the interior can be rearranged in any way desired at any future time—as the needs of the future unfold.

It was only late in the second building conference that there came to the surface a problem which was to have great emphasis in the years to come. This is the building program, the exhaustively complete written statement of needs which would tell the architect exactly what was needed and why, but avoid any attempt to translate the needs into provisional plans. The minutes report: "Someone suggested that the lack of . . . clear outlines is a perennial cause of misunderstanding and friction between architects and librarians. We librarians have, in general, not learned to do that kind of thing. We might perform a real service by showing how librarians ought to develop their programs, state their problems, and convey them to their faculties and their architects clearly and intelligently." And later, emphasis was laid on the fact that architects design many university buildings, including libraries, but the designs are basically buildings, not libraries. Keyes Metcalf of Harvard is quoted: "I am perfectly sure that we can tell the architect a great many things," and Julian Boyd of Princeton, "The better we can state our problems, the more clear [*sic*] we can bring out what we want, the better the architect can do his work. And to know how to say clearly what we want . . . we have to know that what we ask for can be done."[6]

These two conferences merit historical notice principally as first beginnings; it was the third, held in the unlikely location of Orange, Virginia, which really set in motion developments of greatest importance. Why Orange? The invitation came from Angus Snead MacDonald, President of Snead and Company, located in Orange, the principal developer and supplier of multi-tier stacks. But aside from his business interests, MacDonald combined education as an architect with the zeal of a missionary for radical innovation in library building planning. More than a decade before he had published an article promoting such innovations as: eight-foot ceiling heights in study areas; luminous ceiling lighting; temperature and humidity control plus an air-filtering system; acoustical ceilings combined with noise-deadening flooring; informal seating; free-standing shelving; stack oases, i.e., small study areas scattered throughout the stacks; infinite flexibility through the use of demountable panels for walls with critical fixed facilities such as stairs and rest rooms concentrated together. He was outspoken against "the traditions of regal display at the expense of utility and good reading conditions; of chained books in their arrangements for close supervision."[7]

The year of publication, 1933, was not a good one to promote such extreme change because virtually no university library building was contemplated at that time, the depth of the depression. But the situation was different at the end of World War II, and MacDonald spoke out again, this time with his fully developed proposal for modular construction.[8] Again, all space arrangements were to be flexible except stairs, lavatories, etc., but this time the supporting columns were to be hollow, and thus able to carry ventilation and wiring which previously had always been placed in walls and ceilings. Spacing of columns was suggested as eighteen feet in one direction, twenty-four in the other. The earlier basic recommendations for acoustics, ceiling height, lighting, etc., remained the same. So it was that the president of the company that had developed the multi-tier stack to the relative perfection of the twenties rejected it completely in the forties in favor of freestanding shelving and flexibility of reader-book storage and, to a certain extent, staff space. These basic principles of more than a century of library planning were discarded almost overnight.

The Orange Conference of October, 1945 is notable principally because it is the first conference to involve architects and engineers along with a select group of the leading research librarians of the country. Defined as important were: the detailed statement of program which every librarian should set down on paper as his requirements for the architect to translate into building plans; the merits of modular, flexible space; recognition of the dead hand of architectural monumentality; the importance of further studies, with the assistance of experts, of air-conditioning, lighting, acoustics, floor surfaces, interior decoration, etc.

Mr. MacDonald had constructed a mock-up of his module (2 stories high, 13.5' × 19.5'). This was studied with care for all possible arrangements of tables, carrels, shelving. A principal feature was the hollow column which made possible a simple slab ceiling. This was destined for nearly universal rejection in years to come because of rigid building codes which feared conduction of fire through the hollow center.

The conference was remarkable for other matters as well—fine bourbon, the best steaks, an unforgettable wild ride along the Sky-line drive to a retreat formerly used by President Herbert Hoover for drinks and chicken barbequed before a roaring fire, the intensity of the debate, the great good humor, the zest of all involved. A new world was being born and all felt it. Dozens of ideas conceived there found their way into the brick and steel of new buildings in the next few years, and dozens more were examined, criticized, and tossed on the scrap heap. It was indeed a time to be alive.

With few exceptions, American universities badly needed additional library building when enrollments mushroomed at the end of World War II. The period from the late forties to the middle sixties was one of enormous expansion in every direction and no aspect of university operation needed expanding quite so acutely as the library buildings. The pressure was obvious for shelving on which to put the rapidly growing collections; equally obvious was the need for seats to accommodate the increase in student body. Less obvious but equally important was the obligation to modernize with lighting, air-conditioning, acoustical treatment, special facilities for rare books, for microforms, and many other aspects generally neglected before the war.

The trailblazing Cooperative Committee on Library Buildings phased itself out of existence in 1952 in order for the Association of College and Reference Libraries to take over its assets and responsibilities. The association's Buildings Committee set to work vigorously with a series of building conferences, held nearly every year, and it published the record of each one. Out of these conferences there developed a new procedure that was followed by most universities in planning new library construction. Once funds were in sight, however distant, a library building committee was appointed. Normally, this consisted of several faculty, two or more library staff, and one or several others representing the physical plant, administration, and student body. This group visited other new buildings, read the literature, and finally agreed on the general principles to be followed. At some point a consultant was engaged, normally a librarian of considerable reputation, with extensive building experience. With his help the director of libraries or a principal assistant then prepared a detailed statement of needs. This specified every single function, however small, the space required, and its physical relationship to other functions. In short, it was a statement of precisely what was needed but left the architect to work out how each need was to be met. Of course, an architect was selected at some point, and later, consultants on such problems as air-conditioning and illumination might be used. Once plans were well in hand, it was standard practice for the university to present them for criticism at a building institute.

Typical of these institutes is the Fifth ACRL Building Plans Institute held in January, 1955, at Detroit. In all eighty-three people attended. The composition is typical: fifty-nine librarians, eight architects, eleven from the equipment and furnishings fields, five university faculty or administrators. The library plans of nine institutions were presented and criticized in two days of morning, afternoon, and evening sessions. There was also a paper on the possible future effects of automation technology on library buildings.

It was normal procedure for each library on the agenda to hand out an introductory statement of basic information. Then the librarian (sometimes the architect) showed slides of the building plans and commented briefly on particular features. This was followed by a critical evaluation of the plans by a previously selected guest expert, usually a librarian with much building experience. He also served as leader of the free-for-all discussion from the floor. This discussion was almost always constructive, but it could be merciless to librarians with questionable concepts and to architects carried away by passion for originality of form or for the traditional. It was function, function, function that dominated these meetings. Nearly all discussions led to some modification of plans, and in a few instances plans were virtually scrapped.

Frequently, the program included one or more papers on topics of building interest, such as floor coverings, interior decoration, compact storage, or lighting. A number of librarians developed considerable expertise in building planning and their frank criticism of shoddy work or monumental pretensions reduced some architects and engineers to the verge of tears.

Active in the building institutes, in writing for library publications, and speaking at library conferences were experts in lighting, in acoustical treatment, in air-conditioning and ventilation, in interior decoration, and all types of equipment. For at least two decades there was an extraordinary collaboration among leaders in these and related fields with librarians and with architects specializing in library construction.

From these conferences a number of principles regarding the planning of modern university libraries were firmly established in the minds of librarians but they were not always recognized by architects and trustees. Of vital importance was consideration of the academic program which the library was to serve. Every effort was made to foresee future trends, but since academic programs are all too often no more predictable than the weather, flexibility was essential. For this the ideal was a concentration of essential fixed services either in a corner of the building or in the center of each floor, with the remainder left free, except for supports, as loft space. What few partitions were required should be easily and economically movable. Technology naturally required many special facilities almost unknown a generation earlier: rare book and special collection quarters; microform rooms, both for storage of film and its use; typing and group-study facilities; listening rooms; photographic facilities, and various others.

Flexibility, second only to function, was hammered home as absolutely essential to good planning. To quote a 1946 statement by William M. Randall:

> The buildings which house our libraries today are not bad buildings or inadequate buildings because the men who planned them and who built them were fools. They are bad buildings because what goes on inside them now is different from what was planned to go on inside them. They are unfortunate static elements in an ever-evolving world. They are akin to the dinosaur and the mammoth . . . Feel sorry for them, if you will; have a nostalgic pang for their grand staircases and their monumental reading rooms. . . . but do not condemn them, or their builders—and above all, do not copy them.[9]

Virtually all postwar buildings are of modular construction. In theory this permits infinite flexibility of arrangements, but certain features such as stairs and rest rooms are fixed, and plumbing, heating ducts, etc. introduce complications. While a square module of twenty-two feet, six inches was often used, various other square and rectangular spacing have proved satisfactory. The monumental ceilings of the prewar period were definitely out, replaced by heights in the clear of eight to ten feet, occasionally varied by a sixteen- to eighteen-foot height when combined with a mezzanine. The lowering of the ceiling also lowered the cost of good light and air-conditioning.

An obvious casualty of the new type of construction was the multi-tier stack, universally adopted by larger libraries for two generations. With few exceptions, floors were load-bearing and all stack freestanding. Acoustics, formerly handled by "Silence" signs, came in for major study. Carpeting was found to be often no more expensive than tile when janitorial costs were figured, and carpets were infinitely superior for noise control and aesthetics. Acoustical ceilings became a standard requirement. Lighting for libraries was endlessly debated with experts in several fields. Consensus was reached on many points, but not on the amount of light most suitable for normal reading; the low illumination of the past was discarded in favor of a minimum of thirty footcandles and some favored figures as high as one hundred. Naturally many other considerations are involved, such as type (mercury, incandescent, or fluorescent), diffusion, contrast with surrounding area, floor and desk surface, etc.

The postwar world swung over to the principle of open stack for all. The barriers were kept up for only a few types of material such as that of special value or that in heaviest demand for class assignments. And the seminar collection, but not the seminar room, was a thing of the past.

Easy chairs and sofas had been introduced cautiously in only a few libraries before the war, and were now standard as variant seating for study in
principal reading areas. Carrels were used in greater number. While large
areas continued to be furnished with tables to seat four to eight, smaller
areas for study were scattered throughout new buildings as defense
against distraction.

From all this it should not be inferred that all, or nearly all, university
libraries built in the tremendous expansion of the late fifties and the
sixties embodied the principal features noted. Far from it. Some librarians were denied administrative control, and eager architects, donors, or
chairmen of faculty library committees took over and insisted on features
that were condemned by the knowledgeable. Monumentality reasserted
itself; flexibility was shunted aside by the need to carve out special facilities for entrenched faculty interests, the operational costs involved in
covering a multiplicity of service points were left for the head librarians
to solve. Far too many universities and architects sought originality at the
expense of efficiency. However, the lessons learned in the post-World
War II period were still vivid in the mid-seventies and have been of
incalculable service to higher education and research.

While the focus of this history is on the development of libraries
rather than the individuals involved, it would be wrong to close this
chapter without a word about several who made major contributions to
the building revolution of the twentieth century. Credit for the modular
concept, key to modern library planning, clearly belongs to Angus Snead
Macdonald, president of Snead and Company, the family's iron works,
which specialized in book stacks and related equipment. As noted above,
Macdonald preached the modular gospel with all the zeal of an Old
Testament prophet. Much that he wrote and lectured in the early thirties
had little visible effect, but he carried the day with his ideas later through
the Cooperative Committee on Library Buildings.

A contribution of equal significance but radically different is that of
Keyes D. Metcalf, director of the Harvard University Library. Not only
was he a key figure, with Ralph E. Ellsworth, in postwar building discussions, but in many ways he spoke for the entire profession in such matters. As a consultant for hundreds of academic libraries, he influenced the
incorporation of the new concepts in the building plans. His book, *Planning Academic and Research Library Buildings,* was at once accepted as the
definitive work on the subject from the time of its appearance in 1965.
Its influence will extend into the future.

Nearly as influential as Metcalf as a spokesman and consultant was Ralph Ellsworth, library director at the universities of Colorado and Iowa. Ellsworth was an idea man, brash and original, but an effective consultant to scores of institutions which were planning buildings. Central to the key discussions and agreements of the late forties were such prominent library leaders as Julian Boyd (Princeton), John Burchard (MIT), Charles David (University of Pennsylvania), and Flint Purdy (Wayne State). The leadership of these men with its emphasis on function led naturally to reexamination of virtually all aspects of operation and in so doing made material advances in many which are only remotely related to library buildings.

The contribution of these men and their colleagues is summarized by Walter C. Allen:

> Late in 1945, Macdonald published a paper which he ended with this prophecy: "I think we are entering into the greatest architectural era the world has ever known, and I believe that it will be known to history as the American Era. I also believe that libraries, instead of trailing the procession of progress, will take the lead, consistent with their position as sources of the knowledge whereby culture and civilization advance." It is abundantly clear that libraries have indeed been leaders in the new American architecture which emerged about 1950. Nearly all of the major architectural journals began to feature new libraries, large and small. Countless architects who had scarcely been in a library suddenly found themselves caught up in a new specialty. Nearly all of the nation's greatest architectural leaders became interested, and their projects grace communities throughout the nation.[10]

CHAPTER 11

The Problem of the Departmental Library

Throughout the history of most American universities runs the controversy over centralization of library material, physically by location and administratively by control, versus decentralization in one or both respects. And the problem is not endemic to this country; it is worldwide except as one point of view gains clear ascendancy over the other for a period, or as stark lack of funds virtually eliminates multiple collections. Like poverty, the controversy will apparently be always with us.

Obviously, the problem appeared only as institutions grew in complexity and physical resources. As already noted, in their infancy they operated with a mere handful of faculty, at most a few hundred students, and one or several buildings close together. All the books were in one room, often in only one cabinet. The curricula and teaching methods did nothing to promote the use of the library; indeed, policy often actively discouraged student use. The controversy remained dormant until late in the nineteenth century, when growth of faculties, students, and funds, combined with reorientation of university objectives and teaching philosophy, brought it sharply into the light. Then the picture changed dramatically. First and foremost, there was suddenly a great emphasis on graduate education and original research. The cessation of hostilities in 1865 brought about a great increase in college attendance in the North, to come later in the South, and a consequent expansion of faculties and departmentalization of organization and of studies. Finally, there was a trend away from strict classicism, with greater attention being given to scientific, humanistic, and social studies. Such subjects as physics, chemistry, economics, engineering, agriculture, modern languages, and even English literature suddenly became respectable. Combined with this was the proliferation of professional schools at both the undergraduate and graduate level. This meant far greater use of libraries, and for many the departmental collection seemed the obvious answer. In some institutions it was the practical solution because there was no central library worthy of the name, nor was there a library administration of so much as one person with real responsibility for library developments. Now the chemistry professor wanted his books at his elbow, as did the lawyer, the agronomist, the mathematician, the classicist. Much of the same feeling exists today except as modified by a comprehension of the drawbacks involved in wholesale decentralization by location and administration. In their days of early, rank growth, from collegiate to graduate status, universities seldom had leaders who could assess the pros and cons of decentralization and who were sufficiently respected or forceful to see that the issues were faced clearly by trustees and faculty. The choice was between limiting support to one central library under a director, or providing books in situ for subject departments and schools under the virtual control of the faculty concerned, supplemented by a weak central collection to serve general needs and some humanistic studies.

Before sinking too deeply into the subject, the reader is assured that educators generally agree on the vital importance, the essentiality of books, journals, and related material to most operations of the modern university. Few would dispute the axiom that books should be found in profusion in virtually all corners of the campus. They are considered as essential to university operations as is salt to our food. For the mature scholar, libraries at three levels are desirable: in his own home or office a personal library of the important books and journals bearing directly on his principal research interests; easy access across the corridor or down the hall to a broad scholarly collection of reference books, journals, and individual studies (monographs) of importance to the department of which he is a member; and finally, access within a short distance to a comprehensive collection of scholarship covering all subjects, where the aid of highly skilled librarians is available, together with equipment such as terminals for data base searches and the other apparatus of modern librarianship.

The personal library in some cases may number only a few hundred volumes, and many senior faculty buy these from their personal funds. In several countries of western Europe, notably Italy, it is quite common for every senior professor to have at his disposal a library fund of some size. He alone determines what to buy and from whom, and the books go into what is virtually his own study. There they are available for use by his students, but to others only by special permission.

The departmental library, on the other hand, is the collection that serves a department of instruction or a professional school, such as Social

Administration, Business, or Law. Its location is always convenient to the building where the particular instruction is given, and generally within the same walls. Obviously, the scope is much broader than that of the personal library. It includes general reference works such as language dictionaries and encyclopedias. These collections can grow very large. The largest is probably the Harvard Law Library with nearly one and a half million volumes. As these departmental libraries grow in size, they must have staffs increasing in numbers and in professional background, as well as special equipment. The departmental libraries commonly found in American universities are very similar to the seminar or institute libraries which developed in German universities in the early nineteenth century. They are also found in many French, Italian, English, and other European universities in variant forms and under variations of administrative control. But whether or not a library director has theoretical control of a departmental library, it is obvious that the faculty which uses it daily and in whose building it is located can, and generally does, exercise effective control.

The central library ideally is all things to all scholars. It not only provides volumes on all subjects, numbered in six or seven figures, but a wealth of rare books and manuscripts; microforms; sophisticated reference service; instant access via terminals to computer data bases across the land; private studies or carrels for senior faculty; and through cooperative agreements, loan or photocopies of material in other research libraries at home and abroad.

Here, then, is the scholar's Utopia: a generous study at home or on campus, lined floor to ceiling with publications of special interest to his research; on campus adjacent to his office a fine library of texts and reference books covering his broad discipline and presided over by a librarian with background in that subject; finally a great research library within a few blocks of the office, where virtually any record or inspirational writing can be found and expert bibliographical assistance be had for the asking.

No university has ever had the funds to provide such facilities. The closest approach to them is found at Harvard, where the senior faculty have incomes which at least make possible, granted at some sacrifice, the formation of good personal libraries. Most departments there support comprehensive special libraries, some of which are very large and complete with even rare and expensive source materials; finally, of course, Harvard has the outstanding central university collection in its Widener

Library. The somewhat more than one hundred libraries serving that institution not only are a foundation for the research produced there, but a strong card in faculty recruitment.

Here in the United States, the first departmentalization began around the middle of the nineteenth century, as separate "schools" were established, sometimes at a distance. Thus, at Columbia both the School of Law (founded 1858) and the School of Mines (founded 1864) were at locations remote from the central "college" and they soon established libraries which were, for a time, superior in many ways to the ineffective central library. As institutions grew and as departments, however unofficial, came into existence, books were needed and bought by individual members of the faculty, and up the volumes went on shelves placed for ease of access. There was no library organization to assist in procurement or to protest duplication of effort. At only a few institutions was there any thought given to the problems that might arise from such informal action. So practice solidified into policy, and policy became tradition. At least, this was the general picture; the story is quite different at those institutions which emphasized graduate instruction right from the start, notably Johns Hopkins, Stanford, Chicago, and Cornell.

While the library had little if any role to play in the textbook-recitation method of collegiate instruction, its importance was recognized as research interests developed and as professional schools came into being in the nineteenth century. These schools required books dealing specifically with their field of study and located conveniently at hand. Thus, special libraries were created at some institutions whose main libraries at that time held only a few hundred volumes. Most law schools developed libraries very early in their history. The opposite is true of medicine. Flexner's study of medicine (1910) notes that a number of medical schools had no library worthy of that name, that funds were not made available for books and journals, and that instruction was generally independent of medical literature. However, it was not unusual for departments within colleges of medicine to set up their own libraries despite, or because of, the lack of a general medical library.

A number of state universities found themselves in the 1880s and 1890s with separate libraries of agriculture, because the Morrill Act and later the Hatch Act provided special funds for the subject. In fact some libraries of agriculture developed with considerable independence of any control by, and cooperation with, the central administration. At the University of West Virginia the agricultural library received regular funding from the date of its founding in 1888; ten years later it was the only collection that could support a research project. During the same period at the University of Delaware, the books on agriculture were dispersed in various classrooms, each group being called a "departmental library."

Library literature sometimes draws fine distinctions between college libraries, departmental libraries, seminar collections and divisional libraries. Obviously, some libraries serve a "college" such as law, business, or medicine, and some serve a department, such as romance languages, biology, or geology. Aside from that academic distinction they are here considered one and the same provided they are located in quarters other than the central library building and are serving one or several connected disciplines. They are generally located in the building that is headquarters for the field of study, or adjacent to it. Regardless of administrative organization, the staff works closely with the faculty involved.

A seminar collection or seminar library is, in the United States, usually something quite different. It is located in one or more rooms of the main library. It often serves only a branch of a department as, for example, Art of the Renaissance, or French Literature. It does not have library staff in regular attendance. The space is used as a classroom and is considered very much as their "turf" by the few faculty and graduate students concerned, who guard their prerogatives there most jealously.

Divisional libraries are a later development. They encompass a broad field of literature, such as the sciences, or history in general. They are generally in the central library building and staffed by the central library administration. While responsive to the faculty involved, these staffs are responsible primarily to the central library administration. Unlike departmental and seminar libraries, there are never any barriers to the use of divisional libraries by the general university family.

Illustrative of what happened at many institutions is the record at the University of California at Berkeley, chartered in 1868. To quote the historian of its library,

> Departmental libraries existed at the University before 1900. They were not planned but had evolved over a period of years in response to the particular needs of professors and students. As early as 1875 the president had reported that book collections for agriculture and mechanical arts had been set up in the lecture rooms used for those subjects. In his first report as librarian (1876) Joseph C. Rowell indicated that in addition to the agriculture and circulating libraries there were collections in the "rooms" of five professors. When the

Bacon Library was occupied in 1881, an attempt was made to consolidate all library materials in that building. However, within a few years books were being charged out to heads of departments for "departmental libraries." In time, these collections contained books purchased with departmental funds, as well as those borrowed from the General Library.[1]

At the University of Texas the concept of the separate, departmental collection was as old as that of the general library; the advantages of a library as an integrated whole, physically and bibliographically, were late in gaining recognition. In the 1880s and 1890s the university's books, although few in number, were scattered over a large number of locations. It was only when Phineas Windsor became librarian in 1903 that the library administration gained authority over all library material.

The story of departmental libraries at Columbia is long and complicated. As already noted, in the 1870s there were special libraries of some size to serve the schools of Law and Mines. This was the case at a time when the general library reported, with distress, that it did not even have a copy of Shakespeare suitable for circulation. The turning point for Columbia's library came in 1876 when Professor John A. Burgess united with President F. A. P. Barnard in emphasizing the importance of a central collection and a building to house it. Betts, the librarian of the period, was most unkindly characterized by Burgess as "our mucilagenous librarian . . . the meekest and softest and least masculine of male mankind. Were a sea anemone or a jellyfish endowed with the faculty of speech, it would talk as he does." No such characterization could be leveled at Melvil Dewey, who took over in 1883. Both he and President Barnard were strong believers in a centralized collection; however, under President Low, who took office in 1888, the year following Dewey's departure, the picture changed radically. Now virtually all the major departments of instruction achieved their own individual collections. Some libraries sprouted without official permission and Columbia took formal action toward decentralization in 1896. The trustees then approved a report which sanctioned libraries for all the scientific departments. It stated, in part, "The scientific books are, in effect, a part of the laboratory equipment, and to be useful they must be close at hand. For the most part they are books that specialists only desire to use. If, on the other hand such a book is needed in the general reading room, it can be brought there . . . in a very short time. These departmental libraries will be catalogued by the Librarian and will be as available for the general reading room as though they were shelved in the stack room. Each departmental library will be kept in order, without expense to the administration, by some of the junior members of the department."[2]

Four scientific departments made immediate requests for libraries. They were soon followed by twelve others, among which were included Greek, Latin, Music, Oriental Languages, Pathology, and Psychology. By 1899 there were seventeen departmental libraries on campus outside the new Low Library building, where there were also numerous seminar rooms. As might be guessed, "junior members of the department" were notably uncooperative in keeping the library in order "without expense to the administration." Frictions developed at once over ownership, access, and cataloging. Nor were all the departments cordial to students from other departments who sought to use their books. James H. Canfield, who came as librarian in 1899, struggled to get some of the collections back to the main library, or at least to combine the smallest units in order to provide care and supervision. It was a losing battle, despite Canfield's prestige as a former university president and personal friend of Nicholas Murray Butler. In 1905 President Butler himself gave more than six hundred volumes of his own, not to the general library, but to the Department of Philosophy, as the nucleus for its new library. A large sum was given to set up an historical reading room and to purchase books for it. And so it went. The pattern was set on the Morningside Heights campus, so that when the new central library was built in 1934, provision was made for many special subject rooms in addition to the numerous specialized libraries located in nearby buildings.

At Ohio State University, founded in 1870, departmental collections began to be formed soon after the university could boast of any library. Not only were books drawn from the central repository by the departments, but also their equipment budgets soon included sums specifically for books. Material so purchased was considered to be departmental property. Gifts of private libraries then, as is still the case in modern times, were made to academic departments instead of the library. As elsewhere, Morrill Act money for books went directly to teaching departments. By 1902 the Columbus campus had twenty-nine departmental collections. The library for Greek was separate from that for Latin, Agricultural Chemistry from Agriculture, Horticulture from Botany, etc. Most of this material was not listed in the central catalog. Yet despite this proliferation of collections and lack of administrative control it was "ordered, that the librarian be held strictly responsible for the keeping and care of all the books in the library." These were to be used under rules established by the faculty, not the librarian.

Indiana University and the University of Illinois, two institutions which, metaphorically speaking, spring from the same soil, offer startling contrast in the development of these separate collections. At Indiana around the turn of the century selection and purchase of books were handled directly by the instructors involved. Books went, of course, into the departmental libraries. In 1906 the university's librarian, William E. Jenkins, raised a number of issues which were not faced by the university administration until nearly four decades later. His report for 1906 reads:

> There has arisen in connection with certain measures of library administration a question of very great importance to the library and the University: Are the books bought from the library fund of a particular department to be considered the special equipment of that department, or are they university equipment in a large sense?
>
> If the books are strictly department equipment, they are then on the same basis as other department property and can be used by persons outside the department only with its permission and on its terms. Any measure of general library administration (such as the extension of home-use privileges or the enlargement of the open collection) may be nullified or emasculated by departmental objections.
>
> Details of routine, questions of classification, shelving, etc. are likewise affected. The delivery of library mail directly to departments instead of to the library, the ordering of books without notification to the library—these are minor consequences of the view of department ownership of library property.
>
> As to the first claim of a department to books bought from its library fund, there is no issue, but the claim should be valid only for books actually needed for the department's work at the time, and no department should have the right to lock up indefinitely from general use the entire collection relating to its subjects.
>
> Carried to its logical extreme, this narrow view of library organization would substitute for one central administration as many different administrations as there are departments of instruction in the university, and I believe would result in much less liberal, less efficient and less economical management.
>
> I respectfully ask the consideration of this question by the President and Board of Trustees.[3]

M. H. Lowell comments as follows:

> Librarian Jenkins saw the dangers in the haphazard, unplanned development of departmental libraries and in the departmental control of books funds. Had his farsighted recommendations for centralized administration been accepted, the university community would have profited immeasurably in the years that followed. His advice on this issue was not heeded, the problem was not solved at that time, and the branch libraries continued to develop in a haphazard fashion. Both the central library and the branches suffered as a result. It was not until thirty-five years later (1941–42) that all book funds for the University were administered by a library authority—that year by the Library Committee and in the years since then by the Director of Libraries.[4]

While Indiana did not see fit to control the proliferation of separate collections which were under virtually complete faculty control, Illinois went the opposite way a decade before the Jenkins report. In 1895 when its first separate library building was under construction, the University of Illinois Board of Trustees established a policy that remained in effect for forty years and which, in principle, continues to the present. It reads as follows:

> All books, pamphlets, maps, etc. (other than account books), purchased with University moneys, shall be deemed to belong to the University library.
> All parts of the library shall be in the custody of the Librarian and he shall be responsible for the condition of the same.
> . . . books which are purely technical and relate only to the work of a single department may be taken to that department; but the Librarian shall not thereby cease to be responsible for their safe keeping and proper use.
> The Librarian may make and enforce such rules for the government of the library as are approved by the President.

At the two institutions, time brought great expansion in area for both campuses. With this came a very natural and needful creation of departmental collections. Size of holdings entered the picture, as multi-million-volume collections are not easily housed under one roof. Time also brought student bodies and faculties of a size unimagined before World War I. For such numbers, extensive duplication of material and basic library services must be provided.

But these distances and these numbers were not problems before 1920.

From the vantage point of hindsight, it is apparent that the situation at both Indiana and Illinois called for centralization and emphasis on the main library, at least until the expansion of the 1920s. Equally desirable were administrative control and fixed responsibility for major library development. Indiana went one way, Illinois the other. It was only in the 1960s that Indiana adopted a basic policy for administrative responsibility for all libraries and major emphasis on central university library development.

Typical of smaller universities are events at Delaware. Until recent years, departments had considerable latitude in the purchase and handling of books. Uncataloged collections developed, as units ordered and received their own material without contacting the main library. In theory, such books should be sent in for cataloging, but this was seldom done. Instead, the books went directly to faculty offices, unrecorded. It was not until 1948 that the trustees officially made the librarian custodian of all material with this inclusive ruling:

> All books, maps, charts, periodicals, pamphlets, newspapers, manuscripts, and other printed matter purchased from funds appropriated by the trustees or acquired in any other manner shall be deemed a part of the University Library and shall be marked and cataloged as such except such as are of an administrative nature and such maps and charts as relate to or are used in the internal organization of the several departments. All expenditures for library materials are made under the direction of the University Librarian.[5]

Yale was slow in establishing departmental collections, principally because it was slow in giving recognition to the importance of graduate studies and the new curriculum. There were some departmental collections as early as 1885. By 1901 there were reported to be sixteen departmental "discussion clubs," and each of these had libraries in their special rooms where instructors and their students met. There were no real seminar collections until the Sterling Library was built (1930) with forty seminar rooms.

None of the above institutions went quite so far in departmentalization of collections as did Johns Hopkins at its founding in 1876. At its head was Daniel Coit Gilman, formerly president of the University of California at Berkeley, and before that for nine years the librarian of Yale. Gilman achieved brilliant success by selecting a few potentially great scholars. In his own words, "Every head of a department was allowed the utmost freedom in its development, subject only to such control as was

necessary for harmonious co-operation. He could select his own assistants, choose his own books and apparatus, devise his own plans of study
—always provided that he worked in concord with his fellows."[6] Speaking
at Cornell in 1891 he elaborated his views regarding the library.

> Let me give you an example from the city of Baltimore, partly
> because I am more familiar with it, partly because of certain unique
> advantages it possesses. In the Peabody Institute may be found a
> modern, well-chosen, well-housed, well-arranged, and well-
> catalogued collection of more than one hundred thousand volumes,
> the books of which (with few exceptions) are retained within four
> walls, where any inquirer may find them. Not far away is the library
> of Johns Hopkins University, arranged on the opposite principle,
> under ten roofs, and in even more compartments, so that the teach-
> ers and students of any branch may have at hand in the seminary or
> laboratory the books most important for the prosecution of that
> study. The Assyrian texts which delight one group of scholars do not
> embarrass the chemist, whose journals do not weigh down the
> shelves devoted to classical literature. Crelle's "Journal of Mathe-
> matics" is precious in the sight of another group of students, to
> whom the story of "Aucassin et Nicolette" suggests no attractions.
> Near these scholarly foundations is a free, public, and popular li-
> brary, the gift of Enoch Pratt, with five distant branches. Most of the
> Pratt books are for circulation, and every one who wishes, rich or
> poor, may take home his volume. Around these central institutions
> are special libraries, under different control, for law, medicine, and
> theology. There is also a large historical library and a society library,
> the New Mercantile, where subscribers have free access to the book-
> shelves. Thus, within a circle whose radius is a third of a mile, over
> three hundred thousand books are accessible to any student. Few
> cities in this country supply so well the wants of every class.[7]

President Gilman was loyal to his former calling in public utterances
with comments such as, "The heart of a university is its library. If that is
vigorous every part of the body is benefited." But it is obvious that the
policy was dictated in some part because of the economy that was involved in Hopkins' dependence on the Peabody, the Enoch Pratt and
other Baltimore libraries. Many another urban institution has, at one time
or another, trimmed its budget with the same reasoning. Hopkins' dependence on Baltimore libraries was gradually modified with the passage of
time, but only in very recent years has the university changed its policy
by consolidating the departmental libraries and strengthening the central
library administration.

Cornell under Andrew White, its first president, was a leader in the revolt against traditional methods of education, but Cornell did not follow tradition in respect to departmental libraries, probably because of the centralizing influence of its huge central library, erected in 1891. In the best practice of the day, this had a number of seminar rooms with subject collections. The early decades of the twentieth century brought a plethora of departmental collections, scattered all over the campus, due partly to the filling of the central library, partly to the natural desire of influential faculty to have "their books" right at hand and under their care, and partly to weakness on the part of university and library administrators who could not, or would not, control the splintering process.

When President Harper took over the leadership of the University of Chicago in 1891 "he had two central ideas in mind: (1) a librarian in charge of all library services, and (2) departmental libraries to serve in the same way that laboratories served." The historian of the University of Chicago Library, the authority for the above, goes on to comment: "If he had carried out his first idea, his second idea might not have caused the University so much pain in years to come."[8] Undoubtedly at Chicago, as elsewhere, important professors did not readily surrender to any central authority either the forming of their collections or control over their use. The central library, then, was to be primarily for general reference uses and the needs of undergraduates. Interestingly, the library fee assessed undergraduates was assigned to the upkeep of that library while the graduate student's fee was applied to the purchase of books for the library of his chosen studies. By 1895 there were twenty-four departmental libraries, each under the care of a faculty member with the assistance of graduate students who held fellowships.

The deficiencies of this system were realized as the separate collections proliferated; therefore faculty committees began in 1896 a series of studies of the problems involved. As recognized by the first committee, these problems were: the need of students to consult "five or more departmental libraries in preparation for a single course"; the cost of duplication of books and journals to obviate such shuttling back and forth, particularly the cost of rare or otherwise expensive items; and the constant loss from the departmental collections. Not mentioned were such obvious factors as the tendency of scholars to ignore materials in fields related to their specialities, costs of adequate staff services, lack of general reference tools, etc. No easy solution was found by the committee and the planning of a new library building required some decisions, so the trustees appointed a commission to study the matter. Its recommendation, which was followed, was basically for a central library with closely adjoining buildings devoted to major subjects such as philosophy and history and to professional studies such as law and divinity. In each of these buildings attached to the central library would be comprehensive collections appropriate to the studies involved. It was planned to build connecting bridges, umbilical cords as it were to facilitate physical passage to and fro, and thus to provide a two-way conduit for nourishment of advanced studies. The report advocated a somewhat stronger central administrative control over all the libraries of the university. "The departments were like a group of states which, all insistent on their rights, had, nevertheless, come to realize that in union there might be strength." Lack of funds prevented completion of the entire plan, and passage of time and personalities brought erosion of the decisions reached. However, the general plan governed library operations from the time of the completion of the Harper building in 1912 until the erection of the Regenstein Library in 1970.

The revolution of the late nineteenth century in graduate studies brought only gradual change at Harvard. Here there were considerably different conditions. The university already had a well-developed central library and, more important, a tradition for the employment of an able, professional, head librarian. It had long been committed to emphasis on the importance of a strong library. Into this setting stepped Justin Winsor in 1877, the year following the foundation of Johns Hopkins University.

Winsor encouraged a moderate decentralization of book collections but not of administrative control. He did this to encourage effective use; in addition, decentralization via classroom and laboratory libraries also relieved the pressure on the crowded stacks of Gore Hall. An important factor in the growth of separate libraries at Harvard, which has continued up to the present, is the relative independence of departments in the use of funds, the consequence of requiring departments to raise their own funds. "Every tub on its own bottom" is the administrative slogan, if not the motto, of Harvard University. Under these circumstances libraries grew in number and size with few restrictions. A measure of administrative control over their operations has been effected only since World War II.

Keyes Metcalf, the unofficial "dean" of university librarians of the post-World War II period, summarized the arguments for and against decentralization as follows:

In spite of our conviction that we are overly decentralized here at Harvard, we believe in decentralization in a large, physically scattered university—"coordinated decentralization," as we call it. The arguments for decentralization may be summarized as follows:

1. It places the books in convenient locations for those who make the greatest use of them.
2. It broadens the basis of support of the university library system.
3. It gives the various departments a direct interest in their libraries.
4. By breaking down the collections into units by subjects, special library methods can be introduced which give better service at no greater cost.

Some of the objections to decentralization are:

1. Decentralization often results in unnecessary duplication; the various libraries in the biological sciences at Harvard are a good example.
2. The policies of the departmental libraries may get out of line with those for the university library as a whole, in respect to staff organization, salaries, and book acquisition.
3. Departmental libraries offer a ready opportunity for overdevelopment through the interest and promotional ability of a particular librarian or head of a graduate school. Costs then get out of bounds, and subsequent reduction of expenses is difficult because of the bulk of material already at hand. Further, if such reduction is enforced, the collection rapidly deteriorates in relative importance, since gaps in acquisition of new material greatly reduce the value of the collection as a whole and much money previously spent is wasted.[9]

Logical as this statement is, the distressing fact is that logic has had little influence on past action in setting up collections, administratively or physically separate from the central library. The pressures are many and confusing, and tradition has too often been the dominant factor. In the future, budget stringencies may promote administrative consolidation, as pressures of building space influence physical consolidation.

CHAPTER 12

The Growth of Cooperative Enterprise

Cooperative enterprises among research libraries are a major force in the life of university libraries today, but this was not always the case. The first beginnings date from the 1876 founding conference of the American Library Association; little progress was made, other than through basically local agreements, until the mid-1940s. At that time cooperation on a national scale came to be recognized as essential to meet greatly increased responsibilities; thirty years later cooperation was reaching into virtually every aspect of university library operation. Competition continued to exist, of course, competition for collections, competition for staff, competition for services. Without competition there could hardly be healthy growth and accomplishment, but with this went a universal acknowledgement that only through extensive cooperation could libraries effactually perform their assigned duties to the worlds of education and research. These joint projects often required heavy outlays from many separate budgets. This unselfish support of important cooperative projects, both by the assignment of funds and the use of valuable staff talent, reflects enormous credit on the directors of virtually all American research libraries. In some instances support was continued for years before the projects began to pay dividends. This spirit has extended over a quarter of a century and continues as this is written. Few professions can boast a period of unselfish joint action of equal duration and importance.

Cooperation organized by professional associations might be examined under the principal headings: (1) the support of the organizations, especially the professional associations, that promote or administer cooperative activities, and (2) the services themselves that are provided by joint action. In the case of libraries a more specific and practical approach is through several major areas: (1) cooperation in bibliographical control, i.e., in making known what has been published or written on any and every subject and where it is located; (2) collection building, i.e., agreements to specialize so that certain libraries emphasize certain subjects with the knowledge that other libraries will cover other subjects and thereby permit interdependence via loans; (3) interlibrary loan agreements, usually of state or national scope; (4) service and facility agreements, usually of a local nature as for example support of book storage building for little-used material, or for computerized cataloging, and (5) professional organizations, under which much cooperation of national scope is organized, and which foster the discussion and publication which are generally required for the creation of the machinery to activate and administer agreements. A place should also be found in the above analysis for the specific action of the U.S. Congress which, as will be seen, provided support for several major projects.

Cooperation in Bibliographical Control

Vitally essential to the life of a research library is bibliographical control, which is basically knowledge of what has been written or published and where it may be found. From 1900 on, there were hundreds of bibliographical projects of importance to university libraries, but two are of outstanding importance. The first of these chronologically is the National Union Catalog of the Library of Congress, begun in 1901. To this unit the principal libraries of the country sent one catalog card for each new accession; this then became a record of location to answer requests from other libraries as to where a given work could be found, usually with a view to seeking an interlibrary loan. The catalog was of great utility for at least sixty years, but became unwieldy as it grew to gargantuan proportions. Publication of the catalog in book form began in 1956; although an expensive tool, this publication is extremely useful because it provides at hand not only a record of where material may be found, but also reliable bibliographical data for other purposes. In the words of the introduction "It constitutes a reference and research tool for a large part of the world's production of significant books as acquired and cataloged by the Library of Congress and a number of other North American libraries."

A similar tool of great utility was the *Union List of Serials,* which did for serials basically what the National Union Catalog did for books. The *Union List of Serials* was from the very first (1927) in book form and therefore a quick, convenient source of information in constant use at all scholarly libraries.

There followed a number of important tools of the same character, union lists of library holdings of American newspapers, international congresses and conferences, serial publications of foreign governments, etc.; also many union lists of holdings in metropolitan areas, states, and regions. With these developed many minor and a few major union catalogs in card form, principally in the mid-thirties. Major financing of these came from federal funds for the relief of the widespread unemployment that existed at that time. The three most important are the Union Catalog of Pennsylvania located in Philadelphia, the Pacific Northwest Bibliographic Center in Seattle, and the Bibliographical Center for Research in Denver.

The cost of these catalogs escalates as size increases into the millions of cards and the need for them diminishes as more records of ownership become available via computer. For example in 1975 the Philadelphia catalog was "closed" (no more cards to be interfiled) and the record made available on microfilm at a price easily within the reach of university libraries. The enormous record of book ownership in memory units of the Ohio College Library Center computer is available to hundreds of libraries through their terminals. This service provides location information for material purchased in recent years. More and more records of this sort will be phased out in card form partly because of increase of expense with size and partly because computer record becomes regularly more sophisticated and economical.

Reference has already been made to cooperation on a local scale in collection building. After World War II most university libraries had some understandings with neighbors which specified fields of collecting in which each would depend largely on one of the group. This aspect of cooperation eventually led to the several major national programs to be discussed shortly.

Cooperation through the Loan of Material

The important traffic of books on loan from one library to another originated from a proposal made in the first issue of the *Library Journal*. In a letter dated September 4, 1875, Samuel S. Green of the Worcester Free Public Library proposed "an agreement . . . to lend books to each other for short periods of time . . . It happens not infrequently that some book is called for by a reader . . . which he finds in the catalogue of another library, but which does not belong to his own collection . . . It would take time to get it through ordinary channels." Green then cited the practice of the Boston Public Library to allow students, properly introduced, to borrow books even though they were not citizens of Boston. He then suggested loans from library to library as preferable because of local control. In the phrasing of the day "There would be a certain increase in the sense of safety in the consciousness that a library knows the peculiarities of its own readers better than they can be known to the officers of a distant institution. I should think libraries would be willing to make themselves responsible for the value of the borrowed books, and be willing to pay an amount of expressage." Green cited the practice of loans by European libraries and suggested that the 1876 conference, about to convene, should formulate a "definitely-formed plan."[1]

While the "plan" recommended came considerably later in the form of an interlibrary loan code, the idea caught on immediately. Justin Winsor of Harvard offered loans to other libraries almost at once. His report for 1877–78 states "I see no good reason why, in regard to books not in common demand, there cannot be greater reciprocity of use among these neighboring libraries. With an express at our service, I have found no unwillingness in my confrères of other institutions to engage in some interchanging of this sort during the past year, and have even extended the service to remoter libraries."[2] His 1894–95 report lists 570 volumes so loaned over the previous two years.

Loans began at Columbia under Melvil Dewey in the mid-1880s. Chicago established formal loan agreements with a number of local libraries in 1899. The practice was followed, informally if not formally, at most larger libraries by the turn of the century.

For such traffic there had to be some commonly accepted rules of conduct. These came in 1916 from the Committee on Co-ordination of the American Library Association as "Regulations for the Conduct of Inter-library Loans"; a year later when formally adopted, the regulations were dubbed the "Code of Practice." This code was liberal in that its stated purpose was "to augment the supply of the average book to the average reader" as well as "to aid research . . . by the loan of unusual books not readily accessible elsewhere." It did exclude current fiction and other easily obtainable publications, rarities and fragile material. It specified that the borrower assume the cost of the postage both ways, recommended a term of loan of four weeks, and certain other provisions concerning the treatment of borrowed books, acknowledgement of receipt, and similar matters.[3]

As the traffic in loans increased over the years, the code was periodically reviewed and tightened, notably in 1940 and 1952. A major change was the recommended restriction of loans for the advancement of research, but including the needs of graduate students. The 1952 revision was one of the major early accomplishments of ALA's division, the Association of College and Reference Libraries after it established a secretariat. A principal contribution of the 1952 code committee was the preparation of a standard Interlibrary loan form which was gradually approved for use by other library associations. The code was again revised in 1968 to introduce distinction in practice for basically local loans and those made on a national level.

From the date of the first loans, the traffic in books between libraries has increased steadily. In 1976 it was estimated to exceed ten million volumes annually. Statistics published by the Association of Research Libraries show that its ninety-nine member libraries made 2,158,000 loans in 1974–75, borrowing 477,000 items in the same period. A lack of balance between loans and borrowing was recognized as a heavy burden on the larger libraries, since these transactions are expensive in staff time as well as in wrapping, insurance, and similar costs. Therefore a few university libraries began charging a standard fee for each loan made, and the practice was spreading in 1976. There are obvious restrictions on fees charged by state-supported libraries to other in-state libraries.

The National Commission on Libraries and Information Science has prepared plans for a National Periodicals System to expedite the furnishing of periodical articles, which are a significant portion of the interlibrary traffic. If adopted, this could lead later on to a lending operation involving books as well as journals, along the lines of Great Britain's highly successful British Library Lending Division.

Cooperation through National Organizations and Consortia

In 1949 ten midwestern universities entered into a pact to create a new libraries' library in Chicago, named the Midwest Inter-Library Center. The principal function originally was that of relieving the shelves of member libraries, crowded with little-used material, such as old college catalogs, house organs, foreign dissertations, and old textbooks. The center was to keep single copies, pulp the duplicates, and loan to members on request. To this was soon added the function of filling gaps in collections by purchase.

In the early sixties the center took a considerable change of course. It opened its membership to the research libraries of the nation under the new name of Center for Research Libraries; it invited associate memberships from smaller academic libraries; it de-emphasized and virtually gave up the acceptance of collections from members and concentrated its funds and attention on procurement of important but generally lesser-used research materials. By 1975 it had more than one hundred regular members and several score associates. The annual budget for 1976–77 was $1,625,993.

Somewhat similar to the center in composition and size of membership is the Association of Research Libraries, organized in 1932 by forty-three of the largest research libraries. It was for more than a decade little more than a debating society and a social gathering dominated by eight or ten senior library directors. It developed no real program until it tackled the problems of collection development arising from World War II. It then gradually became a "working and planning center for cooperative movements among university and research libraries." To it goes much credit for the Cooperative Acquisitions Project for Wartime Publications and virtually all the credit for the Farmington Plan.

Those two projects were the only accomplishments of note in the first three decades of ARL operations. In the words of the association's historian, "For thirty years, prior to its organization and incorporation in 1962, the Association was essentially an informal discussion group of librarians who had reached the top of their profession. Its policy was to undertake only those few projects that other groups could not, or would not, accept. . . . Nearly all of the Association's business was conducted by less than half of the representatives. A self-perpetuating advisory committee and an autocratic executive secretary selected by the committee may prove efficient but policies and procedures are likely to reflect a narrow point of view." The relative lack of accomplishment of ARL during those years undoubtedly stems from lack of use of available talent by involvement of more of its members.

Things changed abruptly in 1962 when ARL nearly doubled its membership, set up a paid secretariat, and became incorporated. From that date on it became the principal spokesman for research libraries in national councils and with foundations. It has been extremely effective in influencing federal legislation. ARL works with the ALA Washington

Office in testifying before congressional committees and in other contact work with key government officials.

The American Library Association was founded in 1876 and for a generation was the only professional organization of importance to serve the profession. As it grew in size it began a natural process of subdivision into interest groups but the only unit of importance to the general needs of research libraries was the Association of College and Reference (later "Research") Libraries which did not achieve a supporting staff and office until 1946. In addition, various ALA committees and round tables did address themselves to research library problems and make important contributions. ACRL was overshadowed by the Association of Research Libraries; its principal focus was on the academic library in general rather than on "research."

The founding of the American Library Association was followed shortly by other groups, national, state, and local; their number is legion and still on the increase. A few, such as those for librarians in medicine, law, and art, are of considerable importance to a degree that the state and local groups generally are not. Then there are the consortia, a relatively recent phenomenon. Some have secretariats and perform the most important functions for members in cataloging and similar essential tasks. One of the earliest and most important of these is the New England Library Information Network (NELINET). The idea caught on and NELINET was followed by SOLINET (in the Southeast), PALINET (for the Pennsylvania area), and others. Some consortia are limited by state boundaries; of these NYSILL serving all the libraries of New York State and MINITEX serving Minnesota are of outstanding service; however, they are both of principal benefit to nonresearch operations. In Colorado a complete book-processing center is operated for the state academic libraries. In short, by 1970 most large university libraries were involved in half a dozen or more of these consortia, some local and relatively informal, others national with paid staff and therefore expensive. There are nearly two hundred consortia today which are concerned principally with academic library operations.

Cooperation via Major National Acquisition Programs

While librarians had played an active role with the military during World War I, interest then had centered on service to the troops rather than problems of procurement of research materials. In 1940 and 1941, as the United States built up its military force, strategic intelligence on a worldwide basis became of increasing national importance. It was then dreadfully apparent that maps, photographs, research reports, and publications of all kinds that were urgently needed were nowhere to be found. The war effort shone a spotlight on great deficiencies in the collections of research libraries. So, in 1941, the military set up its own procurement operation to serve intelligence purposes under the peaceful title of "Interdepartmental Committee for the Acquisition of Foreign Publications." Most of its material came in microfilm through neutral sources, but friendly hands in enemy territory also did their share.

Toward the end of the war Verner Clapp of the Library of Congress spoke for all librarians when he wrote, "For nearly five years the disorganization of the world book trade has been such that American libraries have had to depend upon sporadic, casual, and accidental sources both for information about foreign books and for the books themselves." Certainly the leading librarians were smarting over the stigma of being unable to provide so much material needed earlier, and they were desperate to fill the gaps in European and Asiatic book and journal production of the last five years.

Out of this situation grew an enterprise, unique in history, the Cooperative Acquisitions Project for Wartime Publications, led by the Library of Congress and involving more than a hundred and fifty research libraries. This was the first of a series of major cooperative, collection-building enterprises involving large research libraries across the country.

The national need had been brought to the attention of the Secretary of State in urgent terms early in 1943, but nothing could be done at that time. It was renewed late in 1944, and again in June, 1945, each time on the initiative of the Association of Research Libraries with the Library of Congress. As the war in Europe drew to an end the stars were at last propitious: Archibald MacLeish had just moved from the Librarianship of Congress to the Department of State as Assistant Secretary; Luther Evans, his replacement at the Library of Congress, had all the uninhibited energy of a Texan plus a strong sense of international responsibility. So there were cautious approvals; after much careful spadework by committees it was agreed that the War Department would recognize the Library of Congress as the representative of research libraries; in return the Library of Congress would assist the War Department with problems concerning the disposal of captured library material.

Thus, for more than two years beginning in August, 1945, teams of American librarians and other specialists were in Europe to assist the army in the disposition of materials and, of course, to channel a huge flow of books, journals, and documents to the States. When available, fifty copies of books and at least three copies of journals, pamphlets, maps, and so forth were sent back. Into this stream also was fed much foreign material previously picked up by the military organizations for the prosecution of the war.

Naturally, once the shipments were received at home there were problems of distribution. Committees were established, 254 categories of material were agreed upon, and for these libraries made application. More than a hundred institutions participated initially, and one-half that number stayed with the project to the end. Participants were assessed a portion of the costs. In all, some two million pieces were distributed, all to universities except the Library of Congress, the Army Medical Library, and the New York Public Library. The mission also led in the difficult negotiations with the Russians regarding the release of publications held by German dealers in the Russian zone for their American customers. The mission was scrupulous in returning any material seized from legitimate enemy libraries. In many ways it was the voice of reason in the re-establishment of order and justice in the war-torn book world.

A small but delightful vignette of this very successful enterprise is that of Harry Miller Lydenberg leading the initial big push. Lydenberg, the former director of the New York Public Library, at the age of seventy the venerated dean of research librarians, a short, slender, soft-spoken man, rode his jeep, with David H. Clift at the wheel, through war-torn Europe with all the dash and verve and presence of a General Patton. To him goes much of the credit for the success of the effort.

Robert B. Downs summed up the accomplishments of the Cooperative Acquisitions Project as follows:

> It brought to the United States an unsurpassed collection of European wartime publications, far richer than would have been possible if dependence had been placed on individual institutions. The undertaking demonstrated several important facts: (1) American libraries could look to their national library for leadership in large cooperative activities; (2) research libraries were able and willing to support a broad program for the improvement of library resources; (3) the idea of libraries combining for the acquisition of research materials

is feasible and desirable; and (4) the research resources of American libraries, as represented by their holdings, are a matter of concern to the federal government.[4]

As the Cooperative Acquisitions Project was winding up its operations in the fall of 1947 its place was taken by the Farmington Plan, a more ambitious project planned and put into operation by the leading libraries of the country under the sponsorship of the Association of Research Libraries.

The plan takes its name from a meeting held on October 9, 1942, in Farmington, Connecticut at the home of Wilmarth S. Lewis, a noted bibliophile. In attendance were nearly a dozen librarians representing the Library of Congress and its Executive Committee of the Librarian's Council. The meeting was called to discuss the National Union Catalogue and a proposed National Institute of Bibliography. Apparently the agenda topics developed only inconclusive discussion; then, led by Luther Evans of the Library of Congress and Keyes Metcalf of Harvard, the group turned its attention to a proposed agreement whereby libraries might specialize in order collectively to cover all current book production. Mr. Metcalf was appointed chairman of a committee (with Julian Boyd of Princeton and Archibald MacLeish of the Library of Congress) to draft the proposal. And so began the plan that was to have such a decisive influence on American research library collections.

Like most births, this one depended on previous action. Nor was the project born all at once, complete, and lovely like Venus rising from the sea. Behind it lay the several years of growing concern and professional discussions about the country's deficiency in all manner of publication and related materials which had been urgently needed by the military for defense purposes. The wartime curtailment on travel had cut scholars off from research sources that had too long been taken for granted. In addition there was worry about the possible destruction of vast amounts of research material by military action. So, in December of 1939, two years before the attack on Pearl Harbor, the prestigious American Council of Learned Societies and the Social Science Research Council took formal action to promote the speedy acquisition of important printed materials by the Library of Congress. Other learned societies cooperated in the movement.

In 1940 two conferences of librarians focused on the need for research libraries to specialize in acquisitions to insure coverage of significant printed material; the Library of Congress had set up an Experimental Division of Library Cooperation to assist in the effort. Both the ALA's Board on Resources and the Association of Research Libraries had studied aspects of the problem. Other committees were involved. In short, cooperative specialization by research libraries was front and center on the library stage for at least two years prior to the meeting in Farmington.

The Metcalf Committee which had been assigned the task of drafting the plan soon accomplished its task. Its "Plan for Library Cooperation" provided for "the acquisition, promptly after publication, by some library in the United States, of one copy of every book . . . in the Latin alphabet, which might conceivably be of interest to a research worker." These were to be cataloged promptly and listed in the Union Catalogue of the Library of Congress. The plan also suggested something which never came to fruition, "a new classed catalogue from which, sooner or later, subject catalogues of limited fields for which there is a demand may be published in book form . . ." It is emphasized that this was a proposal for a project to be shared by many American libraries, necessarily nearly all of them university libraries.

The plan had the principal attention and support of the leading librarians of the country for a considerable period. Financial support was sought from the Carnegie and Rockefeller foundations in 1943 and, surprisingly, was not funded despite the endorsement of senior figures in university circles. But interest was sustained and the Association of Research Libraries took the development on as its principal responsibility early in 1944. Need for the plan was underscored by a study which showed that sixty American research libraries had acquired only 39 percent of the books published in eight foreign countries; from some countries less than 25 percent had been imported.

Study and planning went on with numerous meetings of various committees, but there was little movement during the hostilities. With peace the Cooperative Acquisitions Project for Wartime Publications, otherwise known as the Library of Congress mission, took on its important task; nothing could be accomplished through other approaches until the dust of war had settled and commercial bookselling channels were re-established.

The project finally got under way in 1948 with the collecting of books published in certain western European countries. It operated in this fashion:

The entire body of human knowledge, as embodied in Library of Congress classification schedules, had been broken down into over eight hundred segments. Over sixty libraries which were to participate indicated which of these subjects each would be willing to cover, and a table of allocations was drawn up. Allocations were generally supposed to follow the principle of building to strength. . . . A designated agent in each foreign country was to collect all new books and pamphlets published in his country "that might reasonably be expected to interest a research worker in the United States," classify them according to the L. C. classification, and send them, with invoices, to the appropriate American libraries. The libraries agreed to pay for the books, list them promptly in the Union Catalog at the Library of Congress, and make them available through interlibrary loan or photographic reproduction. The agents were instructed to exclude twenty-seven types of material: some, such as reprints, juvenile literature, and sheet music, judged to have little research value, and others such as periodicals and official government publications, felt to represent such special problems that they should be handled outside the Plan.[5]

No sweeping action such as that works perfectly. Agents sometimes had strange ideas as to what might "interest a research worker." So did librarians. A test was made of the latter by having four of their number, all well-known and respected bibliographers, check a volume of the Swiss national bibliography for titles thought to meet the definition. Of the 1,022 items listed, only 110 were selected by all four. They voted three to one on 396 titles, and divided, for or against, on 516. Obviously, with books as with food, one man's meat is another man's trash, if not poison.

The coverage of the plan was extended to countries outside western Europe in successive years until much of the globe was included. The project was largely but not entirely limited to collection of monographs as opposed to journals, government documents, etc. The operating machinery creaked and groaned, tempers flared, a few libraries withdrew in disgust, but the undeniable fact is, the plan really worked successfully until 1973, when it was abandoned. The committee which recommended cessation did so because of the increasing use of blanket orders which duplicated much of the Farmington Plan material, because of the new Library of Congress National Program for Acquisitions and Cataloging, and finally because of budget stringencies in many libraries.

Comment on the plan varied considerably. To Robert Vosper it was "a milestone in American intellectual history." To J. H. P. Pafford, a distinguished English university librarian, it was "a large, costly and rather clumsy sledge hammer to crack so small a nut." Most would agree with a third critic: "In retrospect, the Farmington Plan can be seen as a remarkable attempt by a handful of librarians to organize a national acquisitions program. The central fact is not that the attempt was less than entirely successful but rather the degree to which it succeeded in persuading librarians with limited resources and pressing demands to devote at least part of those resources to the national interest."[6]

Though officially dead, the plan continues in many informal ways as a number of libraries maintain their subject specialities. The trade outlets opened up in the less developed countries continued to supply material much as before. Furthermore, the experience of the plan either led to, or assisted with, the birth of other supplementary joint acquisitions programs.

In 1954 Congress passed legislation best known to the general public as the Agricultural Trade Development and Assistance Act. To librarians this is the famous "Public Law 480," which, because of an amendment in 1958, makes a major contribution to the goal of bringing to the United States the significant literature of the world.

The act, as originally passed, provided for the sale of surplus agricultural products to foreign countries, to be paid for in local currencies "blocked or restricted to the extent that they can be used only for the purchase of such goods and services as the said countries agree to sell for them." The 1958 amendment to the act, shepherded through Congress by Representative John D. Dingell of Michigan, provided for the use of these blocked funds for the purchasing and servicing by the Library of Congress of "books, periodicals, and related materials and their distribution to libraries and research institutions in the United States concerned with the study of the countries and areas of their origin."[7]

To these blocked funds Congress added an appropriation for other expenses, which was in turn increased by small contributions by the libraries involved. The project covered a number of Middle Eastern countries as well as Poland, Yugoslavia, and Indonesia. Several hundred libraries were on the list to receive publications in the English language and approximately two score were recipients of publications in the native languages. The shipments were enormous in size and naturally included much of questionable research value. By the end of fiscal 1972 nearly sixteen million pieces had been distributed.

But P. L. 480 did more than siphon valuable material into American libraries; it undoubtedly helped condition Congress to accept a far more important step in the aid of research libraries, the National Program for Acquisitions and Cataloging (NPAC), which was approved as part of the Higher Education Act of 1965. NPAC has been in operation since that date. It authorizes the Library of Congress to acquire and catalog "insofar as possible all library materials currently published throughout the world which are of value to scholarship." Even today this seems a staggering assignment in the light of the more than half a million books published annually, to say nothing of the journals, newspapers, documents, and myriad of other materials, nearly all of which might be considered of some "value to scholarship." It is a day that Harvard's Sibley and Illinois's Windsor should have lived to see. There are naturally financial limitations. And L.C.'s net, cast worldwide, misses many a worthwhile target. But the project has been of immense value, not just to the Library of Congress, but to all research libraries by providing cataloging copy (printed cards and computer tape) and bibliographic record in other forms. The saving in these costs is enormous and the service to scholarship of major importance.

Not all major cooperative projects required federal sponsorship and funds; in fact, the national government may be blamed for the situation which required the birth of the Documents Expediting Project. As the federal bureaucracy grew in size and complexity from the early 1930s, the volume of documentation increased geometrically, far beyond the capacity of the Government Printing Office to handle, and agencies found GPO prices beyond their means. In any case, a major portion of federal documentation was produced outside that official channel and therefore was not distributed to the restricted list of depository libraries. Procurement became a serious problem. So, in 1946 a group of library associations joined in sponsoring the "Document Expediting Project." The supporting libraries, originally thirty-one in number, grew by 1952 to seventy-six as the project demonstrated its capacity to channel large amounts of useful documentation to members at extremely low cost. As this is written, virtually all libraries with extensive document collections pay an annual membership fee to support the project, which has its own staff but is operated as a unit of the Library of Congress.

Another highly useful organization, created by the joint action of a number of library associations, is the Universal Serials and Book Exchange (USBE), originally titled the United States Book Exchange. Basically this is a self-supporting operation to receive library duplicates and with these to fill, at a fee, orders for materials from this country and especially from abroad.

A whole series of special needs has been met cooperatively, some under the leadership of the Association of Research Libraries, others by the Center for Research Libraries. ARL financed, through membership dues, the purchase of about two hundred of the most important foreign newspapers. Some files go back to 1930, but most began with the project in 1956. The collection, storing, loaning, and financing is handled through the Center for Research Libraries in Chicago. Similarly handled at the center is the Cooperative Africana Microform Project (CAMP), financed independently by certain research libraries collecting heavily from the vast outpouring of literature and documents from the new African nations. Another project of the same variety is the South Asia Microfilm Project (SAMP). Most intriguingly named, if somewhat lesser in scope and support is LAMP (Latin American Microfilm Project).

Of similar objective but quite different in organization and operation is SALALM (Seminar on the Acquisition of Latin American Library Materials). This dates from 1957 when a small group of research librarians and professors met "to discuss and try to solve problems concerned with the selection, acquisition and processing of library materials from the Latin American nations and dependent territories of the Caribbean." What was planned as a one-shot discussion turned into an annual affair and finally a membership organization concerned with all aspects of bibliographical control, acquisition, and effective use of publications from Latin America. The membership now includes many from South America and Central America as well as North America, also institutions, as well as scholars and people in book industries generally.

Lost to fame but nonetheless important are the myriad cooperative studies and programs that flourish in the divisions of the American Library Association, the state associations, and sundry other professional groups. There are also a number of major enterprises, too numerous for inclusion here, which concern all types of libraries. Clearly, cooperation has become the way of life for most professionally alert librarians, not only the administrators, but those down the chain of command. It is a spirit that does honor to the profession.

CHAPTER 13

Systems of Cataloging and Classification

Only second in importance to the actual building of collections is the matter of catalogs. This has been the case from the very beginning. Of all the various functions of the library it has been the most expensive, the most discussed, and the most vexatious.

In the early days of the seventeenth and eighteenth centuries the libraries of a few hundred volumes needed only a catalog that was basically an inventory or record of what was owned, no different from the inventory of the college silver and furniture. As collections increased somewhat in size a need was recognized for a finding list, to indicate the location of what was owned. Late in the nineteenth century attention was given to the students' need for record by subject and in some cases by form of publication. At about the same time the profession realized that the ever-increasing production of the printing press required libraries to describe books in their catalogs in detail sufficient to prevent possible confusion with other books, or editions of the same one. This was the birth of descriptive cataloging.

Along with the problem of the book marches the problem of its classification, or, in simplistic terms, its location. Most libraries at their beginnings simply classified books by broad subjects, such as history, philosophy, ethics, etc., with the number of the shelf on which each book was located, and its order on that shelf. The problem arose when growth required a general shift, or the library was given a new location. With the growth of collections came the need to subdivide by subject, to put the volume on the history of Ethiopia not just under "History," but with other books on African and Ethiopian history. This, then, is the problem of classification, which occupied some of the best minds of the profession for at least two generations.

Still a third problem area related to descriptive cataloging and to classification is that of subject cataloging, or providing an approach to library materials by subject headings, a seemingly simple matter that develops extraordinary complications as collections grow in size. These problems are equally vital to all types of libraries, at home and abroad.

Much of the leadership in cataloging came from the British Museum in the first half of the nineteenth century and from developments in scholarly bibliography on the Continent. While European libraries used somewhat different emphases in their approach to classification and cataloging, conference and agreement across the Atlantic mark the history of these developments. The leadership in the United States has come from all types of libraries, but university libraries have played the principal role. The story of the many developments which have led to the present catalog of any of our largest libraries is so involved that a substantial monograph would be required for adequate coverage. Therefore an account only of the early beginnings of cataloging and the highlights of developments in the twentieth century are given here.

By the dawn of the eighteenth century, no catalog had been printed in the United States but they had been in use for a considerable time in Europe. Ruth Strout summarized the situation in her study of the origins of the library catalog:

> By the beginning of the eighteenth century, catalogs were at last looked upon as finding lists rather than inventories. During this century they were sometimes classified and sometimes alphabetical; indexes were considered useful, though by no means necessary; some catalogs were still divided according to the size of books; authors were now always entered under surname and were often arranged chronologically; the wording of the title page had assumed a certain degree of prestige and was now being transcribed literally and without being paraphrased; imprints were included; "bound-with" notes were used; cross-references were quite common; and some analytical entries were used in most catalogs.[1]

This type of catalog continued to be used in America and in Europe throughout the century. It was as though a plateau had been reached in its development.

The first printed library catalog in the American colonies to survive was that of Harvard, issued in 1723 in three hundred copies. The impetus for this came from Thomas Hollis, Harvard's English benefactor, who "had hinted that we might expect more gifts if well-disposed persons in London knew what we lacked." So Joshua Gee, the Library Keeper of the day, made the rounds noting the authors of folios and setting them down in alphabetical order, then the quartos, then the octavos, etc. The order was at best casual, and an author of several works might be listed in several places. But the catalog did give, in addition to the author, brief title not always as on the title page, place and date of printing, and finally the particular "pluteus" (bookcase) where it was shelved. This finding record, which was commonly called a "fixed location" because it did not allow for growth of collection or change of quarters, remained the principal classification of all early libraries and was given up only late in the nineteenth century.[2]

Yale's catalog of 1743 was an exception to the general eighteenth century practice because of its focus on serving student needs and because it was a listing by location on shelves and a rough subject guide, as well as the traditional record by author. President Clap wrote of it in his history of Yale College:

> Before this Time there never had been any perfect Catalogue of the Books in the Library; for want of which the Students were deprived of much of the Benefit and Advantage of them. The Rector therefore placed all the Books in the Library in a proper order (but in Honour to the Rev. Dr. Berkeley, for his extraordinary Donation, his Books stood by themselves, at the South end of the Library) and put a Number to every Book in its proper Class and Box; and then took three Catalogues of the Books, one as they stood in their proper Order on the Shelves; and another in an Alphabetical Order; and a Third, wherein the most valuable Books were placed under proper Heads, according to the Subject Matter of them; together with Figures referring to the Place and Number of each Book. By which means it might be easily known what Books were in the Library upon any particular Subject, and where they might be found, with the utmost Expedition. This Catalogue was printed, and was a great Incitement to the Diligence and Industry of the Scholars in reading of them.[3]

Princeton's printed catalog of 1760 was a modification of the traditional size arrangement; it was alphabetic by letter, but under each letter arranged by size, first the folios, then quartos, octavos, and so forth, and was apparently designed for use in attracting donations as much as for cultural uses at the college. Its preface states:

> A survey of its literary Wealth, which is exposed to View in the following Catalogue, will soon convince the Friends of Learning and Nassau Hall, how poor it still is in this important article: to which no Additions can be made from the Treasury, which is far from being equal to other unavoidable and more indispensable Exigencies.[4]

Library catalogs were printed by other institutions up to the middle of the nineteenth century but they were expensive, soon superseded as new donations and occasional purchases arrived, and then followed by handwritten supplements. The only development of this period was a noble experiment by Joseph Green Cogswell at Harvard (1821–23). He began a sheaf catalog, with a separate entry on each sheet of paper, and therefore infinitely expandable. Such catalogs still exist in Europe, but they are bulky and cumbersome to untie or to unfasten for new entries, and this one was given up and forgotten.

Ruth Strout's study sums up the situation at the middle of the nineteenth century:

> Up to this time. . . . American cataloging was still following the same general pattern that had characterized European cataloging during the preceding century. For example, of the three catalogs which Harvard printed, one had been divided into three alphabets according to the *size* of books, all three contained the briefest of entries, and none provided much in the way of subject approach. However, in 1850, with the acceptance of Charles C. Jewett's code for the catalog of the Smithsonian Institution, it would not be far wrong to say that cataloging in this country first came to maturity. The unprecedented and still unparalleled interest and activity in cataloging which had flared and flourished at the British Museum for well over a decade now could not help having its effect on American librarians.[5]

Jewett's code was soon followed by two key contributions to the 1876 *Public Libraries in the United States,* namely Dewey's "Decimal Classification" and Charles Ammi Cutter's *Rules for a Printed Dictionary Catalogue.* These publications moved leadership in cataloging and classification across the Atlantic where it was to remain largely thereafter.

Harvard, as the largest academic library, was the first to face the problem of growth, in cataloging and classification as in other areas of operation. The sheaf catalog had been abandoned by Cogswell's successor and by 1848 the manuscript supplements had become so burdensome that Harvard took the advice of Jewett and started a card catalog, the first in this country. It was no model. Clerks simply cut up the entries and pasted each one on a separate card, 2″ × 9 1/2″. New accessions were treated the same way. Access to this record was for staff only, not the public. It was not until 1861 that a separate catalog for public consultation was started at Harvard by the assistant librarian, Ezra Abbot.

This new catalog was innovative in several respects. It was first an "Index of Authors" designed to tell whether a copy was owned and on what shelf it was located; it was not in any respect a bibliographical description, as catalog entries later came to be. Each entry was on a ruled card two inches high and five inches wide, a size maintained for a generation and still well in evidence at Harvard in the 1940s. A second part of the catalog was an "Index of Subjects," which, in Abbot's words, was "to serve as a guide to all the separate works in the library on any particular subject. These catalogues also include the treatises which are contained in Collections, and in the Transactions of learned societies; and they are likewise intended to embrace, as far as practicable, articles in the more important periodical publications."[6]

The subject catalog was "classed," in other words arranged alphabetically, in categories such as Accidents, Acoustics, Aesthetics, Agriculture. Under each of these headings were subdivisions dealing with the topic. An index to the subject catalog was published in 1891. Harvard kept this classed catalog until 1915, when it bowed to almost universal practice elsewhere in the United States in setting up a dictionary catalog (author, title, and subject cards filed together alphabetically).

Abbot not only created the first card catalog for public use, but designed practical cases in which to put it. The earliest card catalogs were only for one or several members of the library staff and could therefore be housed in a few cardboard boxes or any other handy receptacle, to be kept in a desk drawer or on a table. Abbot devised a practical drawer which established the general design which has endured to this day. Principal difference was a shallow depth, sufficient for the two-inch cards then in use, and two rows of cards, not one. He devised a button to prevent accidental withdrawal and consequent spilling of contents. Abbot experimented with wire or cord through the cards to preserve order and to prevent unauthorized removal. For a while libraries used double wires over the tops of cards. O. H. Robinson of Rochester used a wire through a hole in the card as early as 1870. The metal rod which was removable by unscrewing or unsnapping was developed much later. Abbot's provisions had other features, for example thin wooden blocks with labels on the slanting edge to serve as guide cards. He put labels similar to those used today on the front of the drawer, and he devised cases of a height designed to make inspection of all drawers reasonably easy from a standing position. The bottom part of the case was for books and storage. In summary one might say that this young man made several major contributions to the development of academic libraries and indeed to all libraries, before going on to a distinguished career as a Biblical scholar.

In 1896 William Coolidge Lane, librarian of Harvard, summarized

certain principles then generally accepted as practical for a library catalog. There should be a record by subject as well as by author; the author
entry should give full details of name and bibliographic data but only
brief title, while the subject card should give the title in full but other data
might be "in brief." There was then no consensus for or against a dictionary catalog with author, title, and subject cards in one alphabet, or a
divided catalog—usually in two alphabets, one for author and title, one
for subjects. There was still interest in the "classed" catalog although this
would soon disappear; the divided catalog also soon lost out to the
dictionary arrangement only to reappear nearly two generations later in
a goodly number of research libraries. At the same time there was, of
course, much interest in a number of important technical questions, such
as concern over entries for pseudonyms, noblemen, societies, and so
forth; these are far beyond the scope of the present review.

In 1896 Lane would not go so far as to state the catalog in card form
the winner over printed and loose-leaf types; six years later he declared
himself convinced. Actually the contest had long been decided. The 1876
Bureau of Education publication listed no less than 382 book catalogs all
printed since 1870. The card catalog form was obviously still experimental, but by 1896, of fifty-eight typical American libraries, forty-three had
complete card catalogs and thirteen used cards to bring their printed
catalogs up to date. From the very first there was recognition of the waste
involved when the same book in a hundred or a thousand libraries had
to be cataloged a hundred or a thousand times at each location. One
solution was to print and sell catalog cards. This was first proposed by
Jewett in 1847, and finally done by Justin Winsor at the Boston Public
Library in 1872, and later at Harvard. The issuance of Library of Congress printed cards in 1901 had a profound effect on all types of libraries
and effectively sealed the matter.

Before carrying the story of the form of the catalog on into the
twentieth century, it is necessary to consider briefly the development of
policy in determining catalog entries and the classification used to group
like materials together. As previously noted, the first major contribution
of an American to descriptive cataloging was the 1852 publication of
Charles Coffin Jewett of *On the Construction of Catalogues of Libraries, and of
a General Catalogue, and their Publication by Means of Separate, Stereotyped Titles,
with Rules and Examples.* These "Rules" were at once accepted as a basic
guide to practice, only to be supplanted in 1876 by Charles Ammi Cutter's *Rules for a Dictionary Catalogue.*

History has it that back in September of 1898 the infant Stanford University Library cataloged twelve thousand books in a weekend at no cost by putting seventy-eight student volunteers to the task. The student newspaper acknowledged that "many amuzing [*sic*] mistakes were made!" Such solutions of a simpler age were found to be no solutions at all. The average book presents no problem if it has only a simple author (homo sapiens, not a government, industry or association), particularly an author with a truly distinctive set of names all spelled out in full. It should have a simple, straightforward title without variant binding title, series title, running title and so forth, with place, publisher and date nicely spelled out on the title page. Alas, the printing presses have always produced much that has presented perplexing complications in one or more of these elements, and standard practices in handling them had to be devised. With the passage of time the problems were multiplied as new types of material such as microforms, sheet music, audio-visual aids, and the like had to be handled. For the American university library Cutter's "Rules" was the foundation of descriptive cataloging: the accurate description of each book to establish its unique identity, its relationship to other editions and issues, if any, as well as entries for other books, and finally to record such features as index, bibliography, illustrations, size, and so forth, that might be important to the user. Cutter's "Rules" or code was so carefully crafted that it continues to be the basis of present practice.

The 1876 code was revised by Cutter several times. The 1904 edition was the last by his hand. With the distribution of Library of Congress cards came new problems, so the task of preparing rules for general practice was taken up by an ALA committee. This committee collaborated with the Library Association of the United Kingdom in the preparation of the Anglo-American Code of 1908. This emphasized research library needs and was accepted as gospel until the American Library Association published its own revision in 1941, which swelled the 1908 pamphlet of eighty-eight pages to more than four hundred.

The period since 1941 has seen enormous investment of funds, talent, and time in code revisions. Basic principles were restated in *Studies of Descriptive Cataloging* (Library of Congress, 1946), followed by several editions of Library of Congress rules. The American Library Association produced a revised code in 1949. This was attacked in 1953 with devastating logic by Seymour Lubetsky whose *Cataloging Rules and Principles* is considered by many to be the single most important work in English on descriptive cataloging of this century.[7] In 1961 the International Federation of Library Associations published its own principles for cataloging, and finally a new Anglo-American code was published in 1967. In 1979, as this is written, a new Anglo-American code has just appeared. Does it need to be reported that revisions of this are already being studied?

Truly, the effort expended on rules has been enormous. Behind all this is the basic conflict between the broad concept of cataloging as an art in which the practitioner exercises considerable judgment and cataloging as a science with a rule to cover every possible need. One's sympathies are with the former, but the arrival of automation and virtually enforced conformity speak emphatically for the latter.

While the problems of codes for descriptive cataloging seem to have increased with the passage of time, those of classifying books and other material have diminished. It was early recognized that it was not practical to classify books to fixed physical locations because that system made no allowance for growth or relocation of libraries. Further recognition was given to the extreme importance of putting together material on the same topic, and related topics adjacent to each other. The need was for a system based on a classification of knowledge, a subject that has intrigued philosophers certainly from the time of Aristotle, possibly before! It was equally of interest to Francis Bacon, on whose classification of knowledge Thomas Jefferson built the system for his own library. And Jefferson's classification was followed by many early libraries, and influenced the Library of Congress.

Just as the 1876 publication of *Public Libraries in the United States* established the future path for descriptive cataloging as set forth by Cutter, so it presented an equally important classification scheme in outline, namely the Decimal Classification by Melvil Dewey. This not only was adopted by the great majority of academic and virtually all public libraries over the next decades, but it had somewhat similar recognition in Europe where it became the basis of the Universal Decimal (or Brussels) Classification. As the name indicates, this broke knowledge down into nine major classes, with each class subdivided by decimal. There are extraordinarily ingenious provisions for geographic designations and form of material, and it adapted nicely to small as well as large collections. The 1876 publication provided only the outline, which was developed further in later years, and constantly revised.

Many universities, however, did not adopt the Decimal Classification. There was the irresistible attraction of devising one's own scheme, and there was always the question whether a plan, designed for all libraries, however good it might be, was the best possible for a particular collection of books or a particular institution. Harvard, for example, set up its own classification in 1877 under the direction of Justin Winsor. It was a mixture, built partly on the subject headings of Abbot's public catalog, partly on the university's departments of instruction, and partly on notable collections, with principal headings such as "Crus" for "Crusades," and "Nor" for the Norton donation. And Harvard stuck to the classification, with constant revision and expansion at enormous cost, until very recent years. At Indiana University it was the Danforth classification, adopted in 1898. The Cornell scheme was based on the British Museum classification. At a later period Henry Bliss published his own scheme whereby "classes and schedules arrange recorded knowledge in the order that has been found to be satisfactory by the expert scholars in a given discipline . . ." Bliss used it to reclassify the library of the City College of New York shortly after 1900. Although the Bliss classification had apparently only one other "taker" in the United States, it was adopted by a large number of libraries in the British Commonwealth. Still another classification is the Expansive classification of Charles Ammi Cutter (1897). While it was not widely adopted it made its contribution by substantially influencing the Library of Congress classification scheme.

In the Library of Congress classification a single letter designates a major subject. A second letter may be used for a subdivision. After the letters numbers are used for further refinement. Thus P stands for literature, PS for American literature, and PS3537 for twentieth century authors whose last names begin with S. The line below the classification contains letters and numbers arbitrarily assigned by so-called Cutter or Cutter-Sanborn tables in order to group together the material by a particular author.

While the complete classification is obviously the creation of scores of librarians, principal credit for its goes first, of course, to Cutter, but also to Charles Martel and James C. M. Hanson, who launched it at the Library of Congress. It was then described by the Librarian of Congress:

> The system devised has not sought to follow strictly the scientific order of subjects. It has sought rather convenient sequence of the various groups, considering them as books, not as groups of mere subjects.

In other words the base is book oriented, not a philosophical concept. The Library of Congress classification, much more than the Dewey Decimal, was able to expand with the extension of research into new fields. Unlike the Dewey, Cutter, and Bliss methods, the Library of Congress classification was developed exceedingly slowly and full coverage completed only over a period of two generations after publication of the American history schedule in 1901. Work on it actually began in 1898; a considerable portion was finished by 1920 but the last section (K for law) was not published until 1970.

As "LC" was slow in development so also was the library world slow in adopting it, but with the passage of time its superiority over Dewey Decimal became more and more evident. Probably the first university library to use it was Ohio State, which began using both the history schedule and the printed cards early in 1902. Johns Hopkins adopted the LC classification in 1911 and Chicago in 1912, a natural development to follow Hanson's appointment to the University of Chicago library. Rice Institute went LC the same year. California at Berkeley gave up the classification developed by J. C. Rowell, its librarian from 1875 to 1918, for LC in 1913. Cornell attempted reclassification to LC in 1918 but little was accomplished until the matter was attacked with vigor in 1948. Rutgers and Indiana were using the classification by 1917.

The movement away from Dewey to the LC classification picked up in the 1920s as more LC schedules were completed and available in print, and as Dewey proved less adequate for research collections. Michigan began its reclassification to LC in 1923, Brown in 1924, Iowa State in 1925, Emory in 1926, Notre Dame in 1927. The movement slowed in the 1930s, probably because of depression budgets. An investigation published in 1955 reported that of 744 college and university libraries, 84.6 percent still used Dewey, 13.8 percent Library of Congress, and a bare 1.5 percent some other type.[8]

From the late 1950s on it became increasingly clear that the LC classification was a "must" for all large university libraries. The final argument in its favor was the increasing use of the computer for cataloging. It was virtually a matter of adopting LC or sinking under the cost of original cataloging. The directors of libraries with a million or more volumes were understandably hesitant to embark on the mammoth and expensive task of reclassification. Some elected to classify new accessions by LC but only to reclassify as funds permitted. Harvard, the largest library, was one of the longest holdouts.

From the very beginnings of cooperative effort, librarians, particularly those in university libraries, sought some means to make the work of cataloging a book or other material serve all libraries and thus avoid the expense of repetition by each institution owning it. The first attempt dates from 1878 and is known as Cataloging in Publication (CIP). I have before me an 1883 publication of Henry Holt, John Addington Symonds' *Italian Byways.* In the front is a page, blank on one side, with instructions "Slips for Librarians to paste on Catalogue Cards," and a warning as to how to cut it out so as not to damage the binding. Then there is (1) a full entry under author, giving place, publisher, date, size, pagination; (2) a title entry; (3) three different subject entries, each with full information as above, one to file under "Travel," another under "Alps," a third under "Tyrol." It is easy to picture the librarian of that day using the scissors to snip the entries, then pasting them on separate cards, all the work of a minute or two. There is no classification given because there was then no standard classification.

"Cataloging in Source," as it was then called, did not take. It was discussed over the years. Finally, in 1958, rekindled interest led to experimental resurrection of the idea by the Library of Congress. A determined assault brought hundreds of publishers into line in 1970 or 1971 and at the time of writing virtually every book published in the United States contains copy for professional cataloging along with subject headings and numbers for both the Library of Congress and Dewey classifications.

Mention should also be made of still another partially successful project to eliminate the costly work of original cataloging by separate libraries. This is the cards-with-books program of the nineteen sixties, the furnishing of a full set of catalog cards with books sold to libraries. At one time nearly a hundred publishers and distributors were cooperating and in 1967 some ten million cards were furnished by this means.

These projects were all dwarfed by the Library of Congress printed card distribution. The study of land-grant institutions of 1930[9] found that only three libraries were getting their LC printed cards for less than 50 percent of their accessions. A number of universities were using the printed cards for 90 percent or more of their new material. The largest universities naturally had lower percentages because of the volume of purchases in foreign languages; thus Ohio State and Cornell reported LC cards for 54 percent and the University of Illinois a bare 50 percent. Printed cards were also issued selectively for a number of years by California at Berkeley, Illinois, Michigan, Chicago, and Harvard, to name only a few.

While the printing and distribution of Library of Congress cards was the major breakthrough of its time, it is equalled in importance by the dramatic accomplishment of the Ohio College Library Center (OCLC) in 1971 in offering on-line, therefore instantaneous, cataloging data to all subscribing libraries across the country. This enterprise is doubly remarkable because it had little financial assistance from government or foundation sources. It was initiated by a committee of Ohio academic librarians led by Lewis Branscomb, and developed by Frederick G. Kilgour and was by the mid-seventies connected by leased lines to computer terminals in more than a thousand libraries. In each of these a clerk with a book to catalog sits at his terminal, punches in a few numbers or letters from the book on a keyboard similar to that of a typewriter, and thereby calls up on a screen the full bibliographic description of the book, the Library of Congress classification, subject headings, etc. If there is minor variation between the OCLC record and the edition in hand, the corrections are easily made. When all is correct, a lever is pushed which tells OCLC to print a set of catalog cards for that particular library, whose special requirements are entered in the computer and are followed in the printing. The cards are then automatically alphabetized and sent out by mail. Initially the computer would respond to contact with a polite "Good morning" or a "Good afternoon," but gave this up as its service was extended to all time zones!

OCLC has under development a whole series of additional computer services for the nation's libraries, but these are in the embryo stage at the time these lines are written.

While OCLC is the principal vehicle for computer-based cataloging, it is not the only one. Basic to the several such services now in existence is the Library of Congress contribution of machine-readable cataloging data tapes, commonly known as MARC tapes. These in turn depended on the NPAC program of the Library of Congress (National Program for Acquisitions and Cataloging), which seeks to bring promptly to this country all materials of research significance. As this is received it is promptly cataloged and copy made available on LC cards and, even more important, on tape which can be utilized by institutions with sophisticated computer equipment and, of course, by service programs such as OCLC.

In commenting on this program before the Education Subcommittee on Higher Education (May 21, 1970) the Executive Director of the Association of Research Libraries said,

It is an outstanding example of how a modest sum of money spent centrally can create benefits that flow out to users of libraries all over the country. The member libraries of the Association of Research Libraries added 7,500,000 volumes in 1968–69. Reports from these libraries indicate that, on the average, Library of Congress catalog copy is available for 70–75 percent of the books added. In the same year 1968–69, the Library of Congress cataloged 210,000 titles. This production of LC made available to this group of seventy-five libraries cataloging copy for approximately five million volumes. Thus, 210,000 was multiplied almost twenty-five times. If all college, university and public libraries that depend on the LC cataloging were included, these figures would be doubled.[10]

Less well known than OCLC but similar in design and services is BALLOTS, the acronym for a computerized development at Stanford University with the imposing title "Bibliographic Automation of Large Library Operations using a Time-Sharing System." It began to operate in 1972. Relatively few libraries are using BALLOTS, but it was selected by the important network RLIN (Research Libraries Information Network), which comprises, at the time this is written, a number of the largest libraries in the Northeast and is extending its membership. Certainly the use of the Stanford facility is spreading and challenging OCLC for leadership.

BALLOTS is a combined acquisitions and cataloging system. Like OCLC it has the MARC tapes as its base but has built up a large store of non-MARC cataloging data. Serials, standing orders, and approval plan orders are handled. Specifically it supports such functions as placing the order, claims for orders not filled, cancelling, and recording the passage of the volume through library processes until it is ready to be shelved.

A third major computer-activated operation similar to OCLC and BALLOTS is the Washington Library Network.

Still other developments such as CAPTAIN (Computer Aided Processing and Terminal Access Information Network) at Rutgers, the State University of New Jersey, provide printed cards via the computer for local needs. These are also generally designed to produce bookkeeping records and data useful in the ordering process.

Were librarians not so inventive with acronyms this story would not include Oregon State University Library's "Library On-Line Information Text Access," or, of course, LOLITA! It is roughly the same as CAPTAIN, but with a titillating name!

Stephen Salmon sums up the general situation:

> In no other area of library automation has activity been so intense as in the manipulation of cataloging data. A survey conducted by the LARC Association in 1970 revealed a total of 158 cataloging systems and 112 systems involved in the production of special catalogs and bibliographies; there are undoubtedly more . . . The intellectual work of describing the physical book or item and analysing its subject content has been largely untouched, but machines have been used to produce a wide variety of products derived from such description and analysis, to control the clerical and technical processes involved, and to promote the exchange and use of cataloging data regionally and nationally.[11]

At the time this is written it would appear that the standard card catalog may have to give way to other forms of record, if only because of sheer size. Mention has previously been made of the 1944 prediction that if the Yale Library continued normal growth its card catalog would by the year 2044 require eight acres of floor space! Growth brings increased unit costs of filing, using the catalog, and in sundry factors other than floor space and card cabinets. Therefore there is a move back to the book catalog in the form of volumes which reproduce the card catalog. This has been done by several large libraries at their own expense; quite a number of research collections have been published in book form as commercial ventures because of their bibliographic value. Libraries, of course, have always used the codex book to "catalog" special collections of great distinction.

Another form of catalog is card information on microfilm, which is convenient when packaged in cassettes that are ready to be used the moment the cassette is inserted in the reader. Still another form is microfiche, which appears to be more practical than the cassette for many types of need. Some libraries have already turned to the computer to record current accessions. Terminals in the library and at other strategic locations around the institution are used for instantaneous information on library holdings with notations as to whether they are in circulation at that time.

The one certain factor for the future is the essentiality of the library catalog whether it be computer stored with on-line access, recorded on some type of microform, or a card catalog. The governing factor in the choice of instrument by each institution will probably be cost.

CHAPTER 14

The Technological Revolution

In 1972 the Carnegie Commission on Higher Education, certainly no revolutionary-minded body, published a report entitled "The Fourth Revolution; Instructional Technology in Higher Education," much of which dealt directly with fundamental changes in the collection, storage, and dissemination of knowledge—in short, librarianship. It was the conviction of the commission that current developments in this area were of sufficient importance to rank with the "third revolution," the invention of printing from movable type in 1456. Technology had made only minor contributions to library operations before 1945; since then these contributions have increased rapidly in number and importance; at the time this is written technology is creating all the excitement in leaders and in would-be leaders of the profession that comes in time of revolution, be it 1776 or 1848. The possibilities for radical change are virtually limitless but paths must be picked and obstructions cleared.

Verner Clapp, a great leader in many aspects of librarianship but none more so than in its utilization of technology, liked to refer to the seventeenth century admonitions of Gabriel Naude, Cardinal Mazarin's librarian, that the library provide readers with the necessities for note-taking such as tables, pens in the form of quills, knives to sharpen them, ink, and pounce to blot it. The tables have always been with us although they no longer have the sloping surface of earlier centuries. Few libraries still provide the ink, sold for a penny, which was much in evidence until the 1940s. Quills and pounce even antedate the experience of this writer! So there was change, but not a great deal of it until the mid-nineteenth century, when means were devised, as has been seen, to accommodate the card catalog. There were also major developments in housing and the shelving of books, with atmospheric control to minimize decay. The library hand, taught in all library schools as the style to be used for library catalogs, gradually gave way to the typewriter early in this century.

Modern library technology can properly claim Melvil Dewey as its father, an innovator here as he was in so many other aspects. Until the 1880s, libraries depended on stationers and furniture dealers for supplies. Dewey dreamed of a specialty house for all library needs and in 1882 he established the Library Bureau as a private venture. For many years it had the field to itself and it is still in existence although its scope has altered and there are many competitors. The important developments in technology for libraries are those of the last two generations. If the minor ones are included their number is legion; the major developments fall into three categories: (1) those which are basically photographic in nature; (2) those which have to do with the conservation and protection of library materials, and (3) those which depend on automation and computer processes. Each of these groups have made, and continue to make, great contributions to library operations.

Photographic Processes

The photostat machine was invented by Abbé René Graffin in 1900 and came into practical use about 1912. It made possible the photographic copying of manuscript and print, principally because it used paper in place of the glass plates formerly required. But the good Abbé went further; he designed a complete apparatus for reproductions from books, a cradle to hold them, mirrors to reverse the image, etc. This was first used in the United States in about 1912 and by 1929 some two score American libraries had photostat machines. It was an expensive service, sparingly used by scholars.

A related invention, originating earlier, but adopted later and now of great importance to all university libraries, is the microform. The beginnings of this date from 1839, shortly after Daguerre's work on photography, when John Benjamin Dancer reduced images as much as 160:1 and produced a translucent image. This early microfilm achieved fame in 1870 from its use to transmit messages, via carrier pigeon, to and from Paris, then under seige in the Franco-Prussian War. In modern times individual scholars made limited use of Leica or other cameras to make their own copies on microfilm of archival records and manuscripts, but the process first received serious attention from the library profession at the 1936 ALA Midwinter Meeting. At its annual conference the following summer, a full day was devoted to a discussion of microforms and a committee established on Photographic Reproduction of Library Materials. M. Llewellyn Rainey, Director of University Libraries at Chicago was a leader in this movement. Two years later the *Journal of Documentary*

Reproduction was founded. Chicago also had the first laboratory "adequate to produce microfilms of a high quality" which was financed by a Rockefeller grant and operated by the young Herman Fussler. Fussler succeeded Rainey, not only as a national leader in the development of microforms but also as director of libraries some years later.

The general acceptance of microfilm was soon extended to forms other than the translucent roll film. The microcard compressed a hundred or more pages of type on a three-by-five card, and was soon followed by a variant, microprint, and later by microfiche. Most miniaturization is now either in roll form, which is convenient for newspapers and used almost exclusively for dissertations, and microfiche in card format, which is used for reports, documents, and increasingly for book reproduction. Unfortunately each of the four principal forms requires a different reader. The readers have always been much more expensive than seems justified to produce something to hold the material plus a light source, lens, and focusing attachment. The provision of the various readers in adequate numbers entails expenses of purchase, maintenance, and space that are administrative headaches. The problems are multiplied by the requirement of reader-printers for each type to provide hard copy as needed.

There has always been strong resistance from scholars to the use of microforms, because of eye-strain, lack of cheap, portable, or affordable readers, and a variety of other reasons. But the use of film has increased to the point that more material of scholarly value is available in this form than in any other except the book. It has made possible scores of huge projects such as foreign newspaper reproduction, the issue of all English books printed before 1640, nineteenth-century American fiction, early journals, early drama, the Human Relations Area Files, that mainstay of American educational research ERIC, and a host of others, some to be found in most university libraries, other to be borrowed. Truly the scholar of two generations ago would be amazed by the wealth of record and inspiration that is easily placed at the disposal of his successors. Only microforms have made this possible.

The very high reductions, many times more than the normal sixteen or twenty to one, have not had wide acceptance. At least two publishers have put on the market whole libraries in "ultrafiche" form, one in reductions of up to 90:1 and the other as high as 150:1. At the latter reduction some three thousand pages can be reproduced on one four-by-six-inch fiche! Special readers are naturally required. Libraries have no choice but take all the "books" included, even though some are already owned or are unsuitable. Nor is an ultrafiche anything to curl up with on a rainy afternoon! All too often the extreme reductions prove faulty.

No reference to the role of microforms in the research library would be complete without mention of University Microfilms and its founder, Eugene B. Power. He became interested in the potential service of microfilm to research in 1935, while an officer of Edwards Brothers, a firm specializing in the duplication of scholarly materials by offset. With the advice of a committee of leading librarians (Bishop of Michigan, Potter of Harvard, Keogh of Yale, and Lydenberg of the New York Public), he planned a project to microfilm all books printed in England before 1550 for subscribing libraries. The many problems of camera, type of film, source of originals, supervision, and so forth, were worked out in the next two years and the project begun with eleven subscribers, each paying five hundred dollars annually to receive film of approximately one hundred thousand pages. Edwards Brothers set up a separate department, with Power in charge, to handle the new project; this broke away from the parent concern in July, 1938 to become University Microfilms, Inc.

From this one project the company rapidly expanded by setting up filming equipment in several European locations and by offering the scholar microfilm copies of "almost any item he may wish in major European collections at the rate of three and one half cents per page for a positive copy."

At approximately the same date as the founding, Power was promoting his plan to film all doctoral dissertations accepted by American universities, a step of immense importance to research. These two projects, both expanded over the years, have been of the greatest importance to libraries and were the forerunners of a large number of similar major filming enterprises that make it possible today to own, at a modest price, virtually any early printed work, manuscript, or government document, of course in photographic form. The concept of offering film in large, related segments (early American periodicals, American novels published before 1900, etc.) was bold and highly successful both for the company and for the subscribers.

First cousin to the microform and equally important to research is the photocopy machine. This dates from 1938, when Chester Carlson invented the electrostatic dry copy machine that has always been the leader in this field of reproduction. For twelve years the invention was rejected by company after company, was gradually perfected, and finally put on the market commercially in 1950. It became an instant success when the Xerox 914 was made available in 1960. Xerox was put to immediate use for various internal operations and notably for the reproduction of catalog cards. It made possible a great increase in the transmission of material between libraries, and the dozens of coin-operated machines now found scattered throughout the public areas of most university libraries, which collect nickels and dimes by the bucketful daily, bear mute witness to the importance of these "copy machines" to the student body and faculty.

The Conservation and Protection of Library Materials

While Power's contribution was entrepreneurial in nature, progress is more easily made when the priming, indeed the initiating, comes with foundation funds. Of major importance to the development of technological applications to librarianship was a conference held at the Folger Library in January, 1955, which led to the establishment of the Council on Library Resources with a grant from the Ford Foundation. The stated purpose of the meeting was to assist "in the solution of the problems of libraries generally and of research libraries in particular." One of its first major grants, continued for some years, was in support of research by the W. J. Barrow Laboratory into the preservation of paper. Barrow began his work in 1936; at first he concentrated on the preservation of manuscript material. The laboratory soon became the leading independent scientific center for research into paper, books, and other graphic arts components. It was among the first to question the durability of paper, and its investigation of paper deterioration produced data that startled the library world. The nub of Barrow's findings is that 99 percent of the books produced after 1900 had a life expectancy of twenty-five to fifty years. The many factors that contribute to decay—inks, sunlight, dirt, impurities in the air, adhesives, etc.—were all investigated. Much initial experimentation was with lamination and resulted in the invention of a practical, roller-type, laminating machine. However, lamination was not a long-term solution. Research then extended into the causes of paper deterioration and methods to deacidify papers. Barrow invented the first effective spray deacidification formula and device.

The Barrow formula for neutralizing the acid in papers required the disassembly of bound books in order to treat individual pages. Obviously this was quite expensive. Later the laboratory developed a morpholene process for the deacidification of books in bound form. At present a vacuum chamber capable of taking thirty volumes at a time is being utilized.

A development of indirect importance to libraries was the formula for Permalife, a basically wood pulp paper that in theory should last two thousand years.

The Barrow Laboratory was closed in 1977 and the principal work in the field of preservation is now in the Library of Congress under the assistant director for preservation. Among other projects, it has been developing a deacidification method for mass treatment which utilizes diethyl zinc. While carrying on much experimental work on papers, bindings, adhesives, etc., the preservation office also has done much to educate the profession on preventative measures and has been an instant resource for counsel to libraries that suffer disaster of any nature, but particularly water damage. Can it be pure coincidence that its principal authority, as indeed the principal international authority, on damage to books and manuscripts from water is named Mr. Waters and the assistant director for preservation Mr. Poole?

It is only natural for the profession to look to the Library of Congress for greater leadership in measures of conservation and restoration. This should lead to the inauguration of a national program under its leadership and administered through regional centers. In fact one such enterprise which qualifies as a regional center has been in operation since 1972. This is the New England Document Conservation Center, financed by a Council of Library Resources grant to the New England Library Board. The funds were used to establish a workshop to restore, preserve, and maintain the physical condition of books, prints, maps, broadsides, manuscripts, etc.; to conduct studies and tests relating to those functions, and to carry the message of conservation to those who were entrusted with the care of such materials. The center became self-financing through fees charged for work when the grant was exhausted.

While the emphasis of research is on the deterioration of paper and bindings, there are also the constant calamities in the form of Acts of God and the failures of man, which call for extraordinary relief. It may be a flood, a burst pipe, a fire followed by the flow from the firemen's hoses, earthquake, or vandalism. The Florence flood of November, 1966 called for heroic international action to save two million books, and from it came valuable experience in recovery methods. The expedient of freezing books was then applied on a modest scale. Freezing did not restore books but it did prevent further damage until such time as they could be worked on. From this gradually developed a practical method of freeze-drying books in quantity. Freeze-drying is the extraction of water by a vacuum process. It does not achieve complete restoration, but it does produce a usable, if somewhat unhappy-looking tome.

There are foes other than water. A few university libraries have had major problems with insects. These usually come in very old volumes imported from abroad for rare book collections. For these a fumigation chamber is a natural requirement. Unfortunately the law forbids the use of fumigation chambers to handle the most common and the most distressing enemy of books—homo sapiens. This enemy comes in all ages, equally in both sexes, represents varied cultural backgrounds, and ranks from youngest student to senior professor and university executive.

The constant drain on library collections by unrecorded borrowings, a euphemism for book theft, led to the development in the late sixties of mechanisms to give warning when books that were not properly charged were being taken through the exit. The two principal devices bore the names of "Tattle Tape" and "Check Point"; both have special features which make them more attractive for certain needs, less for others. Both employ a type of sensor which is hidden in the book or other material. The one system requires that the material be passed around a barrier by a library attendant stationed at the exit; the other system permits desensitizing when material is charged out, and sensitizing when returned. Both call attention to uncharged material by activating a gong, chime, or buzzer, or by locking a gate. The first installation in a large central university library was at Temple University in 1971. While these devices are not foolproof, they have reduced losses drastically; even more important, in many situations it has been possible in practice to eliminate the position of guard at the exit.

Bindings are of obviously critical importance to libraries, and have been the subject of articles from the 1876 conference right on down to current times. A century ago buckram, the staple covering for library books since that time, was just beginning to be accepted in place of muslin. The American Library Association set up a Bookbinding Committee in 1905. Most library binding has traditionally been "oversewing," first by hand, but since around 1915 by a machine. In simplest terms this involves cutting the signatures (groups) of pages where they are folded and then sewing through the resultant single sheets at the inner margin. Done properly, a very strong volume results, but a rebinding is virtually impossible because of the large number of perforations. This "mutilation" of the book is roundly condemned by collectors and most bibliographers. A more expensive method which required handwork until relatively recent years is sewing through the fold. This eliminates the need to cut and permits rebinding. It is superior in other ways although possibly not so durable, and not all material, particularly journals, can be handled that way except by hand sewing.

The establishment of the Library Binding Institute in 1935, a trade association of commercial binders, resulted in great progress because it was an organized group with which librarians could work in establishing standards of sewing, adhesives, etc. Minimum specifications were agreed upon in 1938 and modified numerous times since then. The Institute holds its members to standards of performance.

A number of contributions to the conservation and protection of library materials have come from the Library Technology Project of the American Library Association. This originated in a 1959 grant of $136,-395.00 to the ALA by the Council on Library Resources. It was a first and, for some years, a principal interest of the council, which viewed it as a professional bureau of standards. To quote Verner Clapp, president of the council, "from these [standards] follow specifications which in turn permit testing. Research and development in the quest of improved supplies, equipment, and systems follow logically, this being the rationale of such agencies as the National Bureau of Standards." The success of the Library Technology Program, as it came to be named, brought sizable grants from the council annually for more than a decade; since 1970 it has been relatively self-supporting by the sale of *Library Technology Reports.*

The scope of the project is naturally much wider than conservation and protection. In the nearly twenty years of its existence the program has tested and evaluated virtually everything used in the operation of libraries. It has addressed its attention to such minor items as stainless steel paper clips (to avoid rust on documents), types of shelving, and record players. It has produced manuals on such topics as fire protection and insurance of libraries. It tests all types of equipment, from electric erasers to photocopy machines, and publishes its findings. It has fostered the development of various equipment for specialized library applications. Some projects worked, others didn't. The most noteworthy was the development of the Se-Lin book labeller, which nearly all research libraries now use to put the classification number on the book spine. It is a combination of a bureau of standards, a Bell

Telephone laboratory, a *Consumer's Reports* and a Nader vigilante group for the library profession.

Automation and the Computer

Historians of automation trace its origins back to French silk weaving in 1725, but a first practical modern application of the principle is traced to a suggestion made by John Shaw Billings, director of the Surgeon General's Library, to Herman Hollerith. This led to the invention of punched cards for tabulations, the foundation of IBM.

The honor of the first practical application of the computer in the form of automated punched cards belongs to Ralph Parker at the University of Texas Library in the mid-thirties. This system used the Hollerith card, on which the borrower filled in all necessary information and which was then filed by call number after the date due for return had been punched in. The whole circulation was run daily to sort out the overdues, which could then be claimed, and a record made of the delinquent borrowers. At the same time, Frederick Kilgour was developing the McBee Keysort system, quite similar except that the sorting was done by hand via rods inserted through holes punched on the edges of the charge cards. This was first used at Harvard's Widener Library in 1938 and was widely adopted elsewhere in the 1940s and 1950s. There were many variations on the McBee Keysort principle by using color and tabs. The essential need was to use one card, filled out by the borrower, to provide two records, one filed by call number, and one to furnish information as to when the charge was overdue.

Another early use of the principle of automation was the tape-driven typewriter; this appeared in a few libraries in the thirties but was used only for correspondence, especially for public relations purposes. In the sixties it was adapted for the producton of sets of catalog cards. As developed, once the main entry information had been entered on the tape, and added entries for subject, joint authors, and so forth, had been punched on a second tape, the machine would produce the unit card, then switch automatically to make all other cards required. The system, known as the Flexowriter, was put into operation at the University of Missouri in 1963 and Washington University in 1964. Further refinements were added later in order to provide automatically typed book cards and spine labels. A number of large university libraries followed suit in the late sixties but all encountered difficulties in keeping the machines in proper repair. Apparently no major library today depends on the Flexowriter for principal card production.

There were several variations on this method. A few libraries used punched cards to achieve the same results. IBM produced a Magnetic Tape Selectric system in the late sixties which used magnetic tape to activate its typewriters. The University of California at Irvine adopted this in 1968, Cornell in 1969.

Some computer facility became essential to university research and operations, and centers to serve such purposes were set up at the larger institutions in the fifties. It was then only a step for libraries to experiment with using the center's services for library records and bibliographical control. To some it seemed the fairy godmother with a magic wand; to others, equally intelligent, it was a grim ogre about to destroy all that is true and beautiful. Listen to Vannevar Bush, one of the half-dozen most distinguished leaders in science of his day, writing in 1945:

> The *Encyclopedia Britannica* could be reduced to a matchbox. A library of a million volumes could be compressed into one end of a desk. If the human race has produced since the invention of moveable type a total record. . . . having a volume corresponding to a billion books, the whole affair, assembled and compressed, could be lugged off in a moving van.

Then, speaking of the desk in which the *Encyclopedia* is stored:

> If the user wishes to consult a certain book, he taps its code in the keyboard, and the title page of the book promptly appears before him, projected onto one of his viewing positions . . . Any given book of his library can thus be called up and consulted with far greater facility than if it were taken from a shelf. He could add marginal notes and comments, taking advantage of one possible type of dry photography, and it could even be arranged so that he can do this by a stylus scheme . . . just as though he had the physical page before him.[1]

The world still awaits the Bush desk, though no one would deny that it could be produced were many billions available to finance it.

Here is the other side of the coin: from Ellsworth Mason, an equally responsible academic and library leader, who investigated computer applications in libraries with a Council on Library Resources grant in 1970:

> The computer feeds on libraries. We actually devote large amounts of talent and massive amounts of money (perhaps 25 million dollars

a year in academic libraries alone) to *diminish* collections and *reduce* services . . . by channeling money into extravagant computerization projects which have little or no library benefits. . . . It is clear that the application of computers to library processes is a disaster and . . . no one is willing to admit it . . . The fascination of the computer, like that of a hooded cobra, lies in its exotic beauty, which fixes its victim for the spurt of poison. On the surface it seems to have many answers. It looks effortless, is pleasantly mysterious, it makes pleasing sounds, it promises great speed, and it has a reputation for performing miracles . . . But when we used the computer it didn't save staff, and it didn't speed processing, and it cost a great deal more to do the same things we were doing by hand.[2]

Mason goes on with detail as to promise and lack of performance.

From Mason's attack it is clear that at that time the great expectations of the fifties and sixties for computer storage of information were unfulfilled. The most notable venture along this line was also the most expensive and in some respects the least successful of major experiments in computer applications to libraries. INTREX (Information Transfer Experiment) at the Massachusetts Institute of Technology, launched in 1965, attempted to assemble and organize an information store of adequate size in a scientific field and to develop the facilities to retrieve and transmit that information. In other words it sought to take the body of knowledge normally found in a library's book and journal collection, store it in the memory units of a computer, and have any and all the data immediately available via terminals (on line) located at points convenient to faculty, students, and librarians. Theoretically the printed material could then be discarded. The user would simply query the central file via his terminal and receive information on a viewing screen. However, there was recognition that for certain needs of full texts, microfiche should be used. The original plan was to include all publications in materials science which involved physics, electronics, and metallurgy; it was scaled down to something less than twenty thousand reports. After an expenditure of nearly four million dollars it was clear that this was far too expensive to be practical. The verdict: "No economical method had been found to interconnect machine-based library systems so as to provide guaranteed rapid access to the full text of documents by electronic means." Some critics maintain the findings well worth the money; to others it was a disaster.

The first computer applications to university library needs were all off-line, that is, based on information keypunched on cards. This meant use of the facility for one purpose at a time and the scheduling of runs, which led to obvious delays and conflicts. The first on-line operations date from the sixties and were institutional in scope. The first practical on-line bibliographic service available country-wide was that offered by OCLC in 1971. Its importance is such that the date may well be used as marking the beginning of a new era in the history of libraries and bibliographical control.

Any attempt to do justice to the first and most successful applications of computers to particular uses in libraries would involve far more detail than is possible in this brief history. Suffice it to say that many research libraries developed reasonably successful control of circulation records by use of computer equipment in the early seventies. One of the earliest and most successful was that installed at the University of Southern Illinois. Basic to most of these is a book card, which has been manually key punched, and a plastic ID card, furnished each student. When the two elements identifying the borrower and the item borrowed are inserted in the terminal, the proper record is transmitted to a central memory. Once the record is made, the computer, if sophisticated, can generate overdue notices, analyze the circulation as to subjects borrowed, status of borrowers, and so forth. Normal to most such records is an enormous printout of all outstanding loans. If done daily the expense is very large; if done only twice a week the record is seriously out of date.

It was not until the mid-seventies that systems became largely or wholly on-line. Probably the first and most complete is that installed at Ohio State by Hugh Atkinson. There one can query the library record from almost any point on that large campus as to ownership of a given book and whether or not it is on loan. If available the book can even be borrowed without entering the library. The request is made by wire, ID number given, and the book is delivered by messenger. Service of this nature is expensive.

In the late seventies the development of the minicomputer held forth promise of library ownership and complete control over the facility in which its records were stored. Several commercial systems were devised, either operating essentially as noted above, or via a light pen scanning device.

Another area of operation apparently adaptable to computer records was that of serials. Why not let the computer record each issue as received, punch out a claim card if it is not received when due, keep a bindery record when the volume is complete, handle financial records, and the like. The first reasonably successful computerized serials control system was that of the University of California, San Diego, in 1961. A few other libraries followed suit in the next few years, but all encountered serious problems, largely due to the frequent changes in this type of publication: of title, editor, and price; delay in issuance, and the like. What had been thought to be more regular and predictable turned out to be just the opposite. Although few have been able to computerize their serial records, a great many have their serial titles recorded on punched cards or magnetic tape along with call number and some record of holdings. This facilitates placing a record of holdings in departmental libraries and other locations where the information is needed. Further, lists can be made by subject, by language, limited to titles currently received, and so forth.

Acquisition procedures are a third area where the computer has proved useful. For a generation most large libraries had used a multiple order form, with anywhere up to nine carbons in a continuously numbered roll, each carbon copy for a special purpose, such as claiming if not promptly received, outstanding order file, requesting Library of Congress cards, and the like. The first extensive use of this was by Nelson W. McCombs at New York University.

This same data lent itself to computer record, generally made by keypunching cards, which transferred the record to magnetic tape or discs. In a typical installation the orders are printed, the file of orders outstanding is maintained, financial records are kept current, bibliographic information is available for use when the order is received, and all manner of statistics made available when and if desired.

These, then, are the principal functions for which the computer has been successfully utilized by research libraries and which are, in a sense, self-generated. There remain a whole series of uses which depend on data procured from a distance via a terminal.

Initial bibliographical uses of the computer, dating from about 1955, were basically indexing operations. For example in 1956 the American Society of Metals set up an Information Searching Service to provide its members with a current awareness service. A computer was used to search abstracts, stored on magnetic tape, which had been coded according to subject. This was the beginning of an extensive use of the computer to match newly published or otherwise available information with computer stored profiles of individuals' interest and thus provide scholars with quick access to the latest findings in their fields. The availability of an increasing number of data bases scattered across the whole country led to the radically new practice of using them for reference service.

In the early seventies most large libraries installed a terminal to query a bibliographic literature-searching system of which there are now three: Lockheed Information Systems, Bibliographic Retrieval Services, and the Systems Development Corporation. For relatively small charges a reference librarian trained in these literature searches can input a query which produces a highly effective literature search. In addition to these three services there is a first cousin in the form of the New York Times Information Bank, which offers instantaneous transmittal of a wide range of current events information. On-line literature searches soon became routine and are used extensively by faculty and graduate students in the physical sciences, engineering, and education.

No discussion of computer applications to libraries would be complete without brief reference to a number of historic cooperative enterprises. Mention has already been made of OCLC and BALLOTS as major factors in the future of libraries. The first network in point of time (1961) and of success is MEDLARS (Medical Literature Analysis and Retrieval System), the brainchild of the National Library of Medicine. This makes possible the rapid printing of the *Index Medicus,* the bibliography of currently produced medical literature; it will produce on demand bibliographies on subjects covered in the *Index Medicus;* at regular intervals it will prepare bibliographies in areas of medical literature for issuance to organizations and agencies. The operation of MEDLARS is by batch processing. The development of MEDLINE (MEDLARS on line) in 1972 gave medical libraries around the country direct, instantaneous access to citations for most current medical literature. All credit should be given to the National Library of Medicine for developing this integrated service for the benefit of the health science professions on a national basis.

Another equally important network-type service by the national government is MARC (Machine Readable Cataloging Project), dating from 1965. Stephen Salmon writes, "If one development were to be singled out as the most significant so far in the entire field of library automation, the MARC Project is clearly the leading candidate." This set the standard for all computer cataloging operations in this country and to a considerable extent abroad. MARC II is the perfected version, which went operational in 1969 by making available to subscribers Library of Congress cataloging on magnetic tape. It not only set the standard, but furnished the base for OCLC, BALLOTS, and others such as MALCAP (Maryland

Academic Library Center for Automatic Processing), and BLC (Books for College Libraries) in Massachusetts. The tapes were also used as the base for numerous book catalog projects.

As this is written it appears that in the near future many research library catalogs will be in the form of COM (Computer Output Microform). Cataloging data will be stored on discs or tapes used to reproduce the data, letter by letter, on a cathode ray tube for automatic transferral to microfilm or microfiche. It will be used in that form. Some use may be made of terminals for on-line query of the computer; this is more convenient but also much more expensive.

From this all-too-brief review of technological services to libraries it should be clear that the rapid progress made in the last two decades will undoubtedly accelerate in the years ahead. Much remains to be done in order to make computer services now operational more effective in virtually all record-keeping operations of the library, but particularly circulation, ordering procedures, and cataloging. A major area still largely untouched is that of instantaneous transmission of the printed page by wire or television from one library to another. Much also remains to be done in the broad area of conservation. Then there is the prospect of research being "published" in forms very different from the conventional journals and codices of past centuries, and this will require major adjustments by all research libraries. It is thus clear that increasingly technology will be required to find solutions to major problems on a scale that will dwarf the remarkable record of the sixties and seventies.

Epilogue

Automation is indeed one of the very strong currents that have dominated recent university library development, and it will continue to be vitally important; another trend, as yet unproductive, is that of photo-transmission of material; other technologies such as those contributing to conservation and preservation will develop further. Cooperative agreements and growth of networks have mushroomed since 1960 and will continue to grow in number and usefulness.

Along with these basically technological and organizational interests there have been strong currents that emphasize librarians' traditional interests in and responsibilities for the book. Consider the field of publishing. On the one hand economic conditions have forced commercial publishers to restrict their acceptance of manuscripts to those which are likely to achieve an ever-increasing sale, while on the other hand the "small press" interest has grown to the point that it now has its own organization, and holds regional and national conferences. The existence of more than six thousand of these, a number that is apparently still increasing, is evidence of the continuing importance of the printed page. Or consider the "book arts," one aspect of which is binding. The exhibition of recent hand binding brought together in 1978 by the San Francisco Museum of Modern Art was conclusive evidence of the consummate artistry of not just a few European masters, but of several score resident throughout the western world.

Until 1940 only a handful of university libraries had space and staff assigned to the formation, care, and use of special collections which emphasize rare books and manuscripts. But after the war this area of responsibility received such wide recognition that virtually all the larger academic libraries, whether serving colleges or universities, have this facility. This movement has resulted in the stimulation of interest in collection building not only by the library but by individuals, many of whom will eventually donate their collections to libraries. The importance of special collections is increasingly recognized as providing unique opportunities for research in the humanities and social sciences, for their influence in stimulating intellectual interests, and for their broad public relations value. As they have grown in number and importance in recent years, so they will continue.

While the past several decades have indeed brought a "Fourth Revolution" in instructional technology, this is principally in the recording and delivery of information as distinct from the awakening of intellectual interests and nurturing of knowledge by reading.

To quote William Ready:

> There is something in the nature of a book that defies analysis, that cannot be transmitted to any other form of communication. The book is but a link in the chain of knowledge. It contains thereby, along with its own dynamic, a quality that remains intrinsical, and cannot be abstracted by other more modern methods of communication that are based on computer technology. . . . As we seek a solution to the library's present and future problems, the computer has come to the fore, but as there is something intangible, irreducible in the earth, in Man, so there is in the Book, and the solution eludes us and always will. . . . This is not to denigrate the use of the machine. We are living in an age of technology. But we will be doing our own kind and the Machine a disservice if we surrender. All of the learning and the wisdom that we amassed from the times past, present and to come, are contained within a book that remains the most convenient and cheapest way of conveying information and can give wonder and delight.[1]

Appendices

A P P E N D I X   1

American College Libraries in 1849

This table is reprinted courtesy of the University of Illinois Press from its publication *Scholar's Workshop, Evolving Conceptions of Library Service* by Kenneth J. Brough, pp.14–15.

Institutions	Year Founded b	Estimated Number of Volumes			Estimated Av. An. No. Vols. Added 1840-1849	Estimated Av. An. Exp. For Books 1840-1849	Number Times Open Weekly	Total Hours Open Weekly	Classes Permitted To Use Library
		College Library	Society Libraries	Total					
Harvard	1636	56,000e	12,000	68,000c	2,040	$1,620	12	30	All
Yale College	1701	20,500c	27,200	47,700e	950	2,500	6	24	J & S
Brown University	1764	23,000	7,200	30,200	1,400				All
Georgetown College	1789	25,000	1,100	26,100		350			...
Bowdoin College	1794	11,600c	9,900	21,500c	130	200	3	3	All
South Carolina College	1801	17,000	1,400	18,400	500	2,000	6	24	All
University of Virginia	1819	18,400	...	18,400	410	550	6	9	All
College of New Jersey	1746	9,000	7,000	16,000		400	2	2	All
Dickinson College	1783	5,100	9,500	14,600	120	100	1	1	All
Union College	1795	7,800	6,800	14,600	470	400	2	2	All
Amherst College	1821	5,700	8,000	13,700	120	300	1		All
Columbia College	1754	12,700	...	12,700	120	200	2	4	So. J, S
University of Vermont	1791	7,000	5,300	12,300	200	60	2	2	All
University of N. C.	1789	3,500	8,800	12,300			5	5	All
Wesleyan University	1831	5,600	5,500	11,100	100	100	2	2	All
Williams College	1793	6,000	4,600	10,600	190	190	2	2	All
Hamilton College N.Y.	1812	3,500	6,800	10,300		60	4	4	All
Franklin College Ga.	1785	7,300	3,000	10,300	130	600	2	1	All
Waterville College Me.	1820	5,200	3,300	8,500	50		2	2	All
Middlebury College Vt.	1800	5,000	3,400	8,400			2		All
Emory and Henry College Va.	1839	2,600	5,400	8,000	250	75	1	1.5	All
Western Reserve College Ohio	1826	4,600	3,100	7,700	130	50	1		All
Georgetown College Ky.	1829	6,500	800	7,300	500		2	1	All
University of Alabama	1820	4,500	2,600	7,100	160	300	2	2	All
Miami University Ohio	1809	3,500	3,300	6,800	200	200			All
Marietta College Ohio	1835	4,300	2,100	6,400	120	...	1	1.5	All

Pennsylvania College	1832	1,800	4,600	6,400	100	90	1	1	All
Geneva College N.Y.	1822	2,000d	3,700	5,700d	80	..	..	..	All
Maryville College Tenn.	1819	3,200	500	3,700	30	..	1	1	All
University of Ohio	1804	1,300	1,500	2,800	..	..	4	2	All
Emory College Ga.	1836	1,000	1,700	2,700	..	..	1	1	All
Bethany College Va.	1840	1,200	1,100	2,300	..	..	1	..	All
Norwich University Vt.	1834	1,000	....	1,000	200	25	1	..	All

a Based on C. C. Jewett,....*Report on the Public Libraries of the United States of America, January 1, 1850* (Washington D.C., 1850).
b Corrected from C. S. Marsh (ed.), *American Colleges and Universities* (4th ed.; Washington D.C., 1940).
c Does not include libraries of departments or professional schools.
d Does not include library of Medical Department (600 volumes).

College and University Library Holdings and Ph. D.s Awarded, 1876–1975

This table is reproduced from Hendrik Edelman and G. Marvin Tatum, Jr. "The Development of Collections in American Libraries" published in *College and Research Libraries* 37:222–45 (May, 1976). Note that slight variations are inevitable in compilations such as this when authoritative sources vary widely. (Reprinted courtesy of authors and publisher)

State / Institution	Year founded	1876 Vol.	1900 Ph.D.	1900 Vol.	1910 Ph.D.	1910 Vol.	1920 Ph.D.	1920 Vol.	1930 Ph.D.	1930 Vol.	1940 Ph.D.	1940 Vol.	1950 Ph.D.	1950 Vol.	1961 Ph.D.	1961 Vol.	1971 Ph.D.	1971 Vol.	1975 Ph.D.	1975 Vol.	Ph.D.
Alabama																					
Auburn	1856	3,000				13,000		23,000		47,000		81,000		150,000		298,000	16		92	733,000	
Alabama	1831	6,000		25,000		30,000		34,000		75,000		250,000		357,000		694,000	29	748,000	236	1,051,000	83
Alaska																					
Alaska	1915									11,000				32,000		59,000	4	304,000	12	358,000	
Arizona																					
Arizona State	1885									14,000		26,000		105,000	3	412,000			151	955,000	124
Arizona	1885			5,000		15,000		52,000		85,000		138,000	2	230,000	2	343,000	28		245	1,723,000	219
Arkansas																					
Arkansas	1871	1,000		15,000		14,000		35,000		98,000		161,000		271,000		459,000	29	684,000	115	752,000	
California																					
Cal. Inst. Tech.	1891			3,000		15,000		9,000	1	25,000	18	53,000	30	75,000	70	129,000	73	238,000	117	293,000	328
Southern Cal.	1879							40,000		127,000	8	274,000	33	566,000	101	963,000	139	1,452,000	468	1,670,000	515
Stanford	1885		2	65,000	2	174,000	5	320,000	6	530,000	41	773,000	42	1,092,000	166	1,691,000	219	3,584,000	580	4,092,000	747
U.C.Berkeley	1868	14,000	2	99,000	2	248,000	6	479,000	23	756,000	83	1,081,000	122	1,665,000	244	2,596,000	369	4,009,000	798	4,649,000	
Davis	1908									23,000		54,000		66,000	38	208,000	38	909,000	179	1,234,000	225
Los Angeles	1907									138,000		347,000		762,000	79	1,568,000	159	3,038,000	572	3,519,000	487
Riverside	1912									5,000		10,000		14,000		150,000		643,000	109		
San Diego												17,000		24,000		45,000		813,000	126	1,102,000	167
Santa Barbara	1891							4,000		15,000		36,000		51,000		149,000		844,000	36	1,126,000	130
Colorado																					
Colorado State	1870			11,000				32,000		64,000		96,000		142,000		210,000	6	768,000	129	935,000	143
Colorado	1861			26,000		52,000		122,000	2	221,000	2	307,000	13	706,000	37	722,000	78	1,401,000	249	1,793,000	263
Denver	1864					12,000				58,000		94,000		263,000	9	315,000	40	565,000	94	802,000	
Connecticut																					
Connecticut	1881					11,000		16,000		23,000		251,000		132,000		423,000	34	808,000	157	1,400,000	193
Yale	1701	100,000	26	309,000	26	575,000	27	1,250,000	28	1,983,000	83	2,219,000	174	3,979,000	174	4,478,000	238	5,829,000	338	6,618,000	348
Delaware																					
Delaware	1743	7,000		14,000		17,000		27,000		41,000		78,000		150,000		328,000	16	766,000		949,000	

District of Columbia																					
Catholic	1887			31,000		40,000	3	123,000	5	300,000	23	286,000	45	405,000	81	594,000	85	854,000	210	968,000	
George Washington	1821	5,000		15,000						86,000		109,000	1	240,000	12	352,000		541,000	76	667,000	
Georgetown	1789	34,000	2	79,000		108,000		140,000		140,000	4	259,000	9	203,000	35	470,000	26	669,000	60	867,000	85
Howard	1867	10,000		14,000		26,000		38,000		54,000		128,000		267,000		376,000		657,000		837,000	34
Florida																					
Florida State	1857					3,000		12,000		36,000		83,000		231,000		568,000	64	916,000	218	1,126,000	336
Florida	1853					12,000		35,000		92,000		109,000	1	407,000	20	917,000	102	1,487,000	273	1,756,000	292
Miami	1925											27,000		232,000		585,000		953,000	56	1,072,000	
Georgia																					
Atlanta	1865	4,000		11,000		12,000		15,000		18,000		65,000		105,000		249,000			2		
Emory	1836	9,000		20,000		30,000		50,000		115,000		178,000		332,000		710,000	24	966,000	76	1,150,000	69
Georgia	1785	19,000		30,000		36,000		66,000		66,000		146,000	2	254,000	1	458,000	4	1,158,000	255	1,522,000	282
Hawaii																					
Hawaii	1907							21,000		50,000		111,000		227,000		348,000	7	1,130,000	89	1,379,000	
Idaho																					
Idaho	1889			4,000		22,000		44,000		91,000		93,000		129,000		213,000		727,000	57	828,000	
Illinois																					
Chicago	1891			303,000	43	500,000	45	599,000	65	915,000	186	1,300,000	163	1,797,000	295	2,142,000	209	3,090,000	418	3,622,000	439
Illinois	1867	11,000		47,000		157,000	12	461,000	29	836,000	70	1,217,000	130	2,383,000	226	3,383,000	409	4,609,000	824	5,509,000	747
Northern Illinois	1895			12,000		12,000		25,000		32,000		50,000		74,000		156,000		604,000	30	749,000	
Northwestern	1851	28,000		70,000		142,000		193,000		280,000	23	637,000	58	1,013,000	109	1,481,000	140	2,364,000	276	2,474,000	369
Southern Illinois	1874	2,000		15,000		20,000		35,000		31,000		48,000		124,000		517,000		1,403,000	166	1,847,000	172
Indiana																					
Indiana	1820	7,000		35,000		77,000		134,000	6	218,000	19	345,000	11	796,000	68	1,414,000	170	2,341,000	380	3,891,000	588
Notre Dame	1842	20,000		52,000		60,000		103,000	1	143,000	4	195,000	12	263,000	21	550,000	33	1,093,000	147	1,220,000	145
Purdue	1865	1,000		13,000		29,000		53,000		110,000	4	154,000	28	286,000	138	535,000	230	964,000	474	1,231,000	367
Iowa																					
Iowa State	1858	5,000		14,000		31,000		77,000	2	180,000	27	297,000	53	413,000	101	518,000	151	831,000	314	1,063,000	207
Iowa	1847	7,000		60,000		80,000	4	162,000	11	366,000	33	473,000	86	633,000	151	1,056,000	147	1,584,000	388	1,879,000	321
Kansas																					
Kansas State	1863	2,000		21,000		36,000		68,000		96,000		125,000	2	160,000	11	255,000	33	600,000	115	716,000	
Kansas	1863	2,000		33,000		76,000	3	132,000	1	232,000	11	320,000	78	424,000	23	925,000	79	1,568,000	261	1,799,000	287
Kentucky																					
Kentucky	1865	13,000		18,000		23,000		41,000		116,000	2	280,000	7	497,000	17	925,000	35	1,153,000	135	1,426,000	151
Louisiana																					
Louisiana State	1860	11,000		21,000		30,000		50,000		77,000		264,000	25	395,000	28	966,000	81	1,348,000	205	1,538,000	148
Tulane	1834			25,000	1	47,000		82,000		141,000	1	242,000	2	342,000	11	743,000	22	1,071,000	133	1,217,000	84
Maine																					
Maine	1865	3,000		24,000		41,000		68,000		84,000		179,000		233,000		319,000		437,000	23	497,000	

State / Institution	Year founded	1876 Vol.	1900 Ph.D.	1900 Vol.	1910 Ph.D.	1910 Vol.	1920 Ph.D.	1920 Vol.	1930 Ph.D.	1930 Vol.	1940 Ph.D.	1940 Vol.	1950 Ph.D.	1950 Vol.	1961 Ph.D.	1961 Vol.	1971 Ph.D.	1971 Vol.	1975 Ph.D.	1975 Vol.	Ph.D.
Maryland																					
Johns Hopkins	1876	5,000	35	194,000		142,000	25	225,000	31	376,000	64	567,000	65	839,000	84	1,185,000	85	2,085,000	194	2,044,000	214
Maryland	1807	1,000		3,000		10,000		8,000	1	66,000	3	142,000	18	239,000	36	458,000	91	1,049,000	346	1,465,000	336
Massachusetts																					
Amherst	1821	37,000		72,000		80,000		125,000		162,000		226,000		279,000		348,000		449,000		506,000	
Boston College	1863	9,000		31,000						125,000	5	175,000	3	232,000		541,000	56	828,000	56	909,000	
Boston Univ.	1839	7,000		25,000		122,000		58,000		142,000	4	207,000	20	319,000	48	521,000	138	831,000	220	1,127,000	266
Brandeis	1948														18	234,000	19	455,000	99	500,000	
Clark	1887	18,000		18,000		55,000	14	95,000	11	126,000	12	162,000	6	200,000	27	233,000	26	282,000	26	336,000	
Harvard	1636	160,000	5	976,000	35	850,000	41	2,028,000	49	2,971,000	105	4,159,000	153	5,397,000	527	6,848,000	344	8,451,000	613	9,206,000	477
U. Mass. Amherst	1863	1,000		21,000		32,000		61,000	3	84,000	3	126,000	12		11	239,000	213	795,000	262	1,362,000	337
MIT	1859	3,000		64,000		86,000		140,000	5	260,000	64	365,000	64	450,000	126	745,000		1,314,000	399	1,573,000	312
Michigan																					
Michigan State	1855	4,000		23,000		31,000		45,000	4	75,000	4	152,000	10	416,000	68	825,000	200	1,759,000	733	2,102,000	603
Michigan	1817	30,000		160,000		270,000	9	432,000	14	784,000	81	1,098,000	141	1,415,000	194	2,912,000	351	4,200,000	784	4,668,000	722
Wayne State	1868			11,000		13,000				50,000		168,000		379,000		754,000	52	1,367,000	208	1,610,000	220
Minnesota																					
Minnesota	1851	13,000		60,000	3	145,000		300,000	1	654,000	67	1,088,000	113	1,528,000	154	2,020,000	218	3,112,000	615	3,559,000	538
Mississippi																					
Mississippi	1844	7,000		17,000		26,000		31,000		50,000		77,000		151,000		336,000	2	464,000	68	519,000	
Missouri																					
Missouri	1839	13,000		36,000		110,000	2	223,000	2	410,000	14	395,000	24	605,000	65	1,043,000	90	1,589,000	158	1,793,000	227
St. Louis	1818	22,000		50,000		60,000	17	75,000		140,000	5	374,000	8	437,000	24	481,000	47	710,000	151		
Washington U.	1853	2,000		5,000	2	109,000		176,000	3	295,000	10	409,000	4	527,000	45	821,000	37	1,421,000	154	1,545,000	162
Montana																					
Montana	1893			7,000		16,000		46,000		183,000		212,000		303,000				561,000	32	676,000	
Nebraska																					
Nebraska	1869	2,000		53,000	1	90,000		147,000	3	256,000	11	353,000		471,000	77	690,000		976,000	223	1,208,000	205
Nevada																					
Nevada	1864			13,000		17,000		35,000		50,000		63,000		90,000		164,000		413,000	23	512,000	
New Hampshire																					
Dartmouth	1769	48,000		105,000		120,000		150,000		250,000	1	512,000		666,000		829,000	21	1,030,000	21	1,172,000	
New Hampshire	1866			6,000		26,000		40,000		66,000		106,000		170,000		295,000	9	560,000	29	698,000	51
New Jersey																					
Princeton	1746	46,000	3	144,000		270,000	9	444,000	31	643,000	31	959,000	43	1,166,000	80	1,689,000	140	2,314,000	255	2,715,000	251
Rutgers	1766	11,000		46,000		61,000	1	106,000		239,000	5	342,000	12	573,000	49	961,000	81	1,164,000	182	1,839,000	258
New Mexico																					
New Mexico	1889			4,000		8,000		13,000		34,000		80,000		184,000	5	326,000	23	720,000	129	886,000	

New York																					
City College	1847	19,000		33,000		39,000		71,000		100,000		245,000		370,000		522,000			112	863,000	
Columbia	1754	17,000		345,000	21	448,000	44	747,000	69	1,222,000	184	1,715,000	198	1,897,000	456	2,939,000	329	4,241,000	505	4,661,000	521
Cornell	1865	39,000		268,000	19	383,000	35	630,000	45	810,000	129	844,000	131	1,463,000	210	2,198,000	239	3,779,000	508	4,272,000	460
Fordham	1841					50,000		100,000	7	110,000	54	198,000	23	260,000	43	401,000	77	927,000	94		
NYU	1831	4,000		54,000	7	100,000	10	153,000	6	319,000	46	592,000	125	888,000	179	1,121,000	307	2,111,000	567	2,456,000	488
SUNY																					
Albany	1844							2,000		15,000		30,000		46,000		65,000		611,000	50	1,007,000	110
Buffalo	1846							29,000		62,000		161,000		195,000		374,000	29	1,575,000	245	1,523,000	241
Stony Brook	1957															35,000		586,000	55	956,000	98
Syracuse	1870	9,000		64,000		78,000	1	109,000	2	195,000	2	322,000	3	348,000	36	559,000	94	1,548,000	231	1,541,000	216
Rochester	1850	12,000		40,000		52,000		83,000		190,000	2	360,000	25	514,000	36	721,000	61	1,179,000	198	1,402,000	200
North Carolina																					
Duke	1838	12,000		16,000		40,000				192,000	8	600,000	23	994,000	46	1,493,000	82	2,231,000	220	2,622,000	155
N. C. State	1891			4,000		8,000		10,000		30,000		55,000		108,000		226,000	48	550,000	203	692,000	
North Carolina	1789	17,000		43,000		58,000		93,000		223,000	27	386,000	34	557,000	100	1,077,000	96	1,819,000	245	2,125,000	332
North Dakota																					
North Dakota	1883			10,000		35,000		58,000		98,000		89,000	2	165,000	2	226,000	10		85	341,000	
Ohio																					
Case Western																					
Reserve	1826	11,000		36,000		90,000		138,000		350,000	5	554,000	25	644,000	33	758,000	51	1,175,000	326	1,558,000	227
Cincinnati	1819	1,000		32,000		118,000	1	125,000	2	256,000	14	491,000	27	649,000	20	813,000	5	1,156,000		1,553,000	147
Kent State	1910											76,000		106,000		204,000		648,000	48	1,066,000	103
Oberlin	1832	15,000		59,000		98,000		204,000		323,000		404,000		486,000		552,000		695,000			
Ohio State	1870	1,000		45,000		95,000		215,000		359,000	68	552,000	97	863,000	229	1,447,000	260	2,539,000	676	3,033,000	649
Ohio Univ.	1804	6,000		17,000		30,000		52,000	2	75,000		127,000		197,000		312,000	5	460,000	108	652,000	
Oklahoma																					
Oklahoma State	1890					14,000		25,000		58,000		139,000	5	275,000	15	619,000	53	1,006,000	217	1,285,000	249
Oklahoma	1890			8,000		16,000		32,000		130,000		217,000		333,000	15	782,000	49	1,158,000	220	1,141,000	213
Oregon																					
Oregon State	1868			3,000		8,000		41,000		93,000		172,000	4	252,000	20	396,000	52	643,000	208	736,000	
Oregon	1872			11,000		30,000		94,000		233,000	2	307,000	2	451,000	12	822,000	49	1,104,000	349	1,266,000	250
Pennsylvania																					
Lehigh	1865	2,000		115,000		125,000		100,000		190,000		245,000		310,000	19	391,000	25	549,000	109	612,000	
Penn. State	1855	3,000		16,000		40,000		75,000		120,000	3	207,000	40	323,000	69	620,000	175	1,165,000	601	1,825,000	340
Pennsylvania	1740	20,000	7	260,000	15	293,000	35	503,000	21	712,000	90	934,000	71	1,194,000	124	1,703,000	157	2,329,000	362	2,640,000	326
Pittsburgh	1787	3,000		15,000		15,000	2	24,000	3	145,000	22	191,000	43	578,000	80	977,000	112	1,456,000	357	1,972,000	412
Temple	1884					8,000		9,000		41,000		149,000	8	322,000	14	527,000	34	1,029,000	147	1,247,000	102
Puerto Rico																					
Puerto Rico	1900							8,000		25,000		73,000		123,000		538,000		879,000			
Rhode Island																					
Brown	1764	46,000		135,000	3	186,000	5	270,000	3	403,000	11	573,000	19	735,000	35	1,059,000		1,390,000	156	1,536,000	145
Rhode Island	1892					17,000		22,000		25,000		60,000		105,000		194,000	3	437,000	45	584,000	

State / Institution	Year founded	1876 Vol.	Ph.D.	1900 Vol.	Ph.D.	1910 Vol.	Ph.D.	1920 Vol.	Ph.D.	1930 Vol.	Ph.D.	1940 Vol.	Ph.D.	1950 Vol.	Ph.D.	1961 Vol.	Ph.D.	1971 Vol.	Ph.D.	1975 Vol.	Ph.D.	Ph.D.
South Carolina																						
South Carolina	1801	30,000	2			43,000		65,000		110,000		156,000		212,000		496,000		934,000	7	1,372,000	80	106
South Dakota																						
South Dakota	1881			8,000		16,000		38,000		70,000		103,000		135,000		182,000		308,000	2	379,000	40	
Tennessee																						
Tennessee	1794	4,000		16,000		29,000		41,000		112,000		169,000		276,000		670,000	12	1,122,000	37	1,229,000	262	253
Vanderbilt	1872	7,000		30,000	1	45,000	2	80,000	2	150,000		374,000	9	567,000	36	809,000	36	1,301,000		1,301,000	189	207
Texas																						
Houston	1934											14,000		72,000		231,000	12	664,000	9	1,192,000	120	192
Rice	1891									81,000		151,000	3	206,000	6	392,000	6	660,000	26	875,000	115	88
Southern Methodist	1910									83,000		112,000		283,000		531,000			9	955,000	49	
Texas Tech	1923									16,000		70,000		100,000		471,000				946,000	102	
Texas	1887			45,000		72,000		194,000		422,000		639,000	19	934,000	46	1,424,000	86	2,427,000	154	3,726,000	438	454
Texas A & M	1876			9,000										175,000		401,000		716,000		926,000	215	234
Utah																						
Brigham Young	1875									67,000		117,000		169,000		330,000				1,267,000	78	58
Utah	1850			30,000		31,000		62,000		102,000		149,000		250,000		438,000		1,178,000	55	1,520,000	242	245
Vermont																						
Vermont	1791	20,000		89,000		80,000		105,000		128,000		152,000		200,000		220,000		579,000		563,000	24	
Virginia																						
Virginia	1819	40,000		50,000	2	70,000	2	120,000	4	172,000	4	338,000	16	592,000	26	1,111,000	36	1,699,000	41	2,006,000	223	172
Virginia Polytech.	1872	1,000		4,000		12,000		30,000		61,000				135,000		289,000		626,000		877,000	154	
Washington																						
Washington State	1890			7,000		23,000		74,000		200,000		406,000	2	600,000	2	750,000	17	853,000	41	1,010,000	142	162
Washington	1861			24,000		41,000		120,000		258,000	2	356,000	13	700,000	33	1,104,000	38	1,876,000	113	2,187,000	154	386
West Virginia																						
West Virginia	1867	4,000		17,000						53,000		93,000	2	232,000	4	461,000	3	684,000	5	814,000	101	
Wisconsin																						
Marquette	1857			10,000		18,000		30,000						172,000	4	310,000				536,000	38	
Wisconsin Madison	1836	8,000		81,000	5	151,000	18	276,000	34	422,000		485,000	130	777,000	160	1,455,000	298	2,417,000	397	2,973,000	913	819
Wisconsin Milwaukee	1908					28,000		30,000		41,000		50,000		78,000		149,000		663,000		938,000	16	
Wyoming																						
Wyoming	1886			14,000		28,000		46,000		75,000		104,000		154,000		284,000		465,000	7		89	

SOURCE: Figures in these tables were drawn from a variety of sources. They are, of course, based on differing counting techniques and are not necessarily compatible at all times. In cases of extreme variations we have omitted the information. The main sources on library collections were: *Annual Report of the Commissioner of Education* for 1876, 1900, and 1910; the *Biennial Survey of Education* for 1918–20, 1928–30 and 1938–40; the *Library Statistics of Colleges and Universities: Institutional Data* for 1960–61 and 1970–71; and the Preliminary Report (December 1975) of the *Survey of Colleges and University Libraries* of the National Center for Education Statistics. Additional data were retrieved from *Public Libraries in the United States of America* (1876). *College and University Library Statistics* 1919/20–1961 (Princeton University Library); the *Academic Library Statistics* 1970–71 and the *ARL Statistics* 1974–75, both issued by the Association of Research Libraries, as well as editions of the *American Library Directory*. Opening dates of universities are quoted from *Webster's New Collegiate Dictionary* (1974). Information on the number of Ph.D. degrees come from the above quoted *Annual Reports* and *Biennial Surveys*; M. Irwin, *American Universities and Colleges*, 6th ed. (1952); *Index to American Doctoral Dissertations* 1960–61 and 1970–71 as well as from *ARL Statistics* 1974–75, accounting for the incomplete data for 1975.

Holdings of the Twenty Largest University Libraries 1876–1978

Sources used: The 1876 figures are from the 1876 report of the Bureau of Education, *Public Libraries in the United States*. Note that two official reports of that year from the Bureau give conflicting figures. The columns for 1900, 1920, and 1940 repeat the figures of Edelman and Tatum given in Appendix 2. Data for 1946 and 1960 are taken from the *Princeton Statistics* (distributed by the Princeton University Library in processed form). The 1977 and 1978 data are from the statistics issued annually by the Association of Research Libraries.

Some variations between the 1977 and 1978 data were caused by recount, withdrawal of material, or lack of inclusion of one or more departmental libraries.

	1876	1900	1920	1940	1946	1960	1977	1978
Harvard	219,550	976,000	2,028,000	4,159,000	4,805,000	6,697,000	9,548,000	9,753,000
Yale	114,200	309,000	1,250,000	2,219,000**	3,540,000**	4,395,000	6,885,000	7,072,000
Illinois	10,600	47,000	461,000	1,217,000	2,004,000	3,288,000	5,829,000	5,623,000
Michigan	27,500	160,000	432,000	1,098,000	1,268,000	2,818,000	4,917,000	5,050,000
California (Berkeley)	13,600	99,000	479,000	1,081,000	1,379,000	2,503,000	4,917,000	5,036,000
Columbia	34,790	345,000	747,000	1,715,000	1,778,000	2,876,000	4,730,000	4,833,000
Stanford		65,000	320,000	773,000	952,000	1,592,000	4,364,000	4,488,000
Indiana	6,000	35,000	134,000	345,000	618,000	1,317,000	4,399,000	4,604,000
Texas		45,000	194,000	639,000	802,000	1,351,000	4,054,000	4,224,000
Cornell	39,000	268,000	630,000	844,000	1,206,000	2,116,000	3,980,000	4,095,000
Chicago		303,000	599,000	1,300,000	1,584,000	2,095,000	3,886,000	4,019,000
California (LA)				347,000	543,000	1,464,000	3,908,000	3,993,000
Minnesota	10,000	60,000	300,000	1,088,000	1,422,000	1,968,000	3,364,000	3,623,000
Ohio State	1,000	45,000	215,000	552,000	710,000	1,369,000	3,258,000	3,372,000
Washington		24,000	120,000	356,000	588,000	1,249,000	3,237,000	3,394,000
Wisconsin	8,563	81,000	276,000	485,000	600,000	1,384,000	3,238,000	3,352,000
Princeton	41,500	144,000	444,000	959,000	1,059,000	1,627,000	2,910,000	3,092,000
Duke	10,900	16,000		600,000	740,000	1,435,000	2,870,000	2,945,000
Pennsylvania	25,573	260,000	503,000	934,000	1,034,000	1,665,000	2,784,000	2,822,000
Northwestern	30,000	70,000	193,000	637,000	789,000	1,429,000	2,595,000	2,655,000

** 1940 and 1946 figures open to question.

Expenditures for Library Materials
and Volumes added, 1947 & 1978

Institution	1946–47 Expenditure for Library Materials and Binding	1946–47 Volumes Added	1977–78 Expenditure for Library Materials and Binding	1977–78 Volumes Added (Gross)
Harvard	410,015	160,516	4,000,219	255,085
Yale	483,692	103,134	3,033,904	182,703
Illinois	267,908	72,590	2,414,208	151,585
Columbia	237,584	60,770	2,246,232	126,679
Chicago	198,591	68,962	1,505,181	144,349
Minnesota	178,248	51,761	2,085,059	123,456
California (Berkeley)	210,689	43,892	2,753,350	142,783
Cornell	121,422	32,729	2,521,023	122,417
Michigan	139,670	34,036	2,402,655	125,901
Pennsylvania	95,805	17,663	1,466,275	74,791
Princeton	109,099	27,360	2,094,227	185,128
Stanford	183,000	39,199	3,449,711	145,360
Duke	144,465	26,208	1,742,943	78,227
Northwestern	180,540	67,277	1,493,316	70,062
Texas	99,169	31,149	3,362,868	227,532

Source: Statistics for College and University Libraries for 1946/47 collected by Princeton University
Library; *ARL Statistics* 1977/78, published by the Association of Research Libraries.

Note that these figures should be used only for the general picture they present, not for
individual comparisons as there are far too many variables not brought out, such as expenditure
for non-book materials, receipt of gifts, purchase of rare books and manuscripts, withdrawals
in the 1946/47 period (believed to be slight) inclusion or exclusion of some departmental
libraries, etc.

Resident, Degree-Credit Enrollment of Colleges and Universities
(Undergraduate and Graduate)

	Undergraduate and Graduate	Graduate Only
1899–1900	237,592	5,831
1909–10	355,213	9,153
1919–20	597,880	15,612
1929–30	1,100,737	47,255
1939–40	1,494,203	105,748
1949–50	2,659,021	237,208
1959–60	3,215,544	341,820
1969–70	7,484,073	(1970) 816,207
1975–76	9,731,431	(1976) 1,030,007

SOURCE: *Digest of Educational Statistics 1978–79*, pp. 85, 84, 90.

Abbreviations

ACLS	*American Council of Learned Societies*
ARL	*Association of Research Libraries*
C & RL	*College and Research Libraries*
DALB	*Dictionary of American Library Biography*
ELIS	*Encyclopedia of Library and Information Science*
Jl. Lib. Hist.	*Journal of Library History*
Lib. Jl.	*Library Journal*
Lib. Qu.	*Library Quarterly*
Lib. Tr.	*Library Trends*

Notes

Full titles of works cited are given in the Bibliography.

CHAPTER 1

1. Morison, *Founding,* p. 208
2. Ibid., p. 269
3. Mitchell, *A Modell,* p. 319
4. Morison, *Founding,* pp. 62–64
5. Ibid., p. 246
6. Ibid., p. 432
7. Ibid., p. 248
8. Shores, *Origins,* p. 214
9. Ibid., p. 5
10. See Jennings, "Notes," in *Bibl. Soc. of America Papers* 41: 239–67
11. Warch, *School,* p. 31
12. Ibid., p. 43
13. Shores, *Origins,* p. 109
14. As quoted in Shores, *Origins,* p. 105
15. Kraus, "Book Collections," *Lib. Qu.* 43: 142

CHAPTER 2

1. Powell, "Development," p. 13
2. White, "Vignettes," *Jl. Lib. Hist.* 1: 66–69
3. McCormick, *Rutgers,* p. 46
4. Franklin, *Gilman,* pp. 78–79
5. Lowell, "I.U. Libraries," p. 71, quoting James A. Woodburn in the *I. U. Newsletter* 12 (July, 1924): 1–2
6. Powell, "Development," p. 99
7. Carlton, "College Libraries," *Lib. J.* 32: 479. This is also the source of many of the short quotations which follow.
8. U. S. Office of Education, *Public Libraries* (1876), pp. 518–19
9. By-laws of the South Carolina College, Columbia, 1848, p. 18
10. Everhart, *South Carolina,* p. 226
11. Carlton, "College Libraries," *Lib. J.* 32: 482–83
12. Ibid., p. 484
13. Lowell, "I. U. Libraries," p. 5
14. Lord, *Dartmouth College,* p. 515
15. See Williamson, "When the Students," *Dartmouth College Library Bulletin* 2: 7–12

16. Cameron, *Emerson,* p. 254
17. Clayton, "The American College Library, 1800–1860," *Jl. Lib. Hist.* 3: 135–36.
18. Brough, *Scholar's Workshop,* p. 21, quoting J. W. Burgess, *Reminiscences of an American Scholar,* pp. 74–75.
19. See Bauersfeld, "University of Delaware Library," p. 1 of Chapter 3 quoting 1932 statement by George A. Harter.
20. Brough, *Scholar's Workshop,* p. 12
21. Ibid., p. 2, quoting from *Outlook,* 71: 248

CHAPTER 3

1. Holley, in *C & RL* 37: 16
2. Wertenbaker, *Princeton,* p. 310
3. Ambrose, "Study," *Lib. Jl.,* 1893, p. 113
4. Brough, *Scholar's Workshop,* pp. 164–65

CHAPTER 4

1. Jencks and Riesman, *Revolution,* p. 14
2. Ellsworth, "Trends in Expenditures," *Lib. Qu.* 14: 1
3. Dyer, *Tulane,* p. 259
4. Wilson, "1930s and 1940s," *C & RL* 1: 121–31
5. Evans, "Research Libraries," *Lib. Qu.* 17: 241

CHAPTER 5

1. DeGennaro, "Austerity," *Lib. Jl.* 100: 917
2. Ellsworth, "Trends in Higher Education," *Lib. Tr.* 1: 8–9
3. Bowker, *Annual of Library and Book Trade Information* 1978, p. 206
4. *ARL Spec Flyer* No. 33 for May, 1977
5. Lathem, Ed., *American Libraries as Centers of Scholarship,* p. 30

CHAPTER 6

1. Potter and Bolton, *Librarians of Harvard College,* p. 40
2. Edelman and Tatum, "Development of Collections," *C & RL* 37: 225
3. As quoted in Brough, *Scholar's Workshop,* p. 80
4. Potter, "Selection of Books," *Lib. Jl.* 22: 43–44
5. Yenawine, "Influence of Scholars," pp. 9–10
6. Edelman and Tatum, "Development of Collections," C & RL 37: 237
7. Butler, *Busy Years,* I, p. 77
8. Powell, "Development," p. 61
9. Lowell, "Indiana University," pp. 391–92
10. Danton, *Book Selection,* p. 133
11. Coney, "The Flooding Tide," *C & RL* 19: 182
12. Peterson, *Berkeley,* pp. 34–35
13. As quoted in Linderman, "Columbia," p. 112
14. Ibid., p. 372.
15. Harris, *Higher Education,* pp. 267, 268

16. Morison, *Three Centuries,* p. 266
17. Babb, "Yale University Library," *Lib. Tr.* 15: 208
18. Vosper, "Collection Building," p. 100

CHAPTER 7

1. Morison, *Seventeenth Century,* I, p. 287
2. Moloney, "Texas University," p. 145
3. McMullen, "University of Chicago," pp. 169–70
4. Lowell, "Indiana University," pp. 75–76
5. Gray, *Minnesota,* p. 530
6. Powell, "Development," p. 63
7. Munthe, *Librarianship,* p. 162
8. Peterson, *Berkeley,* pp. 54–55
9. For this and related material see Logsdon, "The Librarian and the Scholar, Eternal Enemies," *Lib. Jl.* 95: 2871–74
10. Putnam, "The Prospect . . .," *Lib. Jl.* 37: 652–53
11. See Downs, "Status," in *C & RL* 29: 253–58, from which much of these data are taken.

CHAPTER 8

1. Powell, "Development," p. 158
2. Ibid.
3. Works, *Library Problems,* pp. 19–21
4. Ellsworth, "Trends in Expenditures," *Lib. Qu.* 14: 6
5. Millett, *Financing,* p. 125
6. *Changing Patterns of Scholarship,* pp. 28, 31
7. Fussler and Simon, *Research Libraries,* p. 17
8. Stillwell, *Librarians,* p. 101
9. Munthe, *Librarianship,* pp. 165, 167

CHAPTER 9

1. Emerson, *Works.* Vol 7, pp. 191–92
2. U.S. Office of Education, *Survey,* p. 637
3. Brough, *Scholar's Workshop,* p. 69
4. Robinson, "Librarians and Readers," *Lib. Jl.* 1: 123–24
5. Lubans, *Educating the Library User,* p. 83
6. Evan Farber and Thomas Kirk, Jr. in *ALA Yearbook* for 1976, p. 59

CHAPTER 10

1. Quincy, *Harvard University,* Vol. 2, p. 600
2. *Norton's Literary Gazette and Publisher's Circular* 3: 1–2
3. Quincy, *Harvard University,* Vol. 2, pp. 599–601
4. Baumann, *Snead,* p. 64
5. Ibid., p. 75
6. Cooperative Committee *Minutes,* April, 1945, pp. 11–12
7. MacDonald, "Library of the Future," *Lib. Jl.* 58: 971

8. MacDonald, "New Possibilities," *Lib. Jl.* 70: 1169–74
9. Fussler, *Library Buildings,* p. 183
10. Allen, "Library Buildings," *Lib. Tr.* 25: 103

CHAPTER 11

1. Peterson, *Berkeley,* p. 139
2. Linderman, "Columbia," p. 225, quoting Trustees' Minutes of March 2, 1896.
3. Lowell, "Indiana University," pp. 159–160
4. Ibid., p. 294
5. Bauersfeld, "University of Delaware Library," p. 74
6. Gilman, *Launching,* p. 49
7. Gilman, *University Problems,* pp. 247–48
8. McMullen, "University of Chicago," p. 54
9. Metcalf, "Harvard Faces," *Harvard Library Bulletin* 3: 192

CHAPTER 12

1. Green, *Lib. Jl.* 1: 74–81
2. As quoted in Brough, *Scholar's Workshop,* p. 136
3. "Code of Practice," *ALA Bulletin* 11:27–29 (1917)
4. Downs, "Growth," *Lib. Tr.* 25: 62
5. Talmadge, "Farmington Plan Survey," in *C & RL* 19: 376
6. McGowan, "ARL," p. 154
7. *ACLS Newsletter* 19: 1–7 (January, 1968)

CHAPTER 13

1. Strout, "Development of the Catalog," p. 20
2. Morison, *Seventeenth Century* 1: 293
3. Shores, *Origins,* p. 85
4. Ibid.
5. Strout, "Development of the Catalog," pp. 25–26
6. Ibid., p. 33
7. Gorman, "Bibliographical Control," *American Libraries* 11: 202
8. See Holley, "The Trend to L.C."
9. *U.S. Survey of Land Grant Colleges,* p. 624
10. Stephen McCarthy as quoted in McGowan, "ARL," p. 183
11. Salmon, "Library Automation," *ELIS* 14: 350

CHAPTER 14

1. Bush, "As We May Think," *Atlantic Monthly* 176: 103, 107
2. Mason, "Great Gas Bubble," *C & RL* 32: 184, 185

EPILOGUE

1. Ready and Drynan, *Library Automation,* pp. 226–27.

Sources

It would be futile to attempt to trace each statement in a work of this sort to an authority, as one might do with a diplomatic history. In the first place much of the material comes from nearly a half-century of participation in, and observation of, librarianship. Then there are few authorities on exactly what took place. The desire to keep this a readable, interesting account for the mature reader outside as well as inside the profession dictated a minimum of footnotes. For these principal reasons the following plan has been followed:

(1) Footnotes only as essential.

(2) The list herewith set forth, of sources used at various points, arranged alphabetically by institution.

(3) For each chapter a brief statement of principal sources. As with footnotes, these references require consultation of the Bibliography for full identification.

(4) A bibliography with full author, title, and imprint information for all material referred to or used. This is not intended to be an exhaustive bibliography of the subject; one has recently been issued as *American Library History, a Bibliography*, by Michael H. Harris and Donald G Davis, Jr. (University of Texas Press, 1978).

General Sources on Individual Libraries

University of Alabama Library. Benjamin E. Powell. "The Development of Libraries in Southern State Universities to 1920" (Ph.D. dissertation, Chicago, 1946). Hereafter referred to as Powell, dissertation.

Baylor University. Roscoe Rouse. "History of Baylor Library 1845–1919" (Ph.D. dissertation, Michigan, 1962).

Brigham Young University. Hattie M. Knight. *Brigham Young University Library: Centennial Library 1875–1975* (Provo, Utah: Harold B. Lee Library, 1976).

University of California (Berkeley). K. G. Peterson. *The University of California Library at Berkeley, 1900–1945* (Berkeley: University of California Press, 1970); Russell H. Fitzgibbon. *Libraries of the University of California* (1964), pamphlet. Also used for other campuses.

University of California (Los Angeles). Lawrence Clark Powell. "John E. Goodwin, Founder of the UCLA Library." *Jl. Lib. Hist.* 6: 265–74; Robert Vosper. "Books at UCLA." *Pacific Spectator* for 1948.

University of California (Santa Barbara). Correspondence with Donald C. Davidson, University Librarian, Emeritus.

University of Chicago. C. H. McMullen. "Administration of the University of

Chicago Libraries, 1892–1928" (Ph.D. dissertation, Chicago, 1949); Kenneth J. Brough. *Scholar's Workshop; Evolving Conceptions of Library Service* (Urbana: University of Illinois Press, 1953), Illinois Contributions to Librarianship No. 5.

Columbia University. W. B. Linderman. "History of the Columbia University Library, 1876–1926" (Ph.D. dissertation, Columbia, 1959); Brough, *Scholar's Workshop*. See also sources listed for chapter 1.

Cornell University. Rita Guerlac. "Cornell's Library." *Cornell Library Journal*, no. 2 (Spring 1967), pp. 1–33.

Dartmouth College. John K. Lord. *A History of Dartmouth College 1815–1909* (Concord, N.H.: Rumford Press, 1913); Genevieve B. Williamson. "When the Students Owned the Library." *Dartmouth College Library Bulletin* n.s. II (1958): 7–22; article by Richard Morin in *ELIS*. See also sources listed for chapter 1.

University of Delaware. S. H. Bauersfeld. "Growth and Development of the University of Delaware Library . . . 1833–1965" (M.L.S. thesis, Catholic University of America, 1968).

Duke University. Powell, dissertation.

University of Georgia. Powell, dissertation.

Harvard University. Brough. *Scholar's Workshop;* Alfred C. Potter. *The Library of Harvard University. Descriptive and Historical Notes.* 4th ed. (Cambridge: Harvard University Press, 1934); Alfred C. Potter and Charles K. Bolton. "The Libraries of Harvard College, 1677–1877." *Harvard University Library Bibliographical Contributions* no. 52 (1897); Clifford K. Shipton. "John Langdon Sibley, Librarian." *Harvard Library Bulletin* 9 (1955): 236–61. See also sources listed for chapter 1.

University of Hawaii. D. Kittelson. "University of Hawaii Library 1920–1941." *Hawaii Library Association Journal* 30 (1973): 16–26.

Howard University. A. M. Duncan. "A History of Howard University Library, 1867–1929" (M.S.L.S. thesis, Catholic University of America, 1951).

University of Illinois. T. E. Ratcliffe. "Development of the Buildings, Policy, and Collections of the University of Illinois Library in Urbana, 1897–1940" (M.S.L.S. thesis, Illinois, 1949); W. S. Yenawine. "The Influence of Scholars on Research Library Development at the University of Illinois . . ." (Ph.D dissertation, Illinois, 1955).

Indiana University. M. H. Lowell. "Indiana University Libraries, 1829–1942" (Ph.D. dissertation, Chicago, 1957).

University of Kansas. C. S. Griffin. *The University of Kansas, a History* (Lawrence: University of Kansas Press, 1974).

Louisiana State University. Powell, dissertation.

University of Maryland. George H. Calcott. *A History of the University of Maryland* (Baltimore: Maryland Historical Society, 1966).

University of Miami. M. V. Husselbee. "History of the University of Miami Libraries 1928–1960" (M.S.L.S. thesis, North Carolina, 1962).

University of Michigan. R. E. Bidlack. "The University of Michigan General Library . . . 1837–1852" (Ph.D. dissertation, Michigan, 1954).

University of Minnesota. James Gray. *The University of Minnesota 1851–1951* (Minneapolis: University of Minnesota Press, 1951).
University of Mississippi. Powell, dissertation.
University of North Carolina. Charles E. Rush, ed. *Library Resources of the University of North Carolina* (Chapel Hill: University of North Carolina Press, 1945); L. R. Wilson. *Library of the First State University* . . . (University of North Carolina Library, 1960), pamphlet; Powell, dissertation.
Ohio State University. J. E. Skipper. "Ohio State University Library, 1873–1913" (Ph.D. dissertation, Michigan, 1960); G. Schoyer. *History of the Ohio State Libraries, 1870–1970* (Columbus: Office of Educational Services, Ohio State University Library, 1970), pamphlet; correspondence with Lewis Branscomb.
Oregon State University. W. H. Carlson. *Library of Oregon State University . . . A Centennial History* (Corvallis, Oregon: the Author, 1966).
The University of Pennsylvania. E. P. Cheyney. *History of the University of Pennsylvania 1740–1940* (Philadelphia: University of Pennsylvania Press, 1940); see also sources listed for chapter 1.
Princeton University. T. J. Wertenbaker. *Princeton 1746–1896* (Princeton: Princeton University Press, 1946); see also sources listed for chapter 1.
University of Rochester. C. D. Hayes. "History of the University . . . Libraries." *University of Rochester Library Bulletin* 25 (1970): 59–122.
Rutgers University. W. H. S. Demarest. "History of the Library." *Journal of the Rutgers University Library* 1 (December 1937): 3–8; Richard P. McCormick. *Rutgers: a Bicentennial History* (New Brunswick: Rutgers University Press, 1966); see also sources listed for chapter 1.
University of South Carolina. D. W. Hollis. *University of South Carolina* (Columbia: University of South Carolina Press, 1951–56) 2 vols.; F. B. Everhart. "The South Carolina College Library." *Journal of Library History* 3 (1968): 221–41; Powell, dissertation.
University of Southern Illinois. D. M. Manfredini. "A History of the Southern Illinois Library 1874–1950" (M.S.L.S. thesis, Southern Illinois, 1950).
Leland Stanford Jr. University. R. W. Hansen. "Stanford University Library: Genesis 1891–1906." *Journal of Library History* 9 (1974): 138–58.
Syracuse University. W. F. Galpin. *Syracuse University* (Syracuse: Syracuse University Press, 1952–1960) 2 vols.
University of Tennessee. Powell, dissertation.
University of Texas. L. C. Moloney. "History of the University Library at the University of Texas, 1883–1934" (Ph.D. dissertation, Columbia, 1970); various materials were furnished by correspondence.
Tulane University. J. P. Dyer. *Tulane, a Biography of a University* (New York: Harper & Row, 1966).
University of Vermont. R. A. White. "Vignettes of Library History, no. 1: The Library that Saved a University." *Journal of Library History* 1 (1966): 66–69.
University of Virginia. Harry Clemons. *The University of Virginia Library 1825–1950* (Charlottesville: The University Library, 1954); Thomas Jefferson. *Jefferson's Ideas on a University Library; Letters* . . . , ed. E. Cometti (Charlottesville: University of Virginia, 1950); Powell, dissertation.

Washington State University. C. C. Gorchels. "A Land Grant University Library: The History of the Library of Washington State University" (Ph.D. dissertation, Columbia, 1971).
College of William and Mary. J. M. Jennings. "Notes on the Original Library of the College of William and Mary . . . 1693–1705." *Bibliographical Society of America Papers* 41 (1947): 239–67.; see also sources listed for chapter 1.
Yale University, Brough, *Scholar's Workshop;* G. W. Pierson. *Yale: College and University 1871–1937* (New Haven: Yale University Press, 1952, 1955) 2 vols.; see also sources listed for chapter 1.

CHAPTER 1

A principal source for the colonial period is, of course, Louis Shores's *Origins of the American College Library, 1638–1800.* This should be consulted by readers who wish to go further. Most of the material on the Harvard Library is taken from *The Founding of Harvard College* and *Harvard College in the Seventeenth Century,* both by Samuel Eliot Morison. Equally useful have been the articles on the various libraries which have appeared in the *Encyclopedia of Library and Information Science.* Richard Warch's *School of the Prophets, Yale College 1701–1740* is the source of much of the data on the Yale library. For Princeton a chief source is Wertenbaker's *Princeton, 1746–1896.* Helpful in writing of the University of Pennsylvania is the history of that institution by Edward P. Cheyney. For Rutgers I am indebted to material furnished by letter by William Miller, university archivist, and "History of the Library," by William H. S. Demarest (see bibliography). Sources for Dartmouth were Lord's *History of Dartmouth College* and the excellent article by Richard Morin in the *Encyclopedia of Library and Information Science.* An important article on the libraries of this period is that by Joe Kraus, "The Book Collections of Early American College Libraries."

CHAPTER 2

A principal source, recommended for reading, is W. N. C. Carlton's "College Libraries in the Mid-Nineteenth Century." Of equal interest is Brough's *Scholar's Workshop* (1953).

Important statistics for the period are given in C. C. Jewett, *Appendix to the Report of the Board of Regents of the Smithsonian Institution Containing a Report on the Public Libraries of the United States of America,* 1850; also in the fundamental source, the Office of Education's *Public Libraries in the United States of America, Their History, Condition, and Management,* 1876.

Much of the material on Harvard is taken from Shipton's "John Langdon Sibley, Librarian."

The literary societies have been thoroughly researched by Thomas Harding. See his "College Literary Societies . . . 1815–1876" in the *Library Quarterlies* for January and April, 1959. Further treatment is given in his *College Literary Societies* (Pageant-Poseidon, 1971).

For another interpretation of this period, see Clayton, "American College Library 1800–1860."

CHAPTER 3

Many articles noted under other chapters deal with this period, as do the sources for individual libraries, in that section. This chapter is basically a summary of developments given detailed treatment in chapters 6–14.

See particularly Edward Holley's "Academic Libraries in 1876."

Developments in higher education for this period are ably charted in Ernest Earnest's *Academic Procession.*

CHAPTER 4

Much of this chapter is drawn from personal experience and general reading. The final paragraph on the war period is from Evans's "Research Libraries in the War Period, 1939–1945." The library building data is largely from Orne's, "Academic Library Buildings; a Century in Review," which is recommended reading. Data on the several librarians of the period have been drawn from the *DALB*. For a picture of library operations in the early 1920s, see Works's *College and University Library Problems.*

CHAPTER 5

Considerable material is based on experience as assistant librarian in charge of reader services at the University of Pennsylvania, as executive secretary of ACRL, and as director of libraries at the University of Cincinnati and Temple University for the period covered, as well as involvement in many activities of professional associations.

The material on California at Santa Barbara and Ohio State University Libraries was kindly furnished by Donald C. Davidson and Lewis Branscomb, retired directors of the two libraries.

The material on extension is taken from a study done by the author for the U.S. Office of Education in 1961.

The building data are taken largely from sundry studies by Jerrold Orne (see chapter 10).

Compact storage has been widely discussed in professional literature. See Ellsworth, *The Economics of Book Storage.*

For library surveys, see the study by Erickson.

The data on oral history are taken largely from the article by Louis Starr in volume 20 of *ELIS.*

For vandalism, see Davis, "Security Problems."

Data on bulk purchases by libraries are taken from Vosper's "Collection Building and Rare Books."

CHAPTER 6

Data for this chapter came from many sources, much of it from three excellent, comprehensive publications recommended for further reading on the subject: J. P. Danton's *Book Selection and Collections;* R. B. Downs's 1954 lecture "Development of Research Collections in University Libraries"; and Hendrik Edelman and Marvin Tatum's recent "The Development of Collections in American University

Libraries." Robert Vosper has written several perceptive articles on the subject. Other sources are indicated by the footnotes.

CHAPTER 7

For faculty status, see various writings of Robert Downs. The material here is principally from *Faculty Status for Academic Librarians.* For the position of the director, see McAnally and Downs, "Changing role . . ." For the position of women, see Dee Garrison, "The Tender Technicians." The material on Ida Kitter is taken from Carlson's *History.*

CHAPTER 8

For federal assistance, see Low, "Federal Legislation Affecting College and University Libraries." See also Stanford, "Federal Aid for Academic Library Construction." Additional data on governmental support are given in *Library Trends* for July, 1975 (*Federal Aid to Libraries, History, Impact and Future,* ed. by Genevieve M. Casey). See also McNeal, "Financial Problems of University Libraries." Ellsworth, Downs, and Metcalf have written extensively on this subject.

CHAPTER 9

A study of considerable importance is Rothstein's *Development of Reference Services,* the authority for virtually all statements regarding reference here and in other chapters.

Thoreau's reading in college and after is explored in Cameron's "Thoreau Discovers Emerson, a College Reading Record."

For early discussions of the library's responsibility to develop reading interests, see Otis Robinson's chapter on that subject in *Public Libraries of the United States* as well as the *Library Journal* article cited in the footnote.

For undergraduate libraries, see Braden, *The Undergraduate Library.*

CHAPTER 10

Much of this chapter is taken from Boll's dissertation, "Library Architecture . . ." Equally useful has been Helen Reynolds's "University Library Buildings . . . 1890–1939." Those who wish to go further should consult the excellent study "Library Buildings," by Walter C. Allen. This has a full bibliography. See also Ellsworth's "Library Architecture and Buildings," and the several articles listed in the bibliography by Jerrold Orne.

For MacDonald's influence, see Charles Baumann's *The Influence of Angus Snead MacDonald.* . . .

See also Fussler's *Library Buildings for Library Service,* and Davidson's "Significant Developments in University Library Buildings."

The material on the Cooperative Committee on Library Buildings is taken from the Committee's Minutes.

Not historical in treatment but the vade mecum for current practice is Metcalf's *Planning Academic and Research Library Buildings* (McGraw Hill, 1965).

CHAPTER 11

While the literature on this subject is extensive, material for this chapter is taken from publications listed under the individual institutions, except as indicated by footnotes. Those who wish to read further are referred to the two articles by Lundy, McNeal's "Divisional Organization . . .," and Swank's "Educational Function of the University Library."

CHAPTER 12

Much has been published on the various major cooperative programs. The two publications quoted from Downs are particularly useful for the Cooperative Acquisitions Project. See also his "Growth of Research Collections."

For the Farmington Plan, see E. E. Williams, *The Farmington Plan Handbook;* also Robert Talmadge's "The Farmington Plan Survey . . ."; also Hendrik Edelman's "Death of the Farmington Plan."

For the Universal Serials and Book Exchange and for the Documents Expediting Project, see Vosper's "Resources of University Libraries."

Valuable material on the above as well as on ARL itself is given in Frank McGowan's *The Association of Research Libraries 1932–1962.*

CHAPTER 13

As with other chapters extensive use has been made of the *Encyclopedia of Library and Information Science* and the *Dictionary of American Library Biography.* Some material is taken from the general sources on library history used throughout this volume and, of course, from the authorities cited in the footnotes.

Dunkin's *Cataloging U.S.A.* is an excellent summary of the history of library catalogs and the development of the codes; also Strout's "The Development of the Catalog and Cataloging." See also the article on "Catalog and Cataloging" in *ELIS* by Eugene Hanson and Jay Daily; also Tuttle's "From Cutter to Computer."

For the developments at Harvard, see Currier's "Cataloguing and Classification at Harvard 1878–1938."

For cataloging-in-source, see Clapp's "The Greatest Invention Since the Title Page" and Pope's "Cataloging-in-Source" in *ELIS* 4:231–42.

For the shift to LC classification, see Holley's "The Trend to L.C."

Of general usefulness have been Heiss's thesis on the card catalog, McGowan's history of ARL, Lane's "Present Tendencies of Cataloging Practice," and the Office of Education's *Survey of Land Grant Colleges and Universities.*

CHAPTER 14

A number of articles in the *Encyclopedia of Library and Information Science* have been used for this chapter. See particularly "The New England Document Conservation Center," by George M. Cunha; "The Deterioration of Library Materials," by Carl J. Wessel; "Reprography," by William Nazri; "The Library Binding Institute," by Dudley Weiss; "The Massachusetts Institute of Technology Libraries," by Natalie Nicholson (useful for INTREX data); and "Florida Atlantic University," by H. William Axford (for a case history of an installation of automation that did not work).

For further information on the application of computers to library processes from the beginnings until 1974, see the complete and admirably clear article "Library Automation," by Stephen Salmon in *ELIS* 14:338–445. Included is a full bibliography.

For the Library Technology Project, see Clapp's "LTP, the Rattle in an Infant's Fist."

For the deterioration of material, see the Wessel article noted above and also the reports on deterioration in the *ALA Yearbooks* for 1976, 1977, and 1978.

For microforms, see the several articles by Eugene Power, the biography of M. Llewellyn Rainey in the *DALB*, Veaner's article in the *ALA Yearbook* for 1976, and Grieder's "Ultrafiche Libraries."

Much general information is taken from, or has been checked in, Fussler's *Research Libraries and Technology*.

Bibliography

Allen, Walter C. "Library Buildings." *Lib. Tr.* 25(1976):89–112.

Ambrose, Lodilla. "A Study of College Libraries." *Lib. Jl.* (April 1893): 113–17.

Babb, James T. "The Yale University Library." *Lib. Tr.* 15 (1966): 206–14.

Bauersfeld, S. H. "Growth and Development of the University of Delaware Library . . . 1833–1965." M.S.L.S. thesis, Catholic University of America, 1968.

Baumann, Charles H. *The Influence of Angus Snead MacDonald and the Snead Bookstack on Library Architecture.* Metuchen, N.J.: Scarecrow Press, 1972.

Bentinck-Smith, William. *Building a Great Library, the Coolidge Years at Harvard.* Cambridge: Harvard University Press, 1976.

Bidlack, R. E. "The University of Michigan General Library . . . 1837–1852." Ph.D. dissertation, University of Michigan, 1954.

Boll, John J. "Library Architecture, 1800–1875, a Comparison of Theory and Buildings." Ph.D. dissertation, University of Illinois, 1961.

Bolton, Charles K. *American Library History.* Chicago: ALA, 1911.

R. R. Bowker Co. *American Book Publishing Record.* Annual.

———. *Bowker Annual of Library and Book Trade Information.*

Braden, I. A. *The Undergraduate Library* (ACRL Monograph no. 31). Chicago: ALA, 1970.

Branscomb, Lewis. "Libraries in Large Institutions of Higher Education." *Lib. Tr.* 10 (1961): 179–90.

Brough, Kenneth J. *Scholar's Workshop: Evolving Conceptions of Library Service.* Urbana: University of Illinois Press, 1953.

Brown, Dee. *The Year of the Century: 1876.* New York: Scribner, 1966.

Brundin, Robert E. "Justin Winsor and the Liberalizing of the College Library." *Jl. Lib. Hist.* 10 (1975):57–70.

Burgess, J. W. *Reminiscences of an American Scholar.* New York: Columbia University Press, 1934.

Bush, Vannevar. "As We May Think." *Atlantic Monthly* 176 (1945): 101–8.

Butler, Nicholas M. *Across the Busy Years.* N. Y.: Scribner, 1939.

Callcott, George H. *A History of the University of Maryland.* Baltimore: Maryland Historical Society, 1966.

Cameron, Kenneth W. "Thoreau Discovers Emerson: A College Reading Record." *Bulletin of the N. Y. Public Library* 57 (1953):319–34.

———. *Emerson the Essayist.* 2 vols. Raleigh: Thistle Press, 1945.

Carlson, William H. *The Library of Oregon State University . . . a Centennial History.* Corvallis, Ore.: the Author, 1966.

Carlton, W. N. C. and N. Chattin. "College Libraries in the Mid-Nineteenth Century." *Lib. Jl.* 32 (1907):479–86.

Carson, Josephine R. and James E. Bobick. "New Library Buildings, Pt. 6, Science Library Brown University." *Medical Library Assoc. Bull.* 64 (1976):179–86.

Changing Patterns of Scholarship and the Future of Research Libraries. Philadelphia: University of Pennsylvania Press, 1951.

Cheyney, Edward P. *History of the University of Pennsylvania, 1740–1940.* Philadelphia: University of Pennsylvania Press, 1940.

Clayton, H. "American College Library: 1800–1860." *Jl. Lib. Hist.* 3 (1968): 129–37.

Clemons, Harry. *The University of Virginia Library 1825–1950.* Charlottesville: The University Library, 1954.

Coney, Donald. "The Administration of Technical Processes." In *Current Issues in Library Administration.* ed. C. B. Joeckel, pp.163–80. Chicago: University of Chicago Press, 1938.

——. "The Flooding Tide, or 'Where Did You Go? To the Library. What Did You Get? Nothing.' " *C & RL* 19 (1958):179–84.

Cooperative Committee on Library Buildings. *Minutes.* Those for the first three meetings distributed in processed form to participants; those for later meetings made widely available.

Currier, Thomas F. "Cataloguing and Classification at Harvard, 1878–1938." *Harvard Library Notes* no. 29 (1939), pp. 232–42.

Danton, J. P. *Book Selection and Collections: A Comparison of German and American University Libraries.* New York: Columbia University Press, 1963.

Davidson, Donald. "Significant Developments in University Library Buildings." *Lib.Tr.* 18 (1969): 125–37.

Davis, D. G. "Security Problems in College and University Libraries: Student Violence." *C & RL* 32 (1971): 15–22.

DeGennaro, Richard. "Austerity, Technology and Resource Sharing." *Lib.Jl.* 100 (1975): 917–23.

Demarest, William H. S. "History of the Library." *Journal of the Rutgers University Library* 1 (1937): 3–8.

Dix, William S. "Two Decisive Decades: Cause and Effect on University Libraries." *American Libraries* 3 (1972): 725–31.

Doherty, Francis X. "The New England Deposit Library . . ." *Lib.Qu.* 18 (1948): 245–54.

Downs, Robert B. "Crisis in Our University Libraries." *C & RL* 22 (1961): 7–10.

——. (Issue editor) "Current Trends in College and University Libraries." *Lib.Tr.* 1, (July 1952).

——. "Development of Research Collections in University Libraries." *University of Tennessee Library Lectures No. 4–6.* University of Tennessee, 1954.

——. "Growth of Research Collections." *Lib. Tr.* 25 (1976):55–80.

——. "Rare Books in American State University Libraries." *Book Collector* 6 (1957):232–43.

—— and J. W. Heussman. "Standards for University Libraries." *C & RL* 31 (1970):28–35.

——. "Status of Academic Librarians in Retrospect." *C & RL* 29 (1968):253–58.

——. *University Library Statistics.* Chicago: ALA, 1970.

——. "Wartime Co-operative Acquisitions." *Lib. Qu.* 19 (1949):157–65.

Duncan, A. M. "History of Howard University Library, 1867–1929." M.S.L.S. thesis, Catholic University of America, 1951.

Dunkin, Paul S. *Cataloging U. S. A.* Chicago: ALA, 1969.

Dyer, John P. *Tulane, the Biography of a University.* New York: Harper and Row, 1966.

Earnest, Ernest. *Academic Procession, an Informal History of the American College, 1636 to 1953.* Indianapolis: Bobbs-Merrill, 1953.

Edelman, Hendrik. "Death of the Farmington Plan." *Lib. Jl.* 98 (1973):1251–53.

——— and G. Marvin Tatum, Jr. "The Development of Collections in American Universities." *C & RL* 37 (1976): 222–45.

Ellsworth, Ralph. "Architecture, Library Building." *ELIS* 1:491–515.

———. *The Economics of Book Storage in College and Universitity Libraries.* Metuchen, N.J.: Scarecrow Press, 1969.

———. "Library Architecture and Buildings." *Lib. Qu.* 25 (1955):66–75.

———. "Trends in Higher Education Affecting the College and University Library." *Lib. Tr.* 1 (1952):8–19.

———. "Trends in University Expenditures for Library Resources and Total Educational Purposes, 1921–1941." *Lib. Qu.* 14 (1944):1–8.

Encyclopedia of Library and Information Science (ELIS). Edited by Allen Kent and Harold Lancour. New York: Dekker, 1968-.

Erickson, E. Walfred. *College and University Library Surveys, 1938–1952* (ACRL Monograph no. 25). Chicago: ALA, 1961.

Evans, Luther H. "Research Libraries in the War Period 1939–1945." *Lib. Qu.* 17 (1947):241–62.

Everhart, Frances B. "The South Carolina College Library." *Jl. Lib. Hist.* 3 (1968):221–41.

Faculty Status for Academic Librarians; A History and Policy Statements. Compiled by the Committee on Academic Status of the ACRL. Chicago: ALA, 1975.

Fairchild, Salome Cutler. "Women in American Libraries." *Lib. Jl.* 29 (Dec. 1904 Conference Number):157–62.

Fitzgibbon, Russell H. *Libraries of the University of California.* Pamphlet. University of California, 1964.

Franklin, Fabian. *Life of Daniel Coit Gilman.* New York: Dodd Mead, 1910.

Fussler, Herman, ed. *Library Buildings for Library Service, the Historic Development of Library Buildings.* Chicago: ALA, 1947.

Fussler, Herman and J. L. Simon. *Patterns in the Use of Books in Large Research Libraries.* Chicago: University of Chicago Press, 1969.

———. *Research Libraries and Technology, a Report to the Sloan Foundation.* Chicago: University of Chicago Press, 1973.

Galpin, William F. *Syracuse University.* 2 vols. Syracuse: Syracuse University Press, 1952–60.

Garrison, Dee. "The Tender Technicians." *Journal of Social History* 6 (1973): 131–59.

Gilman, Daniel Coit. *The Launching of a University.* New York: Dodd Mead, 1906.

———. *University Problems in the United States.* New York: Garrett Press, 1969.

Gorchels, Clarence C. "A Land Grant University Library: The History of the

Library of Washington State University, 1892–1946." Ph.D. dissertation, Columbia University, 1971.

Gorman, Michael. "Toward Bibliographical Control." *American Libraries* 11 (1980):201–3.

Gray, James. *The University of Minnesota, 1851–1951.* Minneapolis: University of Minnesota Press, 1951.

Green, Samuel S. Letter dated September 4, 1875. *Lib. Jl.* 1:74–81.

Grieder, E. M. "Ultrafiche Libraries: a Librarian's View." *Microform Review* 1 (1972):85–100.

Griffin, Clifford S. *The University of Kansas, A History.* Lawrence: University of Kansas Press, 1974.

Guerlac, Rita. "Cornell's Library." *Cornell Library Journal* no. 2 (Spring, 1967), pp. 1–33.

Hansen, R. W. "Stanford University Library: Genesis 1891–1906." *Jl. Lib. Hist.* 9 (1974): 138–58.

Harding, Thomas S. "College Literary Societies; Their Contribution to the Development of Academic Libraries 1815–1876." *Lib. Qu.* 29 (Jan.–Apr. 1959): 1–26, 94–112.

———. *College Literary Societies.* New York: Pageant-Poseidon, 1971.

Harrer, G. A. "Distribution and Cost of Library Service." *C & RL* 18(1957): 210–12.

Harris, Seymour. *Statistical Portrait of Higher Education.* New York: McGraw-Hill, 1972.

Hayes, Catherine D. "History of the University of Rochester Libraries." *University of Rochester Library Bulletin* 25(1970): 59–122.

Heiss, R.M. "The Card Catalog in Libraries of the United States Before 1876." M.S.L.S. thesis, University of Illinois, 1938.

Holley, Edward G. "Academic Libraries in 1876." *C & RL* 37 (1976):15–47.

———. "The Trend to L.C." *Library Lectures nos 1–4.* Baton Rouge: Louisiana State University, 1967.

Hollis, Daniel W. *University of South Carolina.* 2 vols. Columbia: University of South Carolina Press, 1951–56.

Hopkins, Judith. "The Ohio College Library Center." *Library Resources and Technical Services* 17 (1973):308–19.

Husselbee, M. V. "History of the University of Miami Libraries, 1928–1960." M.S.L.S. thesis, University of North Carolina, 1962.

Jefferson, Thomas. *Jefferson's Ideas on a University Library; Letters . . . to a Boston Bookseller,* ed. Elizabeth Cometti. Charlottesville: University of Virginia, 1950.

Jencks, C. and D. Riesman. *The Academic Revolution.* New York: Doubleday, 1968.

Jennings, John M. "Notes on the Original Library of the College of William and Mary. . . ." *Bibliographical Society of America Papers* 41(1947):239–67.

———. *Library of the College of William and Mary in Virginia, 1693–1793* (Library Contributions no. 6). University Press of Virginia, 1968.

Jewett, C. C. *Notices of Public Libraries in the United States.* Washington, D.C., 1851. Previously published as *Appendix to the Report of the Board of Regents of the*

Smithsonian Institute . . . 31st Cong. 1st sess., Senate Misc. Doc. no. 120. 1850.

Kilgour, Frederick G. "History of Library Computerization." *Journal of Library Automation* 3(1970): 218–29.

Kittelson, D. "University of Hawaii Library, 1920–1941." *Hawaii Library Association Journal* 30(1973):16–26.

Knight, Hattie M. *Brigham Young University Library. Centennial History 1875–1975.* Provo: Harold B. Lee Library, 1976.

Kraus, J. W. "Book Collections of Early American College Libraries." *Lib. Qu.* 43 (1973):142–59. Compressed from doctoral dissertation, University of Illinois, 1960.

————."Harvard Undergraduate Library of 1773." *C & RL* 22(1961): 247–52.

Ladenson, Alex, ed. "Federal Legislation Affecting College and University Libraries." *Lib. Tr.* 19 (Oct. 1970).

Lane, William Coolidge, ed. *Library of Harvard University. Bibliographical Contributions.* IV. Cambridge: Library of Harvard University, 1897–1909.

————. "Present Tendencies of Cataloging Practice." *Papers and Proceedings of the 26th Conference at the Louisiana Purchase Exposition. Oct. 1904.* Chicago: ALA, pp. 134–43.

Lathem, Edward C., ed. *American Libraries as Centers of Scholarship.* Hanover, N.H.: Dartmouth College, 1978.

Linderman, W. B. "History of the Columbia University Library 1876–1926." Ph. D. dissertation, Columbia University, 1959.

Logsdon, R. H. "The Librarian and the Scholar: Eternal Enemies." *Lib. Jl.* 95 (1970): 2871–74.

Lord, John King. *A History of Dartmouth College, 1815–1909.* Concord, N. H.: Rumford Press, 1913.

Low, Edmon. "Federal Legislation Affecting College and University Libraries." *Lib. Tr.* 19 (1970): 200–11.

Lowell, M. H. "Indiana University Libraries, 1829–1942." Ph.D. dissertation, University of Chicago, 1957.

Lubans, John, ed. *Educating the Library User.* New York: Bowker, 1974.

Lundy, Frank. "The Divisional Plan Library." *C & RL* 17 (1956): 143–48.

————. "The Divisional Plan of Library Organization." *ELIS* 7: 242–46.

McAnally, Arthur and R. B. Downs. "The Changing Role of Directors of University Libraries." *C & RL* 34 (1973): 103–25.

McCormick, Richard P. *Rutgers, a Bicentennial History.* New Brunswick, N.J.: Rutgers University Press, 1966.

MacDonald, Angus Snead. "Library of the Future." *Lib. Jl.* 58 (Dec. 1 and 15, 1933): 971–75 and 1023–25.

————. *Morrow's Library.* Pamphlet. Orange, Va., 1948.

————. "New Possibilities in Library Planning." *Lib. Jl.* 70 (1945): 1169–74.

McElderry, Stanley. "Readers and Resources: Public Services in Academic and Research Libraries 1876–1976." *C & RL* 37 (1976): 408–20.

McGowan, Frank M. "The Association of Research Libraries 1932–1962." Ph.D. dissertation, University of Pittsburgh, 1972.

McMullen, C. H. "Administration of the University of Chicago Libraries 1892–1928." Ph.D. dissertation, University of Chicago, 1949.

McNeal, Archie L. "Divisional Organization in the University Library." *University of Tennessee Library Lectures* No. 12. Knoxville: University of Tennessee, 1961.

———. "Financial Problems of University Libraries." *C & RL* 15 (1954): 407–10.

Manfredini, Dolores M. "A History of the Southern Illinois University Library, 1874–1950." M.S.L.S. thesis, Southern Illinois University, 1950.

Mason, Ellsworth. "The Great Gas Bubble Pricked; or Computers Revealed—by a Gentleman of Leisure." *C & RL* 32 (1971): 183–96.

Metcalf, Keyes D. "The Ever-Expanding Demand for Materials and the Threatened Decline of Support. How Shall the Gap Be Filled?" In *Changing Patterns of Scholarship and the Future of Research Libraries*, pp. 27–36. Philadelphia: University of Pennsylvania Press, 1951.

———. "Finances of the Harvard University Library." *Harvard Library Bulletin* 7 (1953): 333–48.

———. "Financial Problems of University Libraries; a Proposal for a Conference." *Harvard Library Bulletin* 8 (1954): 5–13.

———. "Harvard Faces its Library Problem." *Harvard Library Bulletin* 3 (1949): 183–97.

———. "University Libraries Face the Future." *Lib. Qu.* 22 (1952): 5–12.

———. "Why We Need to be Investigated." *C & RL* 15 (1954): 383–87.

Miller, R. A. and J. H. Moriarity. "University Library Development in Indiana, 1910 to 1966." *Lib. Tr.* 15 (1966): 248–57.

Millett, John D. *Financing Higher Education in the United States.* New York: Columbia University Press, 1952.

Mitchell, Jonathan. "A Modell for the Maintaining of Students & Fellows of Choise Abilities at the College in Cambridge. . . ." *Colonial Society of Mass. Publications* vol. 31. Boston: The Society, 1935.

Moloney, L. C. "History of the University Library at the University of Texas, 1883–1934." Ph.D. dissertation, Columbia University, 1970.

Morison, Samuel Eliot. *The Founding of Harvard College.* Cambridge: Harvard University Press, 1935.

———. *Harvard College in the Seventeenth Century.* 2 vols. Cambridge: Harvard University Press, 1936.

———. *Three Centuries of Harvard, 1636–1936.* Cambridge: Harvard University Press, 1936.

Muller, Robert H. "College and University Library Buildings, 1929–1949." *C & RL* 12 (1951): 261–65.

———. "Undergraduate Library Trend at Large Universities." In *Advances in Librarianship*, vol. 1, pp. 113–32. New York: Academic Press, 1970.

Munn, Robert F. "Bottomless Pit, or the Academic Library as Viewed from the Administration Building." *C & RL* 29 (1968): 51–54.

———. "West Virginia University Library, 1867–1917." Ph.D. dissertation, University of Michigan, 1962.

Munthe, Wilhelm. *American Librarianship from a European Angle.* Chicago: ALA, 1939.

Nazri, William Z. "Reprography." *ELIS* 25:230–39.

Nicholson, N. N. "Centralization of Science Libraries at Johns Hopkins University." In *Rutgers University—Studies in Library Administrative Problems,* pp. 133–56. New Brunswick, N.J.: Rutgers University Press, 1960.

Oehlerts, Donald E. "Sources for the Study of American Library Architecture." *Jl. Lib. Hist.* 11 (1976): 68–78.

Oliphant, J. O. *Library of Bucknell University.* Lewisburg: Bucknell University Press, 1962.

Orne, Jerrold "Academic Library Buildings: A Century in Review." *C & RL* 37 (1976):316–31.

———. "Current Trends in Collection Development in University Libraries." *Lib. Tr.* 15 (1966): 197–334.

———. "Library Building Trends and Their Meanings." *Lib. Jl.* 102 (1977): 2397–401.

———. "The Renaissance of Academic Library Building, 1967–1971." *Lib. Jl.* 96 (1971): 3947–67.

———, ed. *Research Librarianship: Essays in Honor of Robert B. Downs.* New York: Bowker, 1971.

——— and J. O. Gosling. "Academic Library Building in 1976." *Lib. Jl.* 101 (1976): 2435–39. An annual *Lib. Jl.* feature.

Peterson, K. G. *The University of California Library at Berkeley, 1900–1945,* Berkeley: University of California Press, 1970.

Pierson, George W. *Yale: College and University, 1871–1937,* 2 vols. New Haven: Yale University Press, 1952.

Potter, Alfred C. *The Library of Harvard University. Descriptive and Historical Notes.* 4th ed. Cambridge: Harvard University Press, 1934.

———. "The Selection of Books for College Libraries." *Lib. Jl.* 22:(Conference Issue, October 1897) 39–44.

——— and Charles K. Bolton. "The Librarians of Harvard College 1667–1877." *Harvard University Bibliographical Contributions* no. 52. 1897.

Powell, Benjamin E. "The Development of Libraries in Southern State Universities to 1920." Ph.D. dissertation, University of Chicago, 1946.

———. "Growth of an Academic Library: Duke University." *North Carolina Librarian* 25 (1967):102–6.

———. "Southern University Libraries During the Civil War." In Marshall, J. D., ed. *American Library History Reader,* pp. 73–82. Metuchen, N.J.: Shoe String Press, 1961.

Powell, Lawrence Clark. "John E. Goodwin Founder of the UCLA Library." *Jl. Lib. Hist.* 6 (1971): 265–74.

Power, Eugene B. "Microfilm and the Publication of Doctoral Dissertations." *Journal of Documentary Reproduction* 5 (1942): 37–44.

———. "Microfilm in Europe." *Journal of Documentary Reproduction* 2(1939):254–58.

———. "Report of Progress in Filming English Books Before 1550." *Journal of Ducementary Reproduction* 1 (1938):45–49.

———. "University Microfilms." *Journal of Documentary Reproduction* 2 (1939): 21–28.

Princeton University Library. *College and University Library Statistics, 1919–1920 to 1943–1944.* Princeton: Princeton University Library, 1947.

Putnam, Herbert. "The Prospect: An Address Before a Graduating Class of Women." *Lib.Jl.* 37 (1912): 651–58.

Quincy, Josiah. *The History of Harvard University.* 2 vols. Cambridge: Harvard University Press, 1840.

Randall, William, ed. *The Acquisition and Cataloging of Books.* Chicago: University of Chicago Press, 1940.

Ratcliffe, T. E. "Development of the Buildings, Policy and Collection of the University of Illinois Library . . . 1897–1940." M.L.S. thesis, University of Illinois, 1949.

Ready, William and Tom Drynan. *Library Automation: A View from Ontario.* Halifax, N.S.: Dalhousie University, 1977.

Reynolds, Helen M. "University Library Buildings in the U. S. 1890–1939." M.L.S. thesis, University of Illinois, 1946. See also in *C & RL* 14 (1953): 149–66.

Rider, Fremont. *The Scholar and the Future of the Research Library.* New York: Hadham Press, 1944.

Robinson, Otis H. "College Library Administration." In *Public Libraries in the U. S.,* pp. 505–25.

———. "Librarians and Readers." *Lib.Jl.* 1 (1876): 123–24.

Ross, Murray G. *The University, the Anatomy of Academe.* New York: McGraw Hill, 1976.

Ross, Norma. *History of Hofstra University Library, 1935–1970.* Research Paper, Long Island University, 1971.

Rothstein, Samuel. *The Development of Reference Services . . .* (ACRL Monograph no.15). Chicago: ACRL, 1955. Also his dissertation for the University of Illinois, 1954.

———. "From Reaction to Interaction: the Development of the North American University Library." *Canadian Library Journal* 29 (1972): 111–15.

Rouse, Roscoe. "History of Baylor University Library, 1845–1919." Ph.D. dissertation, University of Michigan, 1962,

Rowland, Arthur R. *The Catalog and Cataloging.* Metuchen, N.J.: Shoestring Press, 1969.

Rush, Charles E., ed. *Library Resources of the University of North Carolina.* Chapel Hill: University of North Carolina Press, 1945.

Salmon, Stephen. "Library Automation." *ELIS* 14:338–445.

Schoyer, G. *History of the Ohio State University Libraries 1870–1970.* Pamphlet. Columbus: Office of Educational Services, Ohio State University Library, 1970.

Shipton, Clifford K. "John Langdon Sibley, Librarian." *Harvard Library Bulletin* 9 (1955):236–61.

Shores, Louis. *Origins of the American College Library, 1638–1800.* New York: Barnes and Noble, 1934.

Simon, Kenneth A. and M. M. Frankel. *Projections of Educational Statistics to 1984–85.* Washington, D.C.: Department of Health, Education and Welfare, 1976.

Skipper, James E. "Ohio State University Library, 1873–1913." Ph.D. dissertation, University of Michigan, 1960.

Soule, C. C. "Points of Agreement Among Librarians as to Library Architecture." *Lib.Jl.* 16 (1891): 17–19.

Stanford, Edward B. "Federal Aid for Academic Library Construction." *Lib.Jl.* 99 (1974): 112–15.

Starr, Louis M. "Oral History." *ELIS* 20: 440–63.

Stephens, Frank P. *A History of the University of Missouri.* Columbia: University of Missouri Press, 1962.

Stillwell, Margaret. *Librarians Are Human: Memories in and out of the Rare Book World.* Boston: Colonial Society of Massachusetts, 1973.

Strout, Ruth French. "The Development of the Catalog and Cataloging." In *The Catalog and Cataloging,* Arthur R. Rowland, ed., pp. 3–33. Metuchen, N.J.: Shoestring Press, 1969.

Swank, Raymond. "Educational Function of the University Library." *Lib. Tr.* 1 (1952): 37–48.

Talmadge, Robert L. "The Farmington Plan Survey, an Interim Report." *C & RL* 19 (1958): 375–83.

Tauber, Maurice F. *Louis Round Wilson, Librarian and Administrator.* New York: Columbia University Press, 1967.

Thompson, Donald E. "History of Library Architecture: A Bibliographical Essay." *Jl.Lib.Hist.* 4 (1969): 133–41.

Thompson, L. S. "Historical Background of Departmental and College Libraries." *Lib.Qu.* 12 (1942): 49–74.

Tuttle, H. W. "From Cutter to Computer." *C & RL* 37 (1976): 421–51.

U.S. Office of Education. *Digest of Educational Statistics.* Annual.

————. *Survey of Land Grant Colleges and Universities.* 2 vols. (Bulletin 1930 no.9). Washington, D.C.: Government Printing Office, 1930.

————. *Public Libraries in the United States of America, Their History, Condition, and Management.* Washington, D.C., 1876.

Viles, Jonas. *The University of Missouri, a Centennial History.* Columbia: University of Missouri, 1939.

Vosper, Robert G. "Acquisition Policy: Fact or Fancy?" *C & RL* 14 (1953): 367–70.

————. "Collection Building and Rare Books." In *Research Librarianship: Essays in Honor of Robert B. Downs,* ed. Jerrold Orne, pp. 91–111. New York: Bowker, 1971.

————. "Expanding Library Horizons: The Significance for Academic Learning." *Pacific Northwest Library Association Quarterly* 37 (1973): 9–19.

————. "Resources of University Libraries." *Lib.Tr.* 1 (1952): 58–72.

Warch, Richard. *School of the Prophets, Yale College 1701–1740.* New Haven: Yale University Press, 1973.

Weiss, Dudley. "The Library Binding Institute." *ELIS* 2:510–12.

Wertenbaker, Thomas J. *Princeton 1746–1896.* Princeton: Princeton University Press, 1946.

White, R. A. "Vignettes of Library History, no. 1: The Library that Saved a University." *Jl.Lib.Hist.* 1 (1966):66–69.

Williamson, Genevieve B. "When the Students Owned the Library." *Dartmouth College Library Bulletin* n.s. 2 (1958): 7–12.

Wilson, Louis Round. *Library of the First State University: A Review of its Past and a Look at its Future.* Pamphlet. Chapel Hill: University of North Carolina Library, 1960.

———. "The Challenge of the 1930s to the 1940s. A Summary of Developments, Proposals and Objectives concerning College and Research Libraries in the 1930s and 1940s." *C & RL* 1 (March, 1940): 121–31.

Works, George A. *College and University Library Problems.* Chicago: ALA, 1927.

Yenawine, Wayne S. "The Influence of Scholars on Research Library Development at the University of Illinois." Ph.D. dissertation, University of Illinois, 1955.

Index